WESTMAR COLLEGE

Silver Theatre

JAMES STARK
The tragedian who brought Shakespeare to Silver-
land, and helped create the state of Nevada.
Courtesy of Harvard College Library.

SILVER THEATRE

Amusements
of the
MINING FRONTIER
in Early Nevada
1850 to 1864

by

MARGARET G. WATSON

THE ARTHUR H. CLARK COMPANY
Glendale, California   1964

792.09793
W341

PN
2275
.N4
W3

Copyright ©, 1964, by
THE ARTHUR H. CLARK COMPANY

All rights reserved including the rights to
translate or reproduce this work or parts
thereof in any form or by any media.

LIBRARY OF CONGRESS CATALOG CARD NUMBER 64-21209

64394

TO
GEORGE R. MACMINN
without whose faith, counsel,
and warm encouragement this book
would not have been completed

Contents

Illustrations

Preface

"It is entirely false reasoning to suppose that any human being can devote himself exclusively to labor of any description," insisted a newspaper writer on the staff of the *Virginia Evening Bulletin* early in 1864. "It will not do," he repeated. "Man must enjoy himself . . . laugh, sing, dance, eat, drink, and be merry . . . chat with his friends, exercise his mind in exciting gentle emotions, and his body in agreeable demonstrations of activity. The constitution of the human system demands this. It will not remain in health if it cannot obtain that variety . . . that sunshine of the heart . . . as indispensible as the material sunshine to the flower." In short, man "must be amused."

The complete story of Washoe (early Nevada) has never been written; it probably never can be. Nevertheless, this book is an attempt at social history, an attempt to portray one phase of the life and living of the Washoites, their entertainment.

Not merely a rehearsal of plays and players of the theatrical stage, the book includes such political and economic history as relates to the entertainment of bonanza and borrasca times; it deals with many of the means of diversion embraced by the amusement-starved farmers, miners, prostitutes, gamblers and other parasites, business people, children, church members, and all those hardy souls who sought their fortunes in the deserts, the valleys, and up the sides of Mount Davidson to one of the world's greatest mineral-bearing veins, the internationally famous Comstock Lode.

As early as the summer of 1861 the newly created Territory of Nevada boasted seven theatres or entertainment halls, seating from 200 to 1000 people, in Franktown, Genoa, Nevada City (Dayton), Carson City, Silver City, Virginia City, and Fort Churchill Barracks. Before many more months passed, Aurora, Washoe City, and Austin likewise had such buildings to entice local and touring professional troupers. Greater change took place in early Nevada than comes in twenty-five years of growth in normal communities. Time in Washoe, therefore, was measured more by the rapidity of events than in years. Of Virginia City this was especially true. Originally called Ophir, this mining metropolis of the Comstock, boasting at one time as many as four theatres, became one of the important theatrical centers of the West — and hence claims the greatest number of pages in this book.

Silver Theatre, in telling the story of Washoe's search for entertainment, proceeds naturally and chronologically from the entertainment enjoyed by the trappers and the traders, to the first organized professional entertainments of Mart Taylor, the Westwood troupe, the minstrels, the river-boat-playing Chapmans, the tragedian James Stark, and those many Thespians of national recognition who insisted — because of the warm welcome and remunerative attractions — that Virginia City be included in their itineraries. The account thus runs through pre-territorial and territorial years, past statehood on October 31, including the elections and celebrations that followed, to the closing days of 1864, when such popular pioneer players as Virginia Howard, P. M. Westwood, and James Stark returned — as if by plan — and fittingly rang down the curtain on this chapter of Nevada's amusement history.

To keep as far as possible the spirit and tone of the times, the writer has allowed the period to tell its own tale by quoting freely from the newspapers and journals of that day — correcting only such grammatical and typographical errors as seemed most glaring. No attempt has been made to pass moral judgment, to say that this was good or bad, but simply, that it *was*. While it is impossible to work for years with such a research as this and not develop sympathies and affections, no effort has been made to glorify the theatre and the unusual of Washoe; the purpose, rather, has been to re-create so that the reader may understand and enjoy in correct perspective the human character of that day with confidence "that no imagination gilds the tale."

The method of research has been to rely on the earliest known material available in extant files and rare, scattered copies of Nevada and California newspapers, diaries, letters, and photographs as found in the libraries, museums, and historical societies of the universities and cities across the nation. The writer found it an advantage also to visit Nevada's often-called ghost towns founded a hundred years ago, to listen to accounts of old-timers, and to retrieve — even from Comstock mud puddles — such items of historical interest as discarded pieces of wallpaper backed with local, Civil-War-day newspapers containing precious information of Washoe amusement fare.

To entertain and present in a true light has been the aim, but the fact that a work is accurate historically does not necessitate its being stilted and dry. The reader who has no taste for dates and appraisals is encouraged to skim over those sections and proceed with the parts he does enjoy, and is urged to utilize the more spicy and illuminating footnotes as he proceeds through the book. The nearer one comes to understanding the effort expended to build our world of today, the greater the zest and appreciation of those times when the theatre was a vital and lively part of daily living.

Acknowledgments

In gathering material for *Silver Theatre* I became indebted to many kind and generous people, including Dr. William C. Miller, professor of English at the University of Nevada, for bringing to my attention the San Francisco *Weekly Bulletin* for September 15-19, October 4, and 13, 1860, and the *Territorial Enterprise* for August 16, 1864, for supplying information on the photographs of Maguire's Opera House, permitting the use of his Topliffe Theatre Program and his unpublished thesis, and for many other favors, not the least of which has been his continuing and sympathetic interest; Thea Thompson Hill, former librarian at the University of Nevada, for steering me to the files of early Nevada newspapers, and for the photograph of Dan De Quille; Caroline Wenzel, supervising librarian of the California section at the California State Library, and Neal R. Harlow, who lent his personal photographic equipment; and E. C. D. Marriage, Nevada state librarian, for information on Madame Mustache and for locating the *Washoe Times* of April 4, 1863.

My grateful appreciation goes to Helen Harding Bretnor, Elizabeth Bradfield Euphrat, and John Barr Tompkins of the Bancroft Library at the University of California for making available minstrel songs, newspapers, and other rare material and for reproducing several photographs and maps pertinent to this research; to Marguerite L. Sinclair, secretary of the Utah State Historical Society; Margaret G. Hickman, principal librarian of periodicals and newspapers at the Los Angeles Public Library; and to Mary Isabel Fry and Mary Jane Bragg, both of the Henry E. Huntington Library, for locating needed theatrical materials.

I am indebted to the late Walter F. Frear, former governor of Hawaii, for directing me to an appropriate photograph of Mark Twain; and to Anna S. Pratt and the Yale University Library for the use of that photograph in this book. For permission to reproduce photographs of certain actors and actresses I am indebted to Leslie E. Bliss and the Huntington Library; also to Ella I. Brennan and the M. H. de Young Memorial Museum.

I would like to express my appreciation to Ronald Coleman, building inspector for the city of Reno, for scraping parts of hundred-year-old newspapers from the walls of old cabins on the Comstock; to Lucius Beebe for correspondence regarding the Jack McNab-Howard shooting on the opening night of Maguire's Opera House; to the county clerk of Storey County for information regarding Judgment #1496 of Maguire and Burns; to Betty Sheldon for taking notes from the *Gold Hill News* of March, 1864; to Ann Ricks for information from *Valley Tan* on the Westwood troupe; to Belle Roberts of Austin for notes on Artemus Ward; to Arnold A. Miller for information on the Carson Brewery; to W. D. Bray for several suggestions used in Chapter 1; and to Mrs. Percy Train, curator of the Nevada Museum, for quoting an amusement advertisement from the *Aurora Times* of December 28, 1863.

I am grateful to Isobel Field for informative letters regarding the Indian peace celebration of the Comstock; to Mrs. E. Florence Folsom for particulars of the Hank Monk watch; to F. E. Meder for a copy of the sheet music, "The Hank Monk Schottische"; to the late Mrs. Sam Davis for reminiscences of early days in Carson; to Evelyn MacMinn for several chapter title suggestions; to Arthur H. Clark and Paul W. Galleher for their expert assistance in more ways than I can mention; to Lillian McKnight Thorpe for distribution suggestions; to Helen Horton, Gladys Boggess, and Janey Arratia for their assistance in typing parts of the book; to my students Pat O'Brien and Terri Sumida for help in preparing the index; and to my brother Dr. Carl A. Watson for making Ski Haven, his retreat in the Sierra Nevada, available for organizing and writing the manuscript. May I hasten to say that any errors of omission and commission are mine. To all those kind people who endeavored to help by giving of their time, information, and enthusiasm I am grateful.

In closing I wish to express my deep and sincere appreciation for the interest and help given me by Russell Gage, a colleague at Rosemead High School. To him I owe the elimination of many errors. And finally, my grateful thanks go to Professor George R. MacMinn of the California Institute of Technology for sharing with me his knowledge of frontier theatrical history and for the many hours he devoted to reading the original manuscript and helping me solve puzzling problems of form and presentation.

MARGARET G. WATSON

Reno, Nevada
March 1, 1964

Silver Theatre

Tarantula Juice

1

The way a people spend their leisure mirrors their hopes, fears, and desires more clearly than do their working actions. Early Nevada people worked hard because the desert, distances, isolation, and the business of living were hard taskmasters. In their leisure the people could follow their desires to the limit of their imaginations and available facilities. The theatre was an important factor in their lives. And the most prominent actors and actresses of the day — James Stark, Julia Hayne, Virginia Howard, McKean Buchanan, Frank Mayo, Adah Menken, Lotta Crabtree, and many others, who played before the rulers of Europe — were drawn to the candle-, oil-, and gas-lit stages of the desert. But the theatre was only one form of diversion. What did the pioneers do before the theatre arrived?

The story of Nevada entertainment cannot be told without occasionally digressing into the political, economic, social, and general background of the people. No one phase of living exists except in relation to everything else. To understand the kinds of amusements and the types of theatres that attracted the Washoites, a view of the stage in a historical setting is needed so that all aspects of daily living appear in correct perspective.

> "Paint me, in your word-lore,
>   Pictures of the Silver-land;
> Paint me Washoe, as you see it,
>   Tinting with a truthful touch;
> Limn it with a faithful pencil,
>   Do not color overmuch."

The early history of Nevada, the struggle against desert isolation and aridity, and the development of the Comstock Lode are more than history. The intensity of the struggle, the richness of the reward, and the emotional involvements are things out of which drama itself is made. Any account of the amusements of Silverland must progress with the small diggings above Gold Cañon, the discovery of the huge lode, and the development of the richest silver mines in the world.

2

Recreation of the emigrants was usually simple. Perhaps the thrill of each new day of travel could be considered entertainment, that is, when good health and freedom from anxiety of Indian attacks, "breakdowns," condition of cattle, food and water supplies permitted. Story-telling and singing were occasionally enjoyed. At evening with guards posted, the travelers, crouching over their camp fires, were free to visit, read, or write before "turning in" for the night. Some used the precious moments for keeping diaries. One emigrant penned derogatory lines to the Humboldt River: "meanest and muddiest, filthiest stream" — though it had probably saved his life.

However, relief and uncontrolled joy filled man and beast as both plunged into the cool water of the Carson River and dropped in the shade of "those longed-for trees." Behind now were the treacherous mirages, "meanest river" with its "gad-flies, musketoes, and gnats," the unending deserts, the alkali wastes, the swirling dry winds, and parching thirst. No wonder the spot where emigrants reached the Carson — Ragtown, a trading post about 10 miles from present Fallon — became memorable as a bit of heaven.

Amusements of the early traders, trappers, and miners were necessarily primitive. Loneliness was suffered by most; for contacts with the outside world were few. On Sundays the men washed their clothes, cleaned their cabins or camps, and "rested." Like the Indians they made eating an occasion, especially when a rancher from the valley drove up a cow or calf, slaughtered it at some convenient point, and roasted the whole by barbecue.[1]

If the pannings brought good returns, the miners "were not allowed to languish for want of amusement," related mining engineer William Wright (pseudonym, Dan De Quille).[2] Jacob Job, the leading merchant, used to deal faro and Billy Williams, a rancher from Carson Valley, occasionally "dealt for the boys a little game called 'twenty-one.'" Faro and twenty-one usually sent the Johntowners back to their rockers and toms, "each man a financial wreck."

In "Washoe Rambles" — a series of articles published in the *Golden Era* — Dan De Quille spoke of the lively crowd visiting his cabin at Silver City, where "fun was the order of the day and night, too, for the matter of that," especially after

> Mr. Wells (Johnny) of Carson City joined our men . . . and inducted us into the mysteries of a game with cards, called "growl Jack," which came near proving the death of me for I laughed till the tears ran down my cheeks and my sides ached at the singular freaks of the cards, in this most ridiculous of games, and poor Ned's "infernal luck." I am not sure that the game is mentioned in Hoyle, but it should be for the special benefit of dyspeptics.

Saturday evenings most of the boys went into Genoa, where Gilbert's Saloon invited, or to Carson City purportedly to sell their gold and bring back supplies. Upon leaving the stations, the miners inevitably bought a bottle of the infamous Tarantula Juice to assist them back to their diggings. Few men succeeded in varying the staple amusements of eating, sleeping, drinking, and gambling. But a new diversion was in the offing — nondescript dances.

---

[1] *Sacramento Daily Union*, November 8, 1854.

[2] As first historian of Washoe, William Wright has been drawn upon by nearly all later writers. His books, now rare, have perpetuated the facts and spirit of bonanza days.

3

The mining people of Gold Cañon and Hall's Station (Dayton)[3] get the credit for giving the first white man's dance in Nevada. Time: New Year's Eve, 1853; place: the log building over Spafford Hall's Store at the mouth of Gold Cañon. Only nine females, including little girls, attended the party, but possibly 150 men (miners, ranchers, and station keepers) from all over the country were there. When the party was at its height, the Washoe Indians [4] drove off some of the horses and barbecued them in a celebration of their own.

Despite the New Year's mishap, this first white man's dance stimulated other "grand balls" and as there were few women, the miners found it necessary to take in Miss Sarah Winnemucca, the Paiute Princess. "When the orchestra, a yallerbacked fiddle, struck up and the 'French four' was in order, the enthusiastic Johntowners went forth in the dance with ardor and filled the air with splinters from the puncheon floor," [5] never dreaming this same black-haired Princess would in a few years entertain them from the glittering stage of a theatre built in that wilderness.

The dances usually began demurely, but, as the miners became charged with Tarantula Juice, the "Cotillion parties" generally ended in "war dances." "Mines not doing much and times are awfully dull," stated an 1858 diary of Carson

---

[3] Spafford Hall started the little settlement on the Carson River. In 1854 he sold to James McMarlin, who promptly renamed it McMarlin's Station. The next year the Mormons brought about fifty Chinese from California to build a ditch to divert the waters of the Carson into Gold Cañon for mining purposes. The ditch completed, the Chinamen stayed on to mine — under the white man's restrictions, of course — and their camp nearby was known as Chinatown; Dayton as Johntown. Mineral Rapids and Nevada City also served as temporary names until 1861, when Mr. Day surveyed the townsite and the town settled on the name of Dayton. Dayton was the first place in Nevada to have a dance, a divorce, and a marriage.

[4] Most Indians heard the first English words from the emigrant ox drivers. No wonder the natives learned to exclaim, "How do you do. Whoa! Haw! God damn!" When asked about camping conditions on the Humboldt, the Indians told one emigrant party there was some grass for the "whoa! haws! but no water for the God damns!"

[5] Myron Angel, *History of Nevada*, 26-39.

Valley, "but there are plenty of dances here and the charge per couple is five dollars."

After they left Johntown in search of richer fields, the miners found it more difficult to get together for diversion. On Saturday nights some of the boys returned for the parties given by Eilley Cowan, an eccentric individual (later known as the "Washoe Seeress"). Aided by the potency of the Tarantula Juice served, even shy men like illiterate Sandy Bowers grew less restrained while others lunged about the room dancing with each other. When news came of "Gold!" in Six-Mile Cañon, Eilley moved her boarding house to the strike, and when soon afterwards she became Mrs. Lemuel (Sandy) Bowers, the miners noisily "shivareed" the couple, clanging drills on shovels, tossing rocks at the doorstep, and shooting their pistols. Alongside Eilley's restaurant Dutch Nick set up a large tent, from which he dispensed Tarantula Juice that the men drank for "protection" since those snakes or tarantulas biting them "got very sick" — or so the miners declared.

Tarantula Juice had another use too. "About this time," wrote Dan De Quille, " 'Old Virginia' was in camp one night, having a 'little run with the boys,' when he broke his whisky bottle against a rock." Lifting the bottom section of the bottle he solemnly poured the remaining liquid, saying "I christen this camp Virginia!" thus naming the town "in honor of himself and his native state." [6]

---

[6] To show their high regard for "Old Virginny" after he was thrown from a bucking mustang at Dayton on June 20, 1861, and killed, the people gave him an appropriate funeral; then passed a resolution and had it published in the *Enterprise* to say among other things "that James Finney was ever known among the people of this Territory as a generous, charitable, and honest man." — *Sacramento Daily Union*, July 8, 1861. Such high regard was not accorded Henry T. P. Comstock (called "Old Pancake" because he never took time to bake bread), who had forced his name on the great silver lode. Comstock made $10,000 from the mine, but killed himself years later because he was starving. The discoverers of the great Comstock Lode all came to want. Such men as Mackay, Fair, Sharon, Flood, Baldwin, and others, who made millions from the Lode, "were not there at the strike."

4

From over the mountains now came exhilarating news: an assay showed that the heavy black sand the miners had been cursing and throwing away was nearly solid silver. "Almost all of Genoa and Carson Valley have stampeded to the new mines," reported the *Territorial Enterprise* on November 12, 1859. And the *Alta California* noted that rum mills were becoming numerous "as also gamblers, the unual concomitants of a new and rich mineral country."

Snowfalls, however, drove most of the newcomers out of Virginia Town, Monroe City, Virginia Valley, Johntown, Dogtown, Carson City, and Genoa — the leading localities at the time — and back over the mountains. Then Washoe Zephyrs swept the snow in swirling eddies, cutting off all communication with the outside world and even between Gold Hill and Ophir (Virginia) though they were only a mile apart.

During the summer of 1859 Lyman Jones had built a "canvas hotel," including a saloon, of course. The "bar" consisted of an old sluice box; the bar fixtures were a pitcher and a dozen tin cups. It is unnecessary to add that "Jones' place was well-patronized." The side of a wagon box, which had been carried up the gulch on muleback, served as a bar in another saloon.

A few makeshift lodging houses had been thrown together before the snows came. These public places along with the saloons, sagebrush covered leantos, canvas tents, and the entrance to mines made up Virginia that terrible winter of 1859-60. Bean poker and old sledge were the principal amusements besides discussing, between gulps of Tarantula Juice, the great expectation for spring.

5

Almost any subject became a topic of discussion. Tales of achievement, adventure, and skirmishes with the Indians were retold. Snowshoe Thompson's daring feats and tricks performed on skis while carrying the mail into Washoe were recounted to advantage. A philosophical prospector whiled away some time by explaining the puzzling fact that no river of Washoe flows into the ocean. "The way it came about was in this wise," he said:

> The Almighty, at the time was creatin' and fashionin' of this here yearth, got along to this section late on a Saturday night. . . He had traced out the Humboldt river, and Truckee river, and Walker river, and Reese river . . . and he was leadin' of t'm along, calkerlatin' to . . . let 'em empty into the Gulf of Mexico or the Gulf of California, as might be most convenient; but . . . it came on dark and instead of tryin' to carry out the original plan, he just tucked the lower ends of the several streams into the ground, whar they have remained from that day to this.[7]

Not to be outdone, another man endeavored to give an explanation of "Washoe," insisting the word was "derived from a tribe of Indians that originally fed upon sagebrush and manufactured silver bullets." "When John Charles asked the chief, Gwin-ne-much-a, where he obtained the silver in the bullets, the chief replied . . . 'Me *way show* you,' and that being all he said, his tribe was named by Fremont the *Wayshow* tribe. But the *y* being a long letter, the Mormons gradually dropped it, and thus wrote the name afterwards Wa-shoe."

Another, "dissatisfied with this explanation, . . . called upon an aged Pi-ute," keeper of the toll gate at Devil's Gate, who explained that among an enemy tribe was a gigantic Indian, who during hostilities always wore shoes, which thus became known as war-shoes. "By an easy transition, his whole tribe were dubbed 'the War-shoes.' For the sake of euphony the r was dropped — and thus," declared "the aged Pi-ute, with a tear in his eye, you have the true root of Wa-shoe."

Undoubtedly the most popular tale told was the then recent

---

[7] William Wright, *The Big Bonanza*, 19-20.

Hank Monk-Horace Greeley episode,[8] which at length inspired a Nevada musician, John P. Meder (brother-in-law of
J. M. Benton, later owner of the stage line on which Hank
Monk was a driver), to do a piece of music entitled "The
Hank Monk Schottische," the cover of which was adorned
with a photograph of Hank Monk and a sketch of the coach
and the famous quotation.[9] The tale never lost flavor with
retelling and is repeated in Nevada today something like
this: When the editor of the *New York Tribune* crossed
Washoe in the summer of 1859, "the imperturbable Jehu who
handled the ribbons" of the stage coach was Hank Monk.
From Genoa the horses climbed slowly up the steep eastern
side of the mountains, and Horace Greeley, fearing he would
be late for a speaking engagement in Placerville, urged the
driver to hurry, but to no avail. Once over the summit of the
Sierra Nevada, however, the long-silent whip cracked; the
horses broke into a dead run down the steep slopes, the coach
careening around the edges of dizzy precipices. Greeley,
tossing about inside the bounding vehicle with the other
passengers, shouted at the driver that such haste was quite
unnecessary. "Keep your seat, Horace," replied the undaunted
Hank Monk with a fresh crack of the whip. "I'll get you there
on time!"

    According to Richardson's account, the Greeley story so

---

[8] References as basis for the oft-repeated story may be noted in Greeley's *An
Overland Journey from New York to San Francisco in the Summer of 1859.* The
famous humorist, Artemus Ward (Charles F. Browne) was probably the first to
put the tale into print in his *Complete Works* as early as 1862. Albert Richardson
related it in his *Beyond the Mississippi,* 1867. Mark Twain five years later could
not resist repeating it in *Roughing It;* and Dan De Quille, in some ways like his
friend Sam Clemens, felt *The Big Bonanza* would be incomplete without the story.
Walter Leman, the popular character actor, referred to the legend in his *Memories
of an Old Actor,* 1886; and C. C. Goodwin has it in *As I Remember Them,* 1913.

[9] Another such sketch was used on campaign posters when Horace Greeley ran
for the presidency of the United States. Under the stage coach and a team of dashing horses appeared the quotations:

"Coming events cast their shadows before."
"Keep your seat, Horace, we'll get you there on time."

pleased early tellers that they gave Monk a watch beautifully engraved with hunting scenes. Niece of composer John Meder, Mrs. Florence Meder Folsom, insists that the families connected with the stage line all knew Horace Greeley sent Hank Monk "the gold hunting case watch" with the famous quotation engraved inside. However, Greeley's does not appear among the 10 names [10] under the compliment: "Presented to Hank Monk as a testimonial of the appreciation of his friends for his skill and carefulness as a 'whip.' " Below the names is repeated the famous quotation: "Keep your seat, Mr. Greeley, I'll have you there," and the presentation date: "Dec. 1st, 1863." On his death bed Monk gave the watch to J. M. Benton.[11]

6

Besides stories, the dull winter was enlivened somewhat by wind storms, hat races, knockdowns, fist fights, and several bloody gun fights, "just to give a tone to society." When at last Johnny Moore and his gaunt, liquor-laden "Washoe Canaries" broke through the snowdrifts, the men grumbled at having to wait while Johnny put up his tent (15 by 52 feet), laid the first carpet in Virginia, raised the first flag, hung a canvas partition to divide the hotel part from the barroom, made a counter from the sideboard of an emigrant wagon, and unpacked the precious casks. Then the men rushed to the bar, consumed $200-worth of liquor before nightfall, and clamored for more.[12]

Soon the miners were renewing operations. "They are in-

---

[10] One name so engraved is that of George Hearst, father of William Randolph Hearst.

[11] So many people asked to see the watch, Mr. Benton kept it in the safe of the Virginia and Truckee freight office. Since then the watch has passed through many hands, including those of V. L. McBride, proprietor of the Bucket of Blood saloon in Virginia City. A plaque put up April 30, 1938, on the Raffles Hotel in Placerville bears this inscription: "To remember Hank Monk, the world's greatest reinman, who drove Horace Greeley from Carson City to here in 1859, making the 109 miles in 10 hours."

[12] Eliot Lord, *Comstock Mining and Miners,* 66-67.

sane on silver," lamented the *Alta California*. "Go where you will, in the street, in the countinghouse, in the saloon, at home — and we had almost said at church — and the topic is Washoe." Men piled on the Sacramento-to-Folsom train (first railroad in California) to ride twenty-two miles to make stage connections for Placerville and over the Sierras. Some accompanied large saddle trains. Many came as "foot passengers" dressed in heavy shirts of blue, red, or gray, their pants stuffed into leather boots, their blankets and baggage in packs on their backs. William Stewart, Judge Terry, and tunnel-builder Adolph Sutro were among those who now sought their fortunes in Silverland.

And men would have amusement be it drinking "miserable liquors" such as Tarantula Juice at 25¢ per drink; gambling at faro and monte tables, which were "in active operation in every camp"; or smoking a pipe or "stogies." (As for cigarettes, only Mexicans and "the not-nice girls on D Street" smoked them.) Tarantula Juice, "sure death at a thousand yards," was the staff of life in Washoe, the food, raiment, lodging, and amusement.

Mart Taylor

1

Nevada scored theatrically in 1860. That year the Washoites would welcome their first professional entertainer; pack
their own first theatre; and applaud there the first complete
theatrical troupe.[1] With heightened interest the miners now
noted that the "incomparable" Billy Birch and Wells' Minstrels were amusing the near-by California camps and would
"proceed to Washoe"; that Mart Taylor also planned coming;
that he had opened a "theatre, as it is called," for the three
hundred or more miners at Mono Lake Diggings, where songs
"of his own manufacture of local adaption" met with "great
applause." But as yet this pioneer Thespian had not reached
Silverland.

In fact, a stampede had begun back to California as the
Indians were on the warpath and the Pony Express riders
were shouting, "Miller's Station burned by Piutes!"[2] Even
when the Indian trouble was apparently over, men hesitated
while a "grab game of unoccupied claims" went on.[3] As

[1] Except for the Westwood Troupe and a few scattered players, theatrical people
reached Silverland by way of San Francisco.

[2] To replace the burned stations, new buildings were constructed along a 500-
mile line of the Pony Express. Climaxing completion of important Fort Churchill
was a celebration with flags, parading and beer. For accounts of the Pony Express
and the Nevada Indian War of 1860, see the *Territorial Enterprise* for May 5,
1860; the San Francisco *Evening Bulletin* of May 13, 26, 31, and June 25, 1860;
the *Sacramento Daily Union*, August 13, 15, 1860. Because so many stations were
burned, riders were not allowed to leave San Francisco until June, when twenty
picked men accompanied the mail as far as Salt Lake City. Expresses from the
East, brought part way across the prairies by Pony Bob and Bill Cody, also had
been held in the Mormon city.

[3] J. Ross Browne, writing "A Peep at Washoe" for *Harper's Magazine*, reduced
Virginia City and Carson City at this time to the following pungent essences:

summer advanced, business grew better, especially in the saloons and "other houses of entertainment." And as early as February 26 Washoites had read in the *Call:*

> WASHOE. — There is a determination to gratify the population of this now famous locality with dramatic representations, and several companies will be on their way thither as soon as the roads will admit of travelling and suitable transportation.

These companies were evidently deterred the same as "Billy Birch and his negrophilists. It is whispered," chuckled the *Call*, "that Billy lost his scalp in an encounter with the 'battle-ax' Indians. But this is probably a bald hoax." [4]

But Mart Taylor finally arrived. And he brought with him the "Taylor Family — whoever they were, if anybody — or one Joe Bowers and somebody else." Mart may have given the entire program alone; he was versatile enough, singing, acting, reciting, joking, and rhyming for the Washoites, "nevertheless, notwithstanding."

"In the mountain cities, barring the two circuses and a few strolling histrions of no note, we have nothing to record," wrote the theatrical critic in the September 20, 1860, issue of the *Call*, "saving and excepting the following humorous bill, which we consider 'with the powder.' It is characteristic of that mad wag, Mart Taylor, and will forcibly remind our readers of the programme of the renowned Mr. Mullat, as well as show the public to what shifts the mountain strollers have to resort in order to attract attention. Read it:"

THEATRE

THE TAYLOR FAMILY, having just returned from Washoe Valley and Mono Lake, where, for the past six months, they have been

---

"Virginia City — a mud-hole; climate, hurricanes and snow; water, a dilution of arsenic, plumbago and copperas; wood, none at all except sagebrush; no title to property, and no property worth having. Carson City — a mere accident; occupations of the inhabitants, waylaying strangers bound for Virginia; business, selling whisky, and so dull at that men fall asleep in the middle of the street going from one groggery to another; productions, grass and weeds in the Plaza."

[4] San Francisco *Daily Morning Call*, June 3, 1860.

wandering and performing, meeting with sagebrush, Indians, and ducks in abundance, as also the great scarcity of grub and whisky, feel satisfied that a truthful and poetical description of things in Brigham Young's so-styled dominions will be thankfully received and duly appreciated by all those who prefer a candid del--neation of circumstances to time and tune. Yet, however, nevertheless, notwithstanding, but it should be distinctly understood that where-as the performance of this troupe partake not of an extreme political, sectional, religious, or pugilistic nature, it is hoped that the ladies will, by their presence on each and every occasion, inspire the Taylor Family to try and earn a good reputation as well as the four bits charged for admission.

The Taylor Family, assisted by the world renowned URA VIOLINIST and A [hand sign] SOME DOOR-KEEPER, will give one of their purely original, vastly comical, and highly poetical performances at Georgetown, on Saturday evening, August 18th, when will be presented the following

PROGRAMME

Opening Lines	Mart Taylor
Way the Money Goes	Mr. Taylor
Poor Old Mining Gentleman	Mr. M. Taylor
Peep at the Mines (new poem)	Taylor
Benicia Boy Song	M. Taylor
Taylor's Nose	Mart Taylor Esq.
Punning Poem	Mr. Mart Taylor
Ri fol lol	Taylor Family
Pike's Visit to Placerville	M. Taylor, Esq.
Ideal and Real (poem)	Author
My Sister	By her Disconsolate Brother

The whole to conclude with a LOCAL SONG, composed by Mart Taylor and sung by the Taylor Family, in which strictly complimentary mention will be made of the male citizens of this place.

Doors open soon after dark. Performance commences when all get in. Children in arms admitted. Front seats reserved for Ladies. No grumbling at the performance. No counterfeit money taken at the door. The audience is expected to applaud.

Admission. — Dress Circle fifty cents. Parquette four bits. Other parts of the house half a dollar.

Music furnished for dancing.

The hind wagon pays all toll.

Though this was the entertainment bill for Georgetown, a
mining camp 14 miles north of Placerville (Old Hangtown)
on the western side of the Sierra Nevada, what Washoe of
"Brigham Young's so-styled dominions" received in entertainment requires little imagination. Many of the same numbers, no doubt. Yet slanted to affairs and people in Silverland,
Taylor's efforts must have received as unrestrained approval
as at other diggings, where Mart directed his opening song to
"our liberal mining friends" and understandably sang:

> The luring hope of gold, has tempted you to roam
> Far from your friends and relatives, who mourn for you at home.
> 'Tis *hope* that lured you on, 'tis hope that does sustain,
> And hope stands by you while you toil, yes, hope of golden gain.

2

A Monoville placer miner, who in 1859 saw Taylor in
action, remembered him as "the man with the tremendous
nose who . . . travelled from town to town with a variety troupe, and whose strong hold it was to get up a local
song in every camp he visited, bringing in a hit at all prominent characters in the place." In Washoe Bill Stewart, Dan
De Quille, saloon keepers, and mine superintendents probably
took the brunt of Taylor's 20-foot-long song.

Twenty-five years later, upon learning that Mart was still
alive at Red Bluff, California, the Monoville miner would
further recall and inform the *Territorial Enterprise* (August
16, 1884) that at Monoville Taylor held forth in a tent saloon.
"As we were all leaving the camp to winter on the California
side of the mountains, Mart got up a farewell song, and the
whole camp gathered to his tent to hear it. . . Before the
day was ended Mart had very little of his stock of liquors, but
had in lieu thereof a fat sack of gold dust." Mart's local song
always went by the same tune. "He would write it out upon
sheets of foolscap, paste them all to-gether, and when he came
upon the stage would toss the roll from him, showing a song
about 20-feet long. . . Poor old Mart! Alas, poor Yorick."

On those rare occasions in Silverland when women were in the audiences, Mart took special notice of the fact by singing

> The ladies have come in to-night,
>> And I must now address them,
> And say they're beautiful, polite,
>> And lovely, too, God bless them;
> Although they're all hooped up, sometimes,
>> I'll pledge we will not heed it;
> The coopers, all, will tell us that
>> The *weaker vessels* need it.

Sometime during the evening Taylor probably did the eighth number of his Georgetown program, the popular

Ri Fol Lol

> Since singing has become the rage,
> And good attention does engage,
> Whenever brought upon the stage
>> In any town or city,
> I've just come out and made my bow,
> And if you'll listen to me now,
> I'll try and please you anyhow,
>> By singing you a ditty.

SPOKEN. — Now you mustn't expect me to sing as well as Jenny Lind, for she is a real Martingale, but I'll sing you a favorite song of mine, and that is —

> Ri fol lol lol lu ral laddie, ri fol lol ral lu ral la,
> Ri fol lol lol lu ral laddie, ri fol lol lu ri do.

❀ ❀ ❀ ❀

> With present laurels discontent,
> There's many politicians bent
> On being our next President,
>> To rule the Yankee nation;
> Buchanan, Fillmore and Wise
> And Lane and Houston, will arise
> And use the power that in them lies,
>> To get the situation.

SPOKEN. — There are many others who will try to get the situation, no doubt, but I think the best one among them will be he who can best explain the great principles of

> Ri fol lol . . .

Mart Taylor was no amateur in the entertainment world. For a decade or more before his Washoe appearance, he had been entertaining in the interior and at San Francisco, reciting, and composing and singing "to the only tune I ever knew, and in a style I have never heard recommended." The performances, according to the modest preface in one of Mart Taylor's popular booklets, *Local Lyrics* and *Miscellaneous Poems,* "have, upon every occasion, been received with marked favor by the large and respectable audience who have from time to time patronized" the San Francisco Melodeon. At least two volumes of songs — widely used by all outstanding Sons of Momus — attest to Mart Taylor's talent.

3

Where Taylor appeared in Silverland to sing songs from his *Gold Digger's Song Book* is conjecture. Genoa? Most likely. Other than Virginia City, it was the largest and the oldest town in Washoe, though the entertainer had been warned to bring "some kind of vermifuge, for the bed bugs here are the equal to the plague of Egypt." Having for months previously rambled through the mountain camps, often hungry and sleeping on the ground, it is doubtful that the father of the Washoe theatre allowed Genoa bedbugs to stop a performance. Moreover, Taylor, "his musician, and doorkeeper" probably slept in Mr. Gardner's haystack, sharing it with those witnesses who had escaped being shot as they galloped out of Virginia City to testify in Washoe's first important mining trial. When the haystack burned shortly after Taylor left Washoe, the papers considered it "a public calamity" as "members of the court were in the habit of sleeping in it . . . to avoid the bedbugs at the hotels or the payment of lodging."

Momentarily glad to forget bedbugs and differences, judges, attorneys, and witnesses, no doubt, enjoyed Mart's new version of

Bobbin' 'Round

As through the mines I wend my way,
    Bobbin' 'round and 'round and 'round,
I'll tell you what I have to say
    As I go bobbin' 'round.

They follow fashions rather strange,
    Bobbin' 'round and 'round and 'round,
But in their pants there's little *change,*
    A bobbin' 'round and 'round.

The folks at Salt Lake spend their lives,
    A bobbin' 'round and 'round and 'round
Old Brigham Young has seventy wives,
    Which keeps him bobbin' 'round.

From Genoa, Mart Taylor probably went to Carson City. Certainly he appeared on the Lode. With the fresh mining excitement and the rush to the silver camp, how could he have resisted climbing Sun Mountain to sing, dance, and cavort for the amusement-hungry Comstockers? Dressed in Chinese costume complete with smock and cue, he most likely reminded his listeners of

John Chinaman's Appeal

Americans now mind my song
    If you would but hear *me sing,*
And I will tell you of the wrong,
    That happened unto "Gee Sing."
In "fifty-two" I left my home —
    I bid farewell to "Hong Kong" —
I started with Cup Gee to roam
    To the land where they use the "long tom."

    O ching ki ku tong mo ching ching,
      O ching ki ku tong *chi do,*
    Cup Gee Ki ku tong mo ching ching,
      Then what could Gee or I do?

The listening miners might have had stabs of conscience at their mistreatment of the "Celestials," notwithstanding. At the end of the lengthy song, the men broke into "great applause." And thus encouraged, Mart sang "Poor Diggings" or the parody on "We are all a Panning."

Evenings spent with big-nosed Mart Taylor, "one Joe Bowers, and somebody else" were occasions to remember; for the father of the Nevada theatre was far from lacking in dramatic ingenuity, adaptability, or appeal. No record is found, however, of Taylor's returning to Washoe, even during bonanza days. His adaptability was the theatre's loss; for Taylor took up the profession of school teaching, returning only occasionally to the stage as "improvisator to deliver an original poem" or piece before local debating, temperance, or dramatic societies in Stockton and other California towns.

Washoe's First Theatre

1

Now comes one of the choicest pieces of theatre fare. Father-of-the-Nevada-theatre Mart Taylor had scarcely left Washoe — if indeed he had gone — when a group of players as intrepid and bold as Mart himself arrived in the town that was "fast losing its canvas appearance." "Pearlman is putting up a large brick store, running from B to A Street, and" — here one's attention is arrested — "a theatre is in the course of erection above A Street. . ." Thus wrote the *Call's* Virginia City correspondent on the evening of August 25, 1860, the earliest extant newspaper notice regarding the first theatre building in what is now the state of Nevada.[1]

Who was building this theatre? Some enterprising local person? What troupe would dare the uncertainties of a Washoe reception to play in it? The answers to these questions lay in P. M. Westwood and his dramatic company. Though they had to travel through Paiute lands, including the very route of the recent hostilities (yet the minstrels and other troupes — all but Mart Taylor — had been "driven back by the Indians!"), these determined and resourceful players from Utah Territory, undaunted by Indians or reverses, or at finding no theatre in Washoe, set about building one.

That these players were willing to cross six hundred miles

---

[1] Extant newspapers that refer to the building and opening of Washoe's first theatre, chronologically arranged, are:

San Francisco *Daily Morning Call*, August 31, 1860
San Francisco Weekly Bulletin, September 15, 1860
Sacramento Daily Union, October 1, 1860
San Francisco *Daily Morning Call*, October 4, 1860

of dangerous desert to live, build, and perform in a raw mining town tells something of their caliber. Neither amateurs
nor "strolling players" (as Eliot Lord indicates in his *Comstock Mining and Miners*), the Westwood company were
seasoned actors and actresses, who had played in Salt Lake
City until the coming of Johnston's army pushed the theatre
aside.

Forty miles south of the Mormon city, however, federal
troops welcomed theatrical diversion. To Camp Floyd, therefore, went Philip Westwood and the best of the Salt Lake
City players, including the actor's sister Mercy, brother
David, Mrs. Westwood, Mrs. Whitlock, and others. With the
help of Johnston's soldiers the troupe built a crude theatre,
arranged shows for the soldier-audiences for two years, and
received lengthy "theatrical notices" in *Kirk Anderson's Valley
Tan*, which praised Dick White (a camp Floyd sergeant and
former actor, who had joined the Westwood company) as a
"first rate comedian," [2] but neglected to even mention Philip
Westwood.[3] But P. M. Westwood was in Camp Floyd at the
close of the long season; for he it was who led the players to
pioneer a new theatre in the Washoe of Western Utah.

Along with their neighbors, the Tucketts, the Westwoods
had left England for America. Upon reaching St. Louis death
struck in both families and money being scarce, sixteen-year-
old Mercy worked for a time in the household of Roswell
Field.[4] To help the cholera-stricken families, Philip West-

---

[2] Some writers say Richard White, growing restless as a soldier, secured the Salt
Lake actors and opened the Camp Floyd theatre.

[3] This omission seems odd; for Mrs. Lillie Tuckett Freeze (Liela Tuckett),
daughter of Mercy Westwood Tuckett, maintained her uncle Philip went with the
Salt Lake City troupers to play Camp Floyd. It is perhaps possible that P. M.
Westwood, being a leader and of independent nature, started the Military Dramatic
Association and then himself played with another troupe at nearby Spanish Fork —
as Mrs. Freeze once hinted in further recalling for George D. Pyper (*Romance of
an Old Playhouse*) that as a little girl she learned fancy dancing from Sergeant
White at Camp Floyd and appeared between acts of the programs, in which her
mother and Richard White played the leading roles.

[4] Little did Mercy Westwood dream that the story-loving little boy for whom she
cared would become America's greatest children's poet, Eugene Field.

wood, remembering his experiences in the English theatre, organized a dramatic company. His sister Mercy became a member of this group, and though "naive," she seems to have pleased audiences. She pleased Henry Tuckett too, for a time at least — for they married and with the others moved to Utah.

Mercy Westwood Tuckett was the first woman to appear before the footlights in Washoe. The first lady of the Nevada theatre deserves, therefore, a few more words of introduction. Lovely and brown-haired, Mercy was a young actress with a cheerful disposition, sweet voice, and responsive smile; and, like her brother Philip, "showed marked dramatic ability." In fact, Brigham Young, who appreciated theatrical talent, had asked Mercy to entertain the Mormons at the Bowery and at Social Hall. Here, as earlier in St. Louis and later at Camp Floyd, she was pleasantly received as she soon would be on a new stage set high on a silver ledge in the mountain deserts of Washoe.

When the army at Camp Floyd was called East, the Military Dramatic Association reorganized, accepted $275 for their scenery,[5] packed their costumes and families in wagons, bade farewell to their homes and friends at Frogtown (now Fairfield), and headed for Washoe. Unfortunately Mercy was forced to leave behind her two older children. She could care for baby Philip and intended sending for the others. Back in Salt Lake City Mercy's husband, however, took the occasion to divorce Mercy and secure custody of the older children. Mercy's intention when *settled* of sending for her children was clearly in accord with the plan and philosophy of the company. Quite the reverse of "strolling players," the Westwood troupers desired to settle, build a theatre where they

---

[5] The enterprising Mormons bought and hauled the scenery into Salt Lake City for their new stage. Already they had gathered the iron wheels from Johnston's burned wagons and were hammering the iron into nails for constructing the new theatre.

found none, and serve for years the community needs for diversion as they had done at St. Louis, Salt Lake City, and Camp Floyd.

2

Since lots were selling from $200 to $1000 (seldom with a valid title at that) and lumber prices ran from $175 to $300 per thousand, it is hardly reasonable to suppose that Philip Westwood assumed all the financial responsibility and risk. Indicating that a Mr. Howard was financial backer of the enterprise, "the building, a large wooden one above A Street," was called the Howard, which, a Washoe correspondent wrote regarding the troupe, "has been built by their own hands almost, the scenes painted, and all the innumerable adjuncts of a theatre provided within seven short weeks."

"Seven short weeks" to put in foundations; build the theatre, the stage, benches, and "innumerable adjuncts!" Then construct the scenery and paint it — with more, it is hoped, than a solution of mustard and shoe blacking as at Camp Floyd, assemble costumes and stage props! By September first the Carson City *Territorial Enterprise* could announce:

> THEATRE AT VIRGINIA. — A theatre of respectable dimensions and appearance has been completed at Virginia, and will shortly be used for dramatic entertainment. It is the pioneer theatre on the Eastern slope.

Though located on a dusty, and as yet unnamed "street," Nevada's pioneer theatre was finished. Eagerly the Washoites awaited the announcement of its opening.

Soon in a column entitled "Our Washoe Letter," the *Call* gave this intelligence and query:

> . . . And now, sir, there is but one thing more that I would wish earnestly to impress on the minds of your readers in the business: We want light — we want a newspaper. There is probably no town in the whole of the U.S., as large as Virginia City, destitute of a newspaper.

A theatre commences operation to-night. Whoever heard of a theatre before a newspaper? Such an institution would pay well, and no doubt there are many who would willingly engage in the enterprise. . .

Hoping to hear of this intellectual business starting this fall, I remain,

Yours, etc.,
One of the F.F.V.'s

"A theatre commences operation tonight." So a dedicatory address had been written, a program decided upon, and made ready. With only Mart Taylor as a precedent, what had Philip decided best suited Washoe tastes?

On September 28, 1860, the *Sacramento Union* correspondent, who had been in the Washoe mines since early summer, wrote his paper:

> However inappropriate it may have seemed to those who last winter saw a few scattered tents and shanties dubbed with the sonorous title of Virginia City, none will . . . deny that we are fast assuming, if we have not already reached, a size that will fairly entitle us to the name of city. . . The Howard Theatre is also completed and will open to-morrow night with "The Toodles," and the time-honored farce of the "Swiss Swains." The company is one from Salt Lake, where their performances are said to have been received with marked favor. Being the pioneers of the drama on the eastern slope, they will be, doubtless, well received.

Were they? As curtain time neared, the first-nighters struggled up the hill on foot and in carriages. Miners, gamblers, saloonmen, millmen, merchants, mule skinners, prospectors, and, at least, some of the "139 females" of the town (but not Julia Bulette of ill-fame) surged into the new playhouse, filled the 700 available seats and overflowed along the sides.

Accustomed to an overture by the 10-piece orchestra from Johnston's Seventh Infantry Band, the Westwood troupe certainly must have secured some sort of an orchestra for the Howard. No doubt, several selections were played while the

crowd quieted. Then the curtain went up and the Washoites
got their first view of the candle-lit stage. A moment later
Philip Westwood appeared and delivered "the opening address at the opening of the first theatre ever built in Nevada,
viz., the Howard." [6]

One may well assume that the dedication remarks were
enthusiastically applauded; for the Comstockers appreciated
the initiative, courage, and effort of the Westwood troupe.
"Certainly they have been energetic and, if one may judge
from the crowd of last night, are likely to reap a full reward. . . The performance consisted of *Toodles* and *The
Swiss Swains* — the former play, the first ever produced in
Nevada, being exceedingly well rendered," wrote an "Occasional Correspondent" the next day.[7]

3

Undoubtedly, P. M. himself played the inebriate Timothy
Toodles, a role which carried the humor element through an
otherwise serious complication that included double crossing,
lying, and a hanging. The role of a drunkard was under-
standable to a Washoe audience, who could appreciate
Toodles being "drunk in the legs, in the knees, in the heels,
in the hands, and not in merely the preposterous necktie, the
absurd hat, the thumbless gloves," or the coat buttoned in the
wrong places.

The character of the wife also had possibilities; for Mrs.
Toodles, never able to resist an auction sale, was continually

---

[6] San Francisco *Daily Morning Call*, December 2, 1860; *Virginia Daily Union*,
December 2, 1864.

[7] Eliot Lord's review of that first Westwood performance in Virginia City:
"though the fancy of the audience was mightily strained to supply the requisite
stage-setting . . . and the 'star' was of the tenth magnitude. . ." (Lord,
op. cit., p. 93), seems erroneous in light of extant newspaper reviews and the
known background of the Westwood troupe. Also, the Westwood company performed in a theatre — a new theatre, one they had designed, built, decorated, and
dedicated to the drama — and not in a canvas tent, saloon, or store as both Mr.
Lord and Dr. Riegel infer (Robert C. Riegel, *America Moves West*, p. 461).

bringing home "bargains." The emotions in the play were definite: the villain was bad; the heroine pure. Mercy Tuckett probably as "Mary Acron, the good and virtuous daughter, niece, and betrothed bride, suffering for the faults of others," must have elicited the sympathy and admiration of that first Howard Theatre audience.

Then the wicks were trimmed, low candles snuffed or new ones added, and the stage set for the afterpiece of *The Swiss Swains*. Written by comedian B. Webster, this follow-up farce, an operetta in one act, also had been first produced in Haymarket, London. But by 1850 it had reached the United States, where, along with *The Toodles*, it was sweeping the country. The comedy opened on a rustic scene showing Dame Glib trying to marry the "no-account" Swig to her daughter Rosette. When Dame Glib chided Swig on a too-apparent weakness, he replied, "If it's a failing, it's a family one, ever since Adam tasted cider in the juice of an apple. Wine doubles the beauties of women, and reconciles us to the reality when we are sober." Dame Glib had no reply to such reasoning. She could only fuss, "Talk, talk!" But Rosette's lover returned unexpectedly from war and humorous complications arose involving a wine keg and Swig, distraught love, a duel, and bloodshed. All the tricks were there and everything turned out well.[8]

Of course, Dame Glib was not performed as Mrs. Judah would have done her and future productions were smoother; yet a large part of the Howard's audience, though outwardly no cognoscente, were not without theatrical judgment based on the culture they had left behind. And they undoubtedly rewarded the troupe with enthusiastic applause and "financial expressions of appreciation" before making their way happily homeward under a clear, star-studded, autumn sky.

---

[8] F. C. Wemyss, ed., *The Minor Drama*, vol. 15, p. 17.

4

No theatrical troupe came to Silverland for only a one-night stand, least of all the pioneer Thespians from Utah. "If one may judge from the crowd of last night, [the Westwood company] are likely to reap a full reward." This newspaper insertion would indicate future evenings for the new Howard Theatre as would the published sentence of October 12: "The theatre at Virginia City appears to be thriving."

Anxious for more excitement in an already over-stimulated life, the Comstockers, no doubt, enjoyed such plays as had pleased the Mormons and Johnston's soldiers: *The Golden Farmer*, Kotzebue's *The Stranger*, *All That Glitters Is Not Gold*, and *The Widow's Victim*, along with such afterpieces as *The Irish Tutor, My Neighbor's Wife*, and *The Irish Attorney*. It is highly probable, as George D. Pyper indicated in his *Romance of an Old Playhouse*, that Richard White started for California, but joined the Westwood group in Washoe to play opposite Mercy Tuckett as he had at Camp Floyd in such plays as *The Pride of the Market, Sheridan's Rivals*, Schiller's five-act tragedy of *The Robbers*, and Bulwer-Lytton's *The Lady of Lyons*, in which Mercy as Pauline had elicited the following:

> . . . When we consider the high character of the piece, and the manner in which it has generally been produced with . . . Julia Dean, Ellen Tree, Helen Fawcette, and a host of others for Pauline, it is no slight praise to say the piece was well performed.

Even so, some productions at the Howard were undoubtedly "rough in comparison" to those of large city theatres:

> . . . Added to balls, we have also had other pleasures, concerts and theatres, and though rough in comparison to city enjoyments, yet well attended and grateful to those long absent from them.

THE HANK MONK SCHOTTISCHE

Inspired by the Greeley-Monk account, this composition by a Nevada
musician was decorated with a sketch of the dashing team and coach,
and imprinted with the famous quotation:
"Keep your seat Horace, I'll get you thar on time."

HOME FOR THE BOYS

During the dreary winter of 1859-60 the Comstockers left their nondescript hovels, struggled through drifting snows, and pushed into
the lighted and comparatively warm saloons, seeking companionship
and diversion — if of self-created variety.
From a contemporary woodcut.

DIAGRAM OF THE WASHOE SILVER MINES.

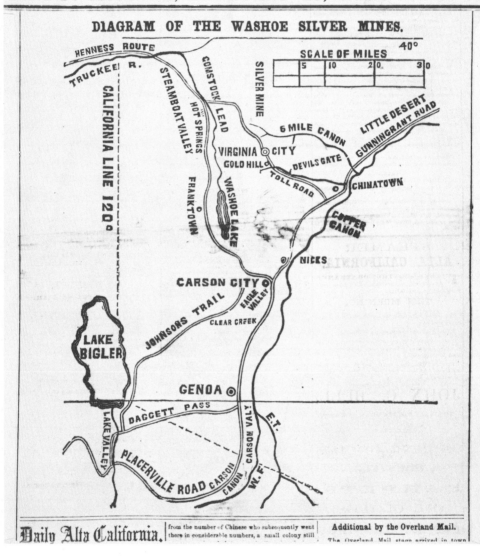

5

As long as the box office did well, the Westwood troupers found living not too unpleasant on the Lode. A new bath house had opened along with ten laundries; two barber shops; two Stationers; a post office, which had "daily dispatches"; ten livery stables; nine restaurants; two fruit stores; four butcher shops; thirty-eight general stores; and twenty-five saloons, which dispensed certain liquids from "clinking glasses, an accompaniment to the whistles of the mills." And there were churches. On Sunday, the day after opening Nevada's first theatre, the players could have attended Father Gallagher's Catholic Church in that same Howard Theatre, the Reverend Rooney's Methodist services at Empire House, or one of any of the other "major denominations." [9]

Unlike some actors who followed them, the Westwoods did not forsake their professions to go mining. They rather reversed the procedure, becoming a part of the community first, building the theatre and performing in it. But — like Washoe's zealous church-goers who, unable to attend theatres, dances, or parties, entertained guests by taking them through the mines — the Thespians undoubtedly visited the Ophir, where a 45-foot vein of ore now lay exposed. Ore, hoisted in cars along an incline track from the rich bonanza heart, fed the quartz mills. Seeming to resent the intrusion of man-made shafts, tunnels, and stopes, the earth began creeping together. Worried mine owners sought brief relief in the dramas performed on the Howard stage. Philip Deidesheimer finally solved the grave problem by devising "square set" timbering, which, however, was so expensive a method

---

[9] The major religious denominations began early vying with each other in the raising of money and in the building of churches. The Catholic Church under construction in Virginia City was blown down by a Washoe Zephyr; hence, Carson City won the race and opened "on Sunday, November 4th, the first Catholic Church in Western Utah."

all prices soared. Flour shot up to $60 a hundred, sugar to 50 cents a pound, and candles to light the Howard cost a dollar a pound.

Exactly how long the Westwood company played Virginia City is unknown. They probably made a tour of Silverland as Dayton had its Spafford Hall seating 250 people; Franktown and Genoa each had halls seating 200 and 280. Washoe's interest in the theatre spurred John Q. A. Moore and his partner Charley Parker to extend their saloon several hundred feet back, making for Carson City a theatre that seated 300 — though the proprietors often crowded in more.

This Saloon Theatre had a stage and proscenium and soon afterwards a drop curtain showing a "well-painted scene" of Yosemite Valley. Reserved seats were comfortable chairs. A door cut through the wall into the alley made entrance easier for ladies and their escorts; lone males generally came in directly from the saloon. As a finishing touch the proprietors painted "Moore's Theatre Saloon" in huge black letters on the "pretentious false front" of the building.[10] To open this new playhouse the saloonkeepers secured the Westwood troupe, who may have found Carson City "a very pleasant place" since the Carsonites insisted they had "all the luxuries that one can get in the cities of California," plus a "watering place," where the weary actors could also go "on bright moonlight nights with beautiful women to dance to the strains of delicious music, or stroll on the surrounding hills while the beautiful valley bathed in a flood of silvery light" lay spread at their feet.[11]

6

Although the fall rains made streets anything but pleasant, the "jovial Comstockers could not resist the fascination which

[10] According to Angel's history, Moore's Theatre was the first playhouse in Carson City.

[11] From a clipping of Carson City, Utah Territory, August 10, 1860, in the Bancroft Library.

Mr. Brown, the able and courteous proprietor of the International, had so liberally opened to their senses" in "A Ball at Virginia." "Who could resist the smiles of beauty and the inspiring sounds of the violin?" when there was "plenty of champagne, plenty of music, plenty of masculines, but *few*, very few of the fair sex (I believe only twelve). However, what they lacked in numbers they made up in agility."

Several weeks later everyone was agile as well as agitated. A fire broke out. Though it was the first in the city's history, destroying only a blacksmith shop, the Comstockers were duly concerned as were the editors of the newly-arrived *Territorial Enterprise*, who called a mass meeting in Howard's Theatre and organized a 40-member fire company, "Virginia Hook and Ladder Company, Number 1."

Early in November while P. M. Westwood and his company were entertaining elsewhere in Washoe, some "first class artists" of the German theatre arrived from "Maguire's beautiful Opera House in San Francisco." Were the Washoites ready for opera? Grand opera! Opera was the Gruenwalds' forte; and they had come to dispense that form of musical entertainment throughout Silverland. Were advance *Enterprise* notices perhaps too enthusiastic? Would Comstockers, like Colorado theatregoers four years later, declare themselves "decidedly disappointed in their expectations"? According to the lone surviving press account, however, such seems not to have been the case in Silverland:

> THEATRICALS IN WASHOE. — There is a large company in Washoe at the head of which is Mr. and Mrs. Gruenwald, the well known popular artistes. They have recently been playing at the Howard Theatre, Virginia City.[12]

No doubt, the "large company" gave opportunity for variety and latitude such as was not possible with "only two performers" at Denver. With the Gruenwald performances

---

[12] San Francisco *Daily Morning Call*, December 2, 1860.

comes the first knowledge of prices charged at the Howard.
Practically a theatrical suburb of San Francisco, it is not
surprising that tickets cost the same as at Maguire's theatre
there: "Dress Circle and Orchestra Seats, $1.00: Parquette,
50¢: Gallery, 25¢: Reserved Seats, 50¢ extra."

Choosing from their San Francisco repertoire, Mr. and
Mrs. Gruenwald sang comic duets in German, which were
"especially enjoyed." Then the "large company" joined in
singing arias, ballads, comic songs, chorus numbers, and
favorite selections from *Romeo, Norma,* and *The Daughter
of the Regiment.*

When five hundred gobbling turkeys strode into Virginia
City — driven all the way from California as an "advance
guard" for Thanksgiving Day, the Gruenwalds decided to
stay on for a drumstick or two and so treated appreciative
audiences of Carson City and other inhabited centers of
Silverland with varied opera programs. Sometime in December the "popular artistes" climbed aboard the westbound
stages and headed back for California, leaving Washoe to
the Westwood troupe.

7

The approach of winter sent the floating population over
the mountains, too. December snows blocked the summits,
damaged stations, and trimmed the branches off hundreds of
trees. Gradually the camps drew into themselves. But Nevadans, remembering New Year's Eve dance of 1853 as the
first, made plans for December 24, 1860, which arrived calm,
white, and splendid to usher in the first Christmas Eve ball
of Virginia, thus starting a Comstock tradition.

Though only twelve had attended the dance at the International Hotel in October, sixteen ladies now appeared in the
splendor of their limited wardrobes — women coming to the
desert usually arranged to have at least one special outfit.
Mr. and Mrs. John Tilton — from their cabin home built by

Tilton himself at D and Union Streets on the site where two and a half years later Thomas Maguire's splendid Opera House would stand and over which a legal battle would rage — also attended the Christmas festivities taking along their nine-month-old daughter, first-born of the town and hence named in honor of it, Virginia. "The sound of sleigh bells mingled with the merry voices of the dancers as Mr. Whipple's new sleigh" — built "expressly for the occasion" — brought fresh loads of participants [13] to San Francisco Restaurant, now a holiday-trimmed ballroom.

Though pack trains continued to arrive, these occasions were sometimes far apart. No wonder men gathered at some of the cabins or went on "flings" at the saloons with their gambling tables, cheap music, and hurdy-gurdy girls. These girls were not necessarily "bad women" such as found in the brothels. Sometimes they entertained by singing or dancing alone. At the conclusion of a dance the man led his partner to the bar, where the girl had the choice of the offered drink or its value in money. She usually chose the "two bits"; hence, some of these houses were known as "Two-bits." Dayton had its "Mineral Rapids" hurdy-gurdy house. Gold Hill, Silver City, Carson, Genoa, and other mining camps provided similar places.

The theatre up on Howard Street may have been dark and cold some evenings, but it also may have glowed with yellow candlelight and sparkled with entertainment during that 1860-61 winter. Eventually the Westwood troupe disbanded in Washoe. Philip and some of the others stayed on the Lode,

---

[13] Angel, *History of Nevada*, 572. Angel states this was the "first" ball held on the Comstock. Such, of course, is not correct. The women who attended the Christmas Ball as listed by Angel included: Mesdames Tilton, Dirk, Delaney, Howard, Paxton, Bryan, Flick, Hastings, Blair, Dill, Adams, Ross, R. J. Smith, Howard, and Charles Barstow, and Miss Leonora Dirks. None of the ladies of the Westwood company are mentioned. Were they perhaps preparing or giving a Christmas performance at the Howard Theatre?

possibly to join Stark's troupe the next year, and finally to cross the Sierras and play theatres of the Golden State, then to return again to Washoe. Mercy, it seems, was the first to go to California, where two years later she married Richard White. The Whites' first child died with its mother. In an unmarked grave in Folsom, California, lies Mercy Westwood Tuckett White, pioneer actress and first leading lady of the legitimate drama in Nevada.

Politics, the Stage, and Circus Ring

1

During 1861 Washoe grew by leaps; miners fought over locations; a national war began, setting miners against each other on the Comstock; Western Utah got a new name and political status; melodeon, minstrel, and circus entertainment arrived; and the climactic event was the advent of the noted tragedian, James Stark. But no theatre production matched the drama-packed scenes between William H. Stewart and David S. Terry, facing each other in a crude Genoa court room, each backed by armed men. Fortunately both lawyers realized the danger and managed to keep matters under control.

Political dissension also arose over the election of city trustees in Virginia.[1] And "fearful gales" started at least one fire and demolished even stone and brick buildings. To add to the discomfort it snowed. Nevertheless, strangers continued to arrive "on horseback, on foot, in wagons — and every stage comes in jam full." As soon as trails opened from the plains, emigrants began pouring in from that direction too, causing some observers to estimate that "the season would reach 30,000." And all would seek diversion, many finding it in the intimate, varied, and light entertainment of the melodeon,

---

[1] Formally incorporated by act of the Utah Legislature in January, Virginia City elected five trustees, but nine candidates competed, though no salary was attached to the position. Many citizens refused to vote; others voted several times. (*San Francisco Evening Bulletin*, February 8, March 12, 15, 1861; *Sacramento Daily Union*, February 21, 1861.)

which early as February had opened its doors in an accessible spot on C Street.[2]

Instead of lengthy dramatic productions, the melodeon specialized in a succession of farces, dances, and songs, sometimes indulging in vulgar humor so that women — except the entertainers and the waitresses — were not allowed. But men who enjoyed smoking and drinking along with "a shapely leg" and "feminine form" crowded the melodeon, where

M — irth, melody and music hold their court,
E — ach evening, at that popular resort.
L — ight hearts and happy faces there are found;
O — n every side their joyous shouts resound;
D — elightful dances, and soul-stirring song —
E — ndless fun delights the laughing throng.
O — n all occasions pleasure reigns supreme;
N — ight glides on smoothly as an angel's dream.[3]

Melodeon farces were often cleverly written and as cleverly presented, local themes and coloring always an added attraction:

Amusements in Virginia City. — There will be a performance at the Melodeon on C Street, to-night, and another on Sunday night. A new farce, entitled, "The Last Chance in Virginia City, or the Speculator and his Jackass," will be presented each evening.[4]

Certain it is the Howard Theatre had a competitor in the Melodeon. And since the price of admission was less than at the Howard, the Melodeon was doubtless packed nightly. The satirical, local farce of *The Last Chance in Virginia City* may very easily have become *The Last Chance in Silver City*

[2] Whether this was the same building listed by J. Wells Kelly in *The First Directory of Nevada Territory* as the "Grunwald Theatre, West side C near Union" is not certain. The *Call* stated that the Gruenwalds appeared at the Howard Theatre up on Howard Street, but the German operatic troupe played some weeks in Washoe, so it is not improbable that they moved to a building that could be more easily heated as well as attract larger audiences during inclement weather.

[3] Thus *The Sunday Varieties, a Chronicle of Life in California* revealed the attractions of the Melodeon.

[4] San Francisco *Weekly Alta California*, March 16, 1861.

or *in Dayton* or *in Carson City* and played on around Washoe's amusement circuit; for at this time Silverland rejoiced in the knowledge of seven theatres besides the Melodeon or Gruenwald Theatre: the Howard, seating 700 people; Genoa, seating 250 persons; Carson with seats for 300; Silver City, 400; Nevada City, 250; Franktown, 200; and Fort Churchill Barracks, as many as 1000.[5]

2

Another form of amusement arrived in the desert on April 25, when Washoite R. M. Evans wrote the *Alta California*, "Ned Bingham came in to-day with a band of minstrels. They played in the Catholic Church, built by Father Gallagher, but not paid for." No doubt, the rent Bingham paid for the use of the building helped remedy the latter condition; for minstrelsy, like the melodeon, became another popular Washoe entertainment.

C. E. (Ned) Bingham was a bundle of energy and enterprise. After serving a stint in the Mexican War, the frontier soldier-actor landed in California in 1849, but not to join the Gold Rush. Instead, Bingham assisted theatricals in Los Angeles and Monterey, and by 1850 was launching Stockton's first dramatic performance.[6] Several years later while enroute to Panama, he became involved in some difficulty, was shot, and his legs left paralyzed.

Though a cripple the rest of his life, Bingham carried on as a man of the theatre, writing plays (being sure to include parts for a crippled soldier) and playing in them. The *Call* of May 26 stated: "The Bingham troupe have been perform-

---

[5] San Francisco *Daily Morning Call*, September 15, 1861.

[6] The next spring playing at San Francisco's Jenny Lind Theatre under the management of Sarah Kirby and James Stark, Bingham was dismissed. Popular as a member of a San Francisco fire company, Bingham's dismissal did not go unnoticed and the fire boys damaged the theatre owned by Tom Maguire. Bingham then opened his own theatre, only to have it burn to the ground. Three months after Downieville's fit-of-justice in the hanging of a woman, Bingham was performing in a new theatre in that wealthy, if notorious, community.

ing in Carson and Silver Cities, Washoe." Considering the
spirit of the man, it is hard to believe that he did not travel
on up to the Lode and serve Virginia City its first minstrel
treat at the Howard Theatre or the Melodeon.

"There are prayer meetings, temperance lectures, and
parties, theatres, minstrels, and gambling, buggy-riding, horse
frolics, and fishing," an Eagle Valley correspondent informed
the *Alta California.* "So you see the folks up here are not
without their amusements," including breweries,[7] "plenty of
liquor," and other recreational needs "good enough for a city
of 80 or 100 houses, one church, two butcher stalls, one
Cheap John, and meals at 50 cents, and 'plenty of men doing
nothing.'" But pack trains and men continued to arrive.

3

Lincoln's inaugural address [8] and the firing on Fort Sumter
heightened the friction between Southern and Northern fac-
tions in Silverland. Judge Terry — it was said — had been sent
to Washoe by Jeff Davis and had three forts ready to take
possession of the mines. One morning when the Secessionists
hoisted the Confederate Stars and Bars — first of four flags
of the Confederacy — over a business building in Virginia
City and stood by with pistols to protect it, a defiant Union
man raised the Stars and Stripes over the other end of the
building. People milled into the streets, many with firearms,
while across the desert John A. Collins frantically rode toward
Fort Churchill. Just before five o'clock, when the whistles
would send the miners and mill workers pouring through the
town, the Secessionists hauled down their Palmetto flag. But
next morning "a company of United States Dragoons"

[7] Carson City had three breweries at this time, but the Carson Brewing Company (founded in 1862) claimed it was "Nevada's oldest business." Old timers
recalled that Chinese, their long cues swinging, carried the heavy kettles on their
backs all the way from Placerville for use in the Carson Brewery.

[8] The fastest time made by the Pony Express was in carrying President Lincoln's
inaugural address to the West.

marched into Virginia, another into Genoa, and still another into Carson. Martial law was proclaimed throughout Washoe and firearms were collected.

Another incident, which helped secure Nevada's loyalty to the Union, was the arrival of Fremont's howitzer abandoned in the mountains 17 years before.[9] Instead of being consoled, Northern men worried, "Without law or government we are in a state of confusion . . . and might secede and what then?" To such fears a Silver City correspondent quickly replied, "Nevada going to secede? Fudge!" He was remembering that a few sacks of Washoe sand carried around the quadrangle at Fort Churchill had silenced many Southern sympathizers. Even so, Northern men met at Howard's Theatre and established the Union Blues: "1200 men good and true . . . ready for any *case of treason.*" Silver City males organized the "Constitution Guards," a military company receiving "arms and equipment as the law directs" from Fort Churchill. Just the same after a Union meeting, the Dixie Democrats took over the speaker's stand to champion a "Secession candidate and compare Jeff Davis with George Washington."

---

[9] According to the *San Francisco Herald* of July 3, 1861, the cannon was a "HISTORICAL GUN. — The Virginia City *Enterprise* of the 29th ult. says: 'A man named Sheldon brought a brass howitzer, which he found on the east fork of Walker's river, to Carson City some day last week, and offered to dispose of it for $200. Failing to find a purchaser there, he brought it up to Gold Hill. Some of our citizens, hearing of its arrival, went down there with purchase money and nipped it before the Gold Hill folks were aware of it. It will be used on the Fourth. There is quite a history connected with that cannon. Fremont, in 1843, when attempting to find a central pass across the Sierras, owing to the reduced state of his animals, was compelled to leave this howitzer [January 29, 1844]. It always was an object of wonder to the Indians in that vicinity. They burnt the carriage and carried off most of the irons, but the cannon was too heavy for them to manage. Captain Truckee, the old Pah-Utah chief, had a wonderful idea of its power and repeatedly requested the whites to go with him and get it. Old Peter Lassen, who was with Fremont at the time it was left, just before his death tried to get up a party to go after it.' "

4

When the telegraph line reached Fort Churchill, cavalry and troops celebrated the occasion. They hoisted the Stars and Stripes to the top of an Overland Telegraph pole while a band played, the troops maneuvered, and the crowd "cheered and toasted with bumpers of sparkling Heidseick." [10]

To properly celebrate any occasion music was needed, and Washoe musicians, stimulated by music-loving Germans, practiced on any available instrument. Soon the larger towns had bands organized to participate in all patriotic circumstances, including the flag raisings of the first territorial Fourth of July. That day Esmeralda "erected a fine Liberty pole" and applauded the "stirring and patriotic orations . . . no less than a half dozen being given." Even the ranchers of Pleasant, Eagle, Jack, and other Washoe valleys left off fighting the grasshopper pests to help raise flags. In the face of the Secessionist threat of a rebel flag-raising, "Carson City kept a guard of twenty-four men out all night to prevent disturbance."

At dawn some five thousand Unionists climbed past the "coyote holes" and, twelve hundred feet above Nevada's first theatre, wedged a twenty-foot pole into the peak of Mount Davidson and fired Fremont's howitzer. Then while the band played and everyone cheered, they raised the flag and let it float "open to the Washoe breeze." Into a near-by rock chimney the celebrators thrust staves with their names and the important date "July 4, 1861 inscribed thereon." (Future actors and actresses in Washoe would do likewise.) The Comstockers turned their attention next to a two-thousand-man parade, the speeches at the Howard, and to dinners and

[10] Instead of "the circuitous route by Panama, half way down the Pacific and half way up the Atlantic," the mail now came via the central, more direct route. Employing "600 horses, 25 stages and wagons, 25 drivers, 12 conductors, and 90 station-keepers," it was an enterprise worthy the processions of cheering citizens, the booming cannon, and the playing bands.

picnics. "Excellent," declared the *Enterprise,* was the "conduct of our population on the occasion, good humor being the prevailing sentiment."

5

Good humor was also the prevailing sentiment upon the arrival of Nevada Territory's jolly first governor. "With three times three tremendous cheers," the Carsonites greeted handsome James W. Nye,[11] a lawyer and former New York City police commissioner, and answered his greeting with "Vociferous applause" and "Longer applause!" The band played again. Then twenty Chinamen serenaded with a discordant mixture of tones, which everyone gravely applauded, but the entertainment committee finally burst out laughing and compared the Celestial serenade with the "caterwaul of cats." Governor Nye, realizing he had been made the butt of a joke, laughed along with the crowd. And a Washoe correspondent wrote afterward:

> Well, the Fourth of July has come and gone, and Gov. Nye arrived and was gloriously welcomed. To use a free and easy phrase, Gov. Nye "takes" . . . He is a "jolly old fellow," a man for the country in the opinion of the masses. . . There will be log rolling as to where we will have the capital and the county seat . . . with three rivals: Carson City, Silver City, and Virginia. Gold Hill stepped aside . . . Carson will probably want them both. — Cosmos

Virginia City also spared nothing to make the governor's arrival on July 15 an occasion of "great pomp and ceremony." By half past two an enlarged procession of bands, fire companies, Guards, and people passed through a "splendid arch" made by the local ladies while "minute guns" fired and the people cheered. Then it stopped at Union Square for the

---

[11] While waiting for his commission and baggage, Nye delivered San Francisco's 1861 Fourth of July oration and was acclaimed "one of the jolliest orators that ever stumped a state."

official welcome and at the Virginia Hotel for the dinner
prepared in the governor's honor. Everything was going
"splendidly," the mining metropolis "duly admiring itself"
until five o'clock, when an impromptu duel took place.[12]

Hurriedly the governor proclaimed the Territory of Nevada [13] (even if instructions for territorial secretary Orion
Clemens were so numerous his brother Sam facetiously remarked that they "had to read a chapter for breakfast every
morning"); established the long-awaited judiciary; arranged
for elections; and appointed Dr. Henry De Groot, the census
marshal. A comparison of De Groot's 1861 census with that
of 1860 shows that Mart Taylor, the Westwoods, and the
Gruenwald troupe entertained in a land having little more
than 6800 people, whereas the melodeon, Bingham's minstrels, Bassett's circus, and the Stark company played to a
territory of over 16,000 of whom a third were on the Comstock. No wonder actors wanted the Lode on their itineraries.

6

Of Dr. Bassett's circus, the first of such entertainment to
reach Silverland, "the Press" spoke "in the highest praise,"
saying "Go see the horse-opera by all means." And the
Washoites must have found the tight-rope walkers, the "elegant and dashing equestriennes," the muscular gymnasts, the
trained trick ponies, the dancing horse, the variety acts, and

---

12 Before the windows of the hotel a man named Butler gave a little speech and
flourished his pistol. Deputy Marshal Williams tried to arrest the man. In the exchange of shots, the marshal hit Butler in the knee and again in the shoulder.
When another bullet scraped his face, Butler surrendered.

13 As superintendent of Indian affairs, Nye called on his red subjects. But upon
unpacking the gifts he had brought from New York, "a fine assortment of hoops
was found among the lot. What disposition the Governor will make of them,
deponent saith not," laughed the *Enterprise*. "The idea of an Indian maiden
threading the forests in full panoply of hoops is a refinement on romance itself."
Hoops did not interest the Paiutes, but telegraph poles did. "One of the chiefs
came into Carson to see our 'Big Injun' about this pole business," a Silver City
correspondent informed the *Bulletin*. "He wanted to know what we were running
such a high fence through their country for and which side was intended for them."

the comicality of the clowns amusing and entertaining. It is probable that the tight-rope acrobat, Mrs. Walter P. Aymar (conceded by some as "one of the most daring experts in such business since the days of Blondin"), gave Comstockers an exhibition of her skill by making an ascent from C Street to the top of the International Hotel — a feat she later would repeat in similar fashion in San Francisco.

"Dr. Bassett's circus is coining money in Nevada Territory, having followed in the wake of Governor Nye," wrote California papers; and again on August 18, 1861:

> Dr. Bassett's United States Circus made a highly successful tour of the State and Nevada Territory, . . . having engaged M'lle Cammille, lately attached to Howes & Cushing's circus in England — a dashing equestrienne; Miss Emma Pastor, one of the finest riders we have had in California, and Mr. George Bartholomew and his trained stud. Then there are the Aymar Brothers, Mrs. Walter Aymar, Little Lottie, and others.

Just what the legitimate theatre offered during the summer months is unknown. But from October first, attention was focused on Silverland's first legislature, which opened at Carson "without trouble" — though all sessions were not so fortunate. The promiscuous granting of monopolies caused Sam Clemens to picture franchises as hanging over the territorial boundary "like a fringe"; and xyz, writing the *Alta California,* taunted, "No legislature will be able to give away a monopoly in Washoe for the next ten years. . . If two men sit down here to play cards, they incorporate the game."

Though seldom observed, a law passed for the "observance of the Lord's Day" stated that "no person shall keep open any playhouse or theater, race ground, cockpit, or play at any game of chance or gain, or engage in any noisy amusement." Then recalling Bassett's full tents, the assemblymen next put license fees at $20 a day on circuses, $20 a quarter on bowling alleys, and five dollars a day on theatres — just in time too, for again Silverland was to be favored with legitimate drama.

THE HURDY-GURDY GIRLS

Coins jingling in their stockings, they entertained in the saloons and "two-bit" houses of early Nevada. From a contemporary woodcut.

VIRGINIA CITY, NEVADA TERRITORY, 1861

From an original drawing by Grafton T. Brown. Courtesy of Warren R. Howell and the Bancroft Library.

October-December 1861

Shakespeare in Silverland

1

During the previous winter after the departure of the Gruenwald troupe, Washoe had been left to a fare of hurdy-gurdy, Tarantula Juice, gambling, dances, and an occasional Westwood performance. By contrast Silverland's 1861-62 season was rich and varied with legitimate productions, thanks to James Stark, "father of the drama in California" and of the Washoe Dramatic Company. Of the actor's new venture, the *Golden Era* of October 27, 1861, wrote:

> At the Placerville Theatre during the past week Mr. James Stark has appeared in several of his popular personations. Mr. Brown, Mr. Griffith, Miss Douglas, Miss Hamlin, Miss Nellie Brown, and others constitute this company, which proceeds this week to Washoe to inaugurate a season of dramatic performances in Virginia City and the other principal towns of Nevada Territory.

Reports of illness, so serious many people feared an epidemic, perturbed Stark no more than did Washoe's apparent disregard for human life (a teamster had been killed at Lake Bigler and the chief engineer of the Bowers' mills murdered, stabbed by the second engineer). But Stark may have wondered how Washoe audiences would receive heavy drama. Taylor's wit and rhymes had been accepted, as had the Westwoods' drama and comedy, Gruenwalds' operatic selections, the melodeon, Ned Bingham's minstrels, and Dr. Bassett's circus. But was Washoe ready for Shakespeare? Stark believed they were.

That the tragedian brought his troupe to Silverland near winter tells the caliber of the man. Toward the end of October James Stark, Miss Nellie Brown, Miss Douglas, Miss Hamlin, Harry Brown, Jimmy Griffith, W. Stephenson, Charles W. Cooke, and others of Stark's theatrical company — without Mrs. Stark, however — stepped aboard stages and proceeded from California over the route recently taken by the Pony Express into Virginia City. Here quartz mills thundered, "furnace fires gleamed" through the "all-pervading dust," and ore cars thundered their "pay rock" into the bins. No wonder the newcomers, gazing around — and upward at the tattered remnants of the Fourth-of-July flag fluttering above the town, were not a little anxious and confused. Well they might be; for now the Washoe Zephyrs tore through the Lode with swirling snow upsetting buildings and blocking roads. Needed stage costumes did not arrive for weeks.

But lights twinkled again in the year-old Howard Theatre — or was it perhaps the more accessible Gruenwald Theatre on C Street? Whatever the location, as if to a new mine strike, the Comstockers struggled through the snowbanks to its doors, filled the seats, and packed the aisles while the *Union* and the *Golden Era* traced the weeks of constant performance:

INTERIOR THEATRICALS. — Mr. Stark with dramatic company is playing at Virginia City.

and again and again:

Mr. James Stark and Company are still playing to very flattering acceptation in Virginia City, and the neighboring localities of Nevada Territory.

What plays did the company present? The papers gave only:

THE DRAMA IN NEVADA TERRITORY. — The daily *Territorial Enterprise*, published at Virginia City, says November 12th: Another full house greeted Mr. Stark's excellent company last evening. The unabated interest with which our citizens view the representations of this troupe shows the strong hold that Mr. Stark has on the community. To-night the great play of "Wm. Tell" will be performed, together with the amusing farce of "Irish Assurance and Yankee Modesty." We are requested to state that persons who clamber over the roof to get in the window will hereafter find somebody there to receive the price of admission — either in tickets or money.

William Tell trod the Howard Theatre boards! What other great characters walked there? Othello? Certainly Hamlet, King Lear, and Cardinal ("one of Stark's best"): roles the young tragedian had played in New York, Europe, and Australia.

2

The Washoites knew that as early as 1850 Maguire's Jenny Lind Theatre of San Francisco had been under the management of the capable James Stark, whose career they had followed through such theatrical criticisms as: "He engages and holds the attention of his whole audience the entire length of his performance. . . Mr. Stark does not rant — he has effectually cured himself of what little predilection he at times evinced for the rugged and severe. He has adopted the true artistic method of natural acting and therein has achieved 'a grace beyond the reach of art,' in the effect produced." According to Professor C. D. Odell in his monumental *Annals of the New York Stage,* James Stark was inferior to no actor.

From his carpenter's shop in Nova Scotia, Stark had drifted down to Boston, where a patron-friend financed him for a three-year study in London under Macready, and on the Continent. First of the stars to reach the West Coast, Stark instilled in his new public a taste for Shakespeare and for good acting so that great actors who followed Stark found appreciative audiences awaiting them. Tragedy was Stark's forte. So intensely did he once portray the Moor that he stabbed himself painfully. And the *Picayune* critic who had previously expressed doubts now gave lavish appreciation:

Mr. Stark's "Othello" was a masterly and finished exhibition of the character. It appeared perfectly evident that he is not a copyist or imitator. . . He does not, therefore, show us Macready's "Othello," or Forest's but Shakespeare's, and we have never seen that in our judgment was a truer or more forcible presentation.

No wonder Stark played to enthusiastic audiences in Washoe as he had in San Francisco, where for the first time *Hamlet, Othello, The Merchant of Venice, Macbeth, Much Ado About Nothing, The Taming of the Shrew,* and *King Lear* were seen and heard. In June of 1851 James Stark and the accomplished actress and theatre manager, Sarah Kirby, who played opposite the tragedian, were married. For years theirs was a happy union — until the Nevada mining fever struck Stark. Well might a California paper praise the Starks as "the first to render the theatre in California an institution worthy of the support of an intellectual and refined public." [1]

And now during the latter part of 1861 James Stark was rendering the theatre in Silverland "an institution," playing the Howard in Virginia City, the Gold Hill Theatre, Chrysopolis Hall in Silver City, Spafford's or some other hall in Dayton, and Moore's Theatre in Carson — thus making the Washoe circuit. And everywhere the people cheered and demanded more. There was no surfeit of the drama in Washoe that winter.

3

Warmly influenced by Stark's dramatic interpretations, Governor Nye gave out his Thanksgiving Proclamation for 1861 in over-optimistic verbosity though only a short time before he had sought help from Washington for the chaotic conditions of his territory. An incident at Moore's Saloon

[1] Stark and Ryder with the first complete troupe to visit Los Angeles gave Southern California a brief season of Shakespeare at the Temple Theatre, a combination Market and Auditorium. Back in San Francisco the summer before coming to Washoe, Stark opened the handsome Metropolitan Theatre, delivering the inauguration address and leading the cast for that enterprising entrepreneur Thomas Maguire — of whom Nevada was to hear much, very much.

Theatre is illustrative. One evening during a performance two "shady citizens," fully charged at the bar and armed with bowie knives and six-shooters, swaggered down the aisle, and commanded the curtain be dropped. Stark refused, but the audience, especially the women and children who made up a small part of it, were stricken with terror. Noting this, Stark dropped the curtain as the greater part of the audience fled, including most of the cast. Then the gunmen put on a show of their own, menacing with the knives and slashing the curtain to ribbons, but eventually were taken and fined $1000 for the local school fund.

It is regretted that daily copies of the *Territorial Enterprise*, read and relished by the Washoites during these months, seem to be nonexistent,[2] but the middle of December the *Era* was again reporting:

> Mr. James Stark with his dramatic company is still playing to crowded houses in Virginia . . .

Comedies and lighter dramas were also on the Stark company's repertoire. An often repeated play was *Ingomar; or, The Greek Maiden*. This five-act play translated from the German was also called *Ingomar; or, The Barbarian*.[3] The rough, calloused Ingomar, leader of a ruthless band of Alemanni, secured possession of a lovely maiden, Parthenia, who had given herself as a sacrifice to save her father's life.

[2] The Virginia *Territorial Enterprise* was published as a daily with the issue of September 24, 1861. Earliest copies of this historic paper located by this investigator include:

> July 30, 1859: facsimile in Thompson and West's *History of the State of Nevada*
> December 15, 1859: one year from date of issue; owned by Joe Farnsworth of Carson City
> May 5, 1860: part of an issue in the California State Library, Sacramento
> June 9, 1860: small-sized issue in the Bancroft Library, Berkeley
> January 10, 1863: in the Nevada Historical Society, Reno
> October 19, 1865: pieces in the author's collection salvaged from a Comstock mud puddle. (The paper pasted over with wallpaper had served as an undercovering in a house in Gold Hill.)

[3] F. C. Wemyss, ed., *The Modern Standard Drama*, vol. 12.

Through act after act ran barbarian complication and conflict, but the tactful, innocent, and womanly Parthenia wove her charm over Ingomar, who by now, helpless in love, forsook his old ways. (So popular a play, *Ingomar* was presented next year also when Mark Twain did a clever, if biting, local version of it.)

Between the high tragedies and such comedies as *Jumbo Jim, Uncle John* (an old comedy), and the *Irish Emigrant* were interlarded a variety of strong patriotic recitations; for Stark was a practiced elocutionist and must have delivered such stirring readings as the *Battle of Bunker Hill* and *O'Flannigan and the Fairies.* That Washoe was unique among mining regions may be noted:

> Interior theatricals are likely to experience a revival. At present only Mr. Buchanan's and Mr. Stark's party [sic] are out.[4]

The weather was miserable with "Cape Hatteras" gales, but the Thespians laughed at the odd sight of "Pi-Utes wearing half a dozen hats after every storm, one wedged on top the other!" Stark may not have intended staying so long; for the *Era* recorded:

> In the Washoe country dramatic performances are still vouchsafed through the continued presence of Mr. James Stark and his theatrical troupe. The season has been so stormy of late, that it is hardly possible for them to get away — in fact the stages, for several days, refused all passengers bound Pacific-ward.[5]

Yet when travel did permit the company's leaving, only Stark went; and the *Era* wrote: "Mr. James Stark has returned from Washoe, and is at his residence in San Jose," trying — though the *Era* neglected to add this — to persuade his wife to accompany him on his return. To appear opposite her husband on the boards of Silverland theatres, yes, said

---

[4] Buchanan was then playing Marysville, California, but six months later he, too, would be in Silverland.

[5] San Francisco *Golden Era*, January 5, 1862.

the lady. But Stark was proposing something more. The Washoe mining fever had entered his blood. The actor was ready to desert his histrionic profession. He wanted to go mining, in fact, had already done so, the *Call* of January 26 revealed:

Mr. James Stark, the tragedian, has gone into silver mining in Washoe, where we hope he may coin more money than it is possible for him (or "any other man") to draw out of the public pocket by anything in the dramatic line, from "high tragedy" to "low comedy."

6

The Sage Struck Galaxy

1

The winter of 1862 was one of the most violent Washoe would experience. Unprecedented snowfall resulted in floods that took out every dam on the Carson River; washed out mills [1] or filled them with debris; dissolved all the adobe houses in Gold Cañon; surged through Carson filling cellars, including Governor Nye's; sent landslides roaring down the Sierra Nevada, covering farms, buildings, and all life in the way; and closed the roads so not even horsemen could get through from California. [2] Washoites found little consolation in being told that "such a deluge will not occur for an entire generation." In fact, the storms "pretty effectually washed out everything pertaining to the drama in the interior," wrote the San Francisco *Call.*

Of the California "interior" the *Call* statement was correct, but not true for Washoe. Though Stark had gone to San Jose, the remainder of his company organized the Washoe Dramatic Company and — much as the Westwood troupers had done — identified themselves with Silverland. The company's leading lady was Nellie Brown. For years she had

---

[1] Though the oldest mill in the territory was "only a little more than two years old," no less than 100 were "in full operation or rapidly approaching completion" at the time of Stark's entry to Washoe. Bringing salt to these mills from the desert salt marshes, heavily-laden camels, crusted with alkali, arrived on the Comstock at night so as not to frighten the teams of horses and mules.

[2] "Silver Mountain, Nevada Territory" — in 1863 the California-Nevada survey put Silver Mountain in California — enjoyed occasional contact with the outside when Snowshoe Thompson came over from Murphy's with papers that told of the floods and enormous destruction of property in Washoe with "consequent stoppage of mills, teaming, and other out-of-door business."

pleased California audiences, was entertaining at the Stockton Theatre with Mrs. Woodward, Harry Brown, and others at the time Stark approached her to play opposite him in the Washoe venture. Ingénue Miss Hamlin, a San Jose girl who had made her debut with the Starks at the opening of Stark's San Jose Theatre, was also a member of the company as was Miss Douglas, Jimmy Griffith, W. Stephenson, sometimes the Comstock residents, Mr. and Mrs. Fairbanks, and others. The male actor mentioned most often was amiable Harry Brown. However, when a "Northern press" proclaimed him "the best actor in the state of California," the *Era* exclaimed, "Shades of the mighty!"

Just what Nellie Brown and the company included in their first programs of 1862 remains unknown. Certain it is, they abandoned the heavy Shakespearean presentations, chose instead, popular plays, and made certain the afterpieces sent the Washoites home laughing. Feeling the need of variety in the humor presented, versatile Dan De Quille wrote a local comedy, about which the *Era* of March 2 wrote:

> "Dan De Quille," of Silver City, Nevada Territory — for years past a regular contributor to the GOLDEN ERA, and recognized as one of the cleverest writers on the continent — is the author of a farce called "The Sage Struck Yankee," which he has presented to the dramatic troupe .   .   .   now performing in the Washoe country.

2

As Nevada's first playwright, Dan De Quille deserves further mention. Born in Ohio, 1829, of Quaker parents, William Wright moved to Iowa, where at age eighteen he worked as a journalist until the cry of "Gold!" lured him to the Mariposa and Mono Lake districts. In 1860 he began mining at the Yellow Jacket in Silver City (where growl Jack was included in his recreation). But Dan could not stop writing. In less than two years he sent more than fifty-four pieces to the *Era*, and by August of 1862 preceded Sam Clemens by a few months to a place on the staff of the *Territorial Enterprise*.[3]

A week after the announcement of Dan's first play, the *Era* noted:

> THE WASHOE DRAMATIC COMPANY. — Nelly Brown, Harry Brown, and others played "Ingomar" at Silver City, February 22d. An original local comedy by Dan De Quille called the "Sage Struck Yankee," in which Mr. and Mrs. Fairbanks volunteered to appear, was also performed for the first time.

That some success marked his first play seems certain; for in less than a month Dan came out with another funny piece of local intrigue:

> "THE WHEELERS IN WASHOE! OR TAKING IN A STRANGER FROM THE BAY" is the title of a new comic drama written by Dan De Quille. . . All who have read Dan De Quille's humorous stories and sketches, contributed to the GOLDEN ERA during years past, feel confident that he has achieved a success in this, his first dramatic composition.[4]

Besides timeliness, *The Wheelers in Washoe* had nearly all the necessary ingredients. "Spudder, P. V.," one of the principal characters, already had a Washoe reputation through Dan's *Era* writings. "Spudder" was particularly intriguing while duping the gullible "Mr. Quartstruck" until that disillusioned character had "enough of mines, miners, and Washoe adventure in general." Heroine Betsy Jane Wheeler was "a Yankee Gal of the right stripe." And Dennis O'Flaherty, personifying "the Hiberian element," added the wit and color needed in a play that "could scarcely fail to prove attractive."

---

[3] Except for several short intervals Dan never left Nevada until well after the bonanzas and borrascas were over and the *Enterprise* suspended publication (1893). Without a regular position then, Dan did free lance writing, but the returns barely kept him. Finally one of the Comstock millionaires, John Mackay, sent De Quille enough to live in comfort a few months at West Branch, Iowa, where he died in 1899.

[4] An error. Editors of the *Golden Era* of March 16, 1862, evidently forgot their Dan De Quille items of March 2 and 9.

3

As early as February 23, 1862, the *Call* let it be known that "the scenery for a new theatre at Aurora, Nevada Territory, has been prepared . . . and the establishment will open in the course of the next two weeks. We are not advised who are the proprietors and what names appear in the company." And diligent search has failed to unearth this information. But what source is found indicates that the Washoe Star Dramatic Company traveled 100 miles southeast of Carson City to the Esmeralda mining district and dedicated Aurora's first house of legitimate drama. These pioneer Thespians would have given the miners a satisfying season of Dan De Quille's comedies, *Ingomar,* and other dramas, which had won popular acceptance elsewhere in the territory.

Although the *Call* of March 23 stated: "Harry and Nellie Brown intend returning to this city shortly from Washoe," Nellie and Harry both stayed on in Silverland. By March 30 the *Era* was commenting, "The Washoe dramatic troupe continues to give occasional performances in the various towns of Nevada Territory." Why not Aurora? And the *Call* of April 6 informed its readers:

IN WASHOE. — The "Star Dramatic Troupe" of Washoe with Harry and Nelly Brown are still in those regions. The company is rehearsing the extravaganza of "Pocahontas" and the colored opera of "Oh, Hush."

Through John Brougham's stage classic of *Po-ca-hon-tas; or, Ye Gentle Savage* the troupe was presenting a humorous, operatic extravaganza, biting and clever. No wonder they held the Washoe boards month after month.

4

After a season of theatrical programs in one town and the Star Dramatic Company's departure to keep an engagement in another, the populace, left to themselves for recreation until the drama's return, held dancing parties that were given the semblance of formal functions by fancy, hand-written invitations, which began "The pleasure of your company is respectfully solicited at a Grand Social Ball . . ." The "Honorary Committee" included such dignitaries as the governor; and the "Floor Managers," "Reception," and "Arrangement" committees were mentioned to assure the success of the affair. At midnight the revelers enjoyed "delicious suppers"; then danced until dawn, at times watching more skilled couples go through intricate steps with grace. One such "Grand Social Ball" was enjoyed at "Union Hall, Genoa" on February 27.

These "grand functions," however, produced gunfights, fist fights, family squabbles, neighborhood quarrels, as well as romances, congenial visiting, and good-humored pranks. A meeting planned with California officials to decide Nevada's boundary had to be postponed because Governor Nye hurt his finger ("got it cut off," said the reporters) in an unintentionally slammed door "the night before at a ball by some ladies with whom he was 'skylarking.'"

Other forms of diversion during that 1862 winter included a billiard match, which "terminated after 32½ hours of uninterrupted play without food or rest" — a record for "endurance if not for skill." A Dayton diversion reached print when "Quartz Ledge" informed his paper:

AMUSEMENTS
Some five hundred people congregated here . . . to witness a grand dog fight. No other fights were scheduled the same day.

Maybe the Washoites needed diversion — even of dogfight variety — for after the floods came mud; then "terrible hurricanes swept the territory." Hotels and restaurants "closed up," unable to get supplies even after offering twenty cents a pound for transportation. Mining supplies, liquor, billiard and monte tables, dice and spinning markers were in demand. And barroom wrangles were natural consequences

of the times. Seeming to overshadow the decent and industrious, the less desirable element swaggered about the towns
or lolled over bars or gambling tables.[5]

Each bar tended, however, to have its special set of patrons:

> Italy has its favorite saloon where Italians "most do congregate"
> to compare "indications," and talk of the happy day when they
> shall return to their fair and fruitful land. France has its *Cafe de
> Paris* and Germany its lager beer cellars, where rotund Germans
> mid clouds of smoke soberly sit and dream of Fatherland, while
> modest little signs, telling of washing or ironing by Si Lung or
> Ski Hi, indicate the presence of the ubiquitous John, pursuing his
> favorite avocation and as remorselessly tearing our linen as in the
> days of yore he did in the Golden State.

Men of some culture frequented fashionable saloons (some
with furnishings valued at $30,000), such as the one owned
by Eleanor Dumont, a beautiful, stylishly dressed woman of
virtue and good humor, who employed an orchestra and
served champagne instead of a lone instrument and cheap
whiskey. Though puzzled by her choice of profession, the
miners declared they would rather lose at *vingt-et-un* with
her than win at a table conducted by a man.[6]

Another female who preceded Madame Mustache and remained after the gambling lady had gone, was the pretty,

---

[5] Such men as Prentiss, "Farmer Peel," and Sam Brown were enemies of law and
order. Brown, a burly 200-pound brute with tawny whiskers parted and tied under
his chin, murdered an underwitted man, who had made a remark Brown did not
like. The supposed supporters of law were often the greatest violators. One such
was Tom Peasley, who killed twice in Virginia street duels, established the Sazarac
Saloon, became foreman of the first hook-and-ladder and the first fire engine companies of Virginia City. Another of the "same ilk," handsome John L. Blackburn,
Deputy U.S. Marshal, forced his own violent death. San Franciso *Alta California*,
May 27, 1860; Lord, *op. cit.*, 76.

[6] In later years Miss Dumont gave up gambling, bought a place in eastern
Nevada, and married, but her husband squandered her fortune including the
ranch, then left her. Broken in spirit and purse, a middle-aged woman with
coarsened features and dark hair growing on her upper lip, a pitiful creature
known as "Madame Mustache," she drifted again to the mining camps. But on a
September morning of 1879, according to Myron Angel's account, "her body was
found about two miles south of Bodie, a bottle of poison lying near. Let her many
good qualities invoke leniency in criticizing her failings."

beautifully gowned Julia Bulette, who also met a violent death. Not a "nice girl," Julie was friend to the lowliest and wealthiest male. During the many fires and other mine disasters, Jule was on hand to help as nurse, cook, seamstress, or comforter. Engine Company of Virginia considered her their special godmother.[7]

Reading rooms opened too, in most Washoe towns for those who sought quiet entertainment in reading, playing checkers or chess, or in "instructive conversation." Here Sam Clemens found diversion in playing cribbage, even spending one restless night with it — and a box of tarantulas.[8]

"Mills still idle," Viator wrote the *Call*. "Capable of turning out from three to eight hundred dollars per day, it is easy to calculate the loss arising from their interruption." Then the Mexican mill burned, a $150,000-loss since insurance was as yet unknown on the Comstock; and an Indian uprising was reported from the Humboldt Sink and Pyramid Lake regions. Fortunately the scare was brief. Governor Nye and the Indian agents with "divers and sundry pack mules laden with a variety of nice things for the Pi-Utes" — no hoops, this time — held a "grand powwow with old Chief Winnemucca," who did much to reduce friction between the races, even paying Nye a formal visit. While in Carson, Winnemucca, noting the White Chief's picture, "had his own Daguerreotype taken, and pronounced it 'heap good!' "

5

Although peace was effected between red men and white, northern and southern sympathizers in Washoe took sides on

---

[7] Down the street from Maguire's Opera House stood Julia's small white house in which she was murdered on the Saturday night of January 19, 1867. For Jule's funeral the mines closed, so did the saloons; the fire department in full dress uniform led the funeral parade; and men wept while their wives seethed with indignation. Another special day for Nevada was the execution of John Milleain, hanged for murdering Jule "for her money and jewelry." — *Gold Hill Evening News*, January 21, 1867.

[8] Samuel L. Clemens, *Roughing It*, 150.

issues the nation was trying to settle in the bloodiest war of
our history. Already by April the Confederate Congress had
passed its first draft law. The North still relied on volunteers;
hence, to encourage enlistment Virginia City early in '62 set
up a recruiting office, secured two drummer boys and a flag
carrier, and started them marching through the Comstock.
Some Secessionists jumped the trio, kicked one drum to
pieces, and were winning the fight until several Unionists
joined the melee, forcing the Copperheads to withdraw.[9] But
the gathering crowd joined the recruiters and "proceeded in
triumph, growing to a grand procession, which marched to
the City Hall, where an enthusiastic Union meeting was
held," the former Justice of the California Supreme Court
delivering "a stirring address."

Though utterances of disloyal sentiment were "painfully
prevalent," the vigilant Loyalists kept matters under control,
and a local paper could not resist inserting in its columns:

An Epitaph

Stranger, behold! here lies the dead;
'Tis John G. Downey, the Copperhead.
Some say that he died from shame and grief;
Others, that he choked on Carpenter's beef.
Anyhow, he lies here, dead as d--nation,
A fearful warning to all who wickedly oppose
Uncle Abe's Administration!

---

[9] The flag carrier was J. H. Matthewson, who was mustered into service early in
1863 taking rank as First Lieutenant of Company b, Nevada Territorial Cavalry
Volunteers.

Though the *Placer Courier* insisted the Secessionists in Washoe were "gamblers
of the lowest stripe, escaped convicts from California," many were men of character who believed in States' rights, but avoided talking of the war. However, the
character-actor Walter Leman and his "secesh" friends did otherwise. Meeting the
actor in a Washoe hotel, an acquaintance would say "with a satisfied tone, 'Leman,
old boy, I'm sorry to hurt your feelings, but we've got great news from Vicksburg,
and Pemberton has knocked h--l's bells out of Grant's wheelhouses.'" Within five
days "the truth came," Leman tells in his *Memories of an Old Actor*, "and meeting
my secesh friend, I said, 'Mr. ----, old boy, I'm sorry to hurt your feelings, but
we've got great news from Vicksburg, and Grant has knocked h--l's bells out of
Pemberton's wheelhouses.'"

WILLIAM WRIGHT
Using the pen name Dan De Quille, he was
Nevada's first playwright and historian.
Courtesy, University of Nevada.

McKEAN BUCHANAN
A tragedian who thundered his stylized
interpretations of Shakespearian roles.
From a contemporary woodcut.

MRS. JAMES STARK

The versatile Sarah Kirkby Stark, pioneer actress of Nevada, and
wife of the famous Washoe tragedian, politician, and mining man.
Courtesy, M. H. de Young Memorial Museum.

7

Tragedians in Washoe

1

James Stark, consoling himself with his wife's promise to join him for the summer theatrical season in Washoe, retraced his way over the Sierras early in May and arrived in Genoa about the time a "tremendous noise like an earthquake" sent everyone rushing out to see "an immense landslide sweep over a fine new" $7,000-sawmill at the mouth of the canyon, mangling and burying men, oxen, horses, and everything in its path.[1] Fortunately the avalanche missed Genoa, but a few weeks later a fire destroyed a large part of the town, including the Grotto Saloon and the Union Hotel — with its bedbugs.

The desire to go mining was still strong, but Stark rejoined his troupe and was soon appearing as Edward Mortimer opposite Nellie Brown in the three-act play of strong dramatic merit, *The Iron Chest*. In its theatrical column the *Golden Era* now informed its readers:

> Mr. James Stark and the Washoe Dramatic Troupe appeared at the Gold Hill Theatre May 19 in the "Iron Chest." Mrs. Stark will soon join her husband in Washoe.

In the meantime Stark and the company presented Coleman's drama in other Washoe towns. "On the 27th of May   .   .   . still doing a good business," the tragedian "appeared as Cardinal in *Richelieu* at the Carson City Theatre," as well as before audiences in Empire City, Ophir, Genoa, Dayton, and the Lode towns.

---

[1] One man jumped behind a large tree. The mill wreck pushed the tree over and slid on down the slope, allowing the man miraculously to crawl out unhurt.

With the advent of James Stark's new leading lady in Washoe's theatrical life, Nellie Brown climbed aboard a westbound stage.[2] Sarah Stark scarcely needs an introduction. Her versatility, energy, and talent were well known to the Washoites. What she chose as a vehicle for her professional entry to Silverland is unknown. That she appeared first at Ophir City, where the troupe held "a highly remunerative engagement," is certain. And the troupe found the Gold Hill Theatre "entirely refitted and considerably enlarged." By latter June the company were still "winning golden opinions, as well as golden profits." [3]

Camille; or, The Fate of a Coquette had aroused theatrical controversy in San Francisco.[4] Although Alexander Dumas *fils* had written *La Dame aux Camelias* on a French theme, it had been adapted and readapted to the American stage so may have lost much of its wickedness — or Washoites had become more educated in theatrical art. Be that as it may, *Camille* was produced "with great success at Gold Hill," Mrs. Stark's performance drawing "from the *Territorial Enterprise* the remark that 'her Camille is hard to be surpassed.' " (Even Julia Hayne's "admirable" Camille at Maguire's Virginia City Opera House the next summer elicited no such praise.) Mrs. Stark was a measure by which the Washoites would judge other actresses.

Whatever had happened to the Howard Theatre during the time James and Sarah Stark were playing along the desert circuit is unknown, but the *Call* of July 6 announced in a special item:

NEW THEATRE. — A new theatre is being built in Virginia City. . . It is so far completed that a ball took place there on the 4th of July.

---

[2] A few days later Nellie Brown was appearing with Walter Bray, the "great banjoist Sam Pride," and others of a "strong, complete and talented troupe" for applauding San Franciscans.

[3] San Francisco *Daily Morning Call*, June 29, 1862.

[4] See George R. MacMinn, *Theater of the Golden Era in California*, 253-308.

Mr. Topliffe, considering accessibility important, constructed his "said to be a fine building" on C Street — as the Gruenwalds had theirs.

Who would officially open the new Topliffe Theatre? Stark, with his excellent company playing Washoe since October, 1861? Or would a new company be imported for the honor? To these questions one finds conflicting answers. The *Golden Era* on July 13 said "McKean Buchanan and daughter" opened the "Virginia City Theatre" on July 5; the *Call,* however, insisted, "A new theatre (Topliffe's) was opened at Virginia City, Nevada Territory, on the 26 July" with Mr. and Mrs. James Stark. Considering the reception they had been receiving in Washoe, it seems more than likely that the Stark players officially dedicated Topliffe's, Buchanan playing there previously, on the fifth before the building was even finished. Buchanan did not remain long in Silverland. There was a reason.

2

A well-known actor in the Golden State even before 1856, when he sailed out through the Golden Gate, Buchanan and his daughter traveled over 250,000 miles and "Buck" gave over 1000 performances in Australia, Great Britain, eastern United States, and back to California. Buchanan was a "good worker" and his daughter, specializing in the juvenile business, was "a young lady of decided promise, who had made her *debut* in England." Though not yet seventeen, Virginia Buchanan, a Downieville critic insisted, "acquitted herself admirably," and added, "This beautiful young lady is an ornament, and an honor to the profession, and is becoming the pride of her father's life."

Since Buchanan's return to the Pacific Coast, July 4, 1861, the newspapers had followed his energetic career from San Francisco to "the interior floods" and the *Call* could not resist reporting:

"McKean Buchanan has reached the banks of the Merced River, and like

> Zacheus he
> Did climb a tree

to escape the raging floods, and at the last accounts was still lingering among the branches with Othello's sword in one hand and the drum on which theatrical thunder has so often sounded in the other. Bloggs says he hopes he may stay there until he dries up."

Walter Leman, a member of Buchanan's stock company giving the miners "illustrations of the drama, as it had never been seen before, and, as the bills declared, 'would never be seen again,'" told of an emergency and how "Buck" met it. In descending a divide of the American River the mule team hauling the baggage became

> frightened and ran down the mountain scattering baggage and wardrobes on the greasewood and manzanita bushes . . .
>
> Any other man than Buchanan would have abandoned the idea of playing that night, for it was dark before we reached the hotel; but he was a man that never lost a night, "rain or shine," and he sent men back on the road to gather up what they could, got the curtain up — the curtain in that particular "temple of the drama," I remember, was composed of four blue blankets, basted together — made a speech to the audience, which was a good one, and all the better for the mishap which had befallen us, and after the performance won enough at poker to repair damages.

The Washoites admired the grit and resourcefulness of such a manager, but of his acting they were not so sure. Unlike Stark, who had developed his own subtle and realistic interpretation, Buchanan thundered out the heavy verses of Shakespeare, tore into scenes, and ended them in a "walk around" that was "apt to be headachy" even for a Washoe audience; or, aping the old schools, the tragedian made much of postures and attitudes, always overacting.

3

To compete with Stark now for the patronage of Silverland, Buchanan arrived with his daughter, a small troupe, a drum, a sword, and a boxful of printed handbills announcing the "Great Dramatic Novelty of McKean Buchanan . . . for ONE NIGHT ONLY IN COMEDY AND TRAGEDY . . ."[5] According to one of these dodgers, a choice item in the Nevada State Historical Society, the troupe appeared at Dayton on June 26, 1862. How Buck was received is uncertain. But of his next appearance, at Carson, where Stark had just finished a successful season, the *Enterprise* reported that Buchanan was "meeting with poor reception at Carson City and Empire City." "A gentleman who saw them at the latter place — which has been termed 'the head of navigation in our Territory' — has resignedly seated himself to await the arrival of the next 'steamboat,'" a *Call* critic taunted; then added:

> McKean Buchanan understands his business; in fact he is a genius in his way. A couple of weeks ago he was playing at Empire City, Nevada Territory. The house was quite thin, consisting mainly of a few married people who had brought their urchins along. Buck didn't require more than a bird's eye view to discover the fact that there were not adults enough in the house to pay expenses; so he laid a tariff on the brats, making the indignant parents come out with a half dollar for each and every young one, thereby getting even with Empire City.

Disgusted, Buchanan tore on up the canyon to the Lode towns and played the new Topliffe Theatre on July 5, where according to the *Era*, which may have simply copied Buchanan's handbills,[6] the tragedian assisted by Virginia gave scenes

---

[5] Buchanan's handbills were published in "San Francisco by commercial steam presses." Soon most of such printing would be done on the Comstock for local circulation. Not until July 31, 1863, was the *Territorial Enterprise* published by steam presses in Virginia City.

[6] It is of passing interest that *Richard III* is the historical play listed on the oldest known American playbill (presented in New York on November 12, 1753); however, most authorities agree that the first play given in America was *The Merchant of Venice*, September 5, 1752, at Williamsburg, then capital of Virginia.

from Shakespeare, interspersed with music by the orchestra and the band — one group serving as both — and ended the evening with the eccentric trifle, "a laughable comedy in one act entitled *Flirtation; or, A Morning Call.*" Though they paid only "one dollar admission," the Comstockers did not find this afterpiece too "laughable," nor Buchanan one of the "Greatest Living Actors." Buck headed for Carson and back to California.

Buchanan's failure was not so much a lack of talent or even that Washoites had been educated for months by a greater tragedian, but a difference in temperament and character. Buck actuated himself in an atmosphere of his own creation, impatient with others.

4

Where, specifically, Stark played during the brief invasion of Buchanan is not known, but Mrs. Stark took a benefit at the Gold Hill Theatre that was "largely attended." By July 26 the Stark troupe were opening the new Topliffe Theatre at 49, 51, 53 North C Street with a perennial favorite, *The Lady of Lyons,* Mrs. Stark appearing as Pauline, the role in which she had made her debut to the California stage twelve years before.

According to Bulwer's five-act play, an ignorant gardener's son fell in love with the daughter of his father's boss, and determining to win her, learned to paint and write poetry because, as the boy insisted, "art became the shadow of the starlight in those haunting eyes." Although there was nothing in the verses that "a serf might not send to an empress," Pauline refused the amorous epistles. She also rejected the advances of a score or more other suitors, two of whom planned revenge by furnishing Claude Melnotte (James Stark), another disgruntled suitor, with money and clothes to impersonate a prince, win the girl, marry her, then force her to live in a hovel.

Taking Pauline to the wretched house on the wedding night, Claude, now contrite, admitted being a fraud, expressed his remorse, agreed to a divorce (although Pauline still loved him), and rushed off to war. After becoming a general, he returned to find Pauline being sold to an old rejected suitor for her bankrupt father's debts. Claude "planked up thrice the sum" and clasped Pauline in his arms as the curtain fell, leaving the audience to dry their eyes and go home in a "haze of sentiment."

Topliffe audiences demanded repeat performances; and in August the *Era* informed its theatrically-minded readers that "Mr. James Stark with a *corps* of excellent assistants is still entertaining the Washoe Virginians." Did the Thespians perhaps remain too long in reckless, bewildering Washoe? Discord entered the ranks of the Stark company.

5

Seemingly without preliminary "the entire concern dissolved." What caused the breakup of the Stark troupe is not clear. From the brief account in Carson City's *Silver Age* one would assume that Harry Brown was wholly or partly responsible. Swaggering into Comstock bars he proceeded to "do himself brown by drowning his good reputation as an actor in that of a bummer." The remainder of the troupe used their talents elsewhere. Miss Douglas, the "solid" actress, returned to California as Nellie Brown already had done in May.[7] Miss Hamlin probably returned to San Jose. W. Stephenson joined a troupe of minstrels formed from a breakup in the ranks of the Hussey Minstrels.

---

[7] By winter Nellie Brown was still reaping laurels and "dimes" as a popular member of a minstrel team. The next August the Washoites would learn that their favorite of the Washoe Dramatic Company was marrying the actor, Charles Taylor in the California mining town of Dutch Flat. Less than two years later as an unfortunate member of her husband's "Failure Company," she would "die of nostalgia" in far-off Shanghai. Taylor then joined the rebels, was captured by the Imperialists, and along with several Chinese was beheaded.

What became of Harry Brown? After several weeks of dis-
sipation, he finally discovered that saloons were not so attractive as theatres, returned to his profession, and by the next
summer would again be in Washoe as "an invaluable accessory to the Great Star Company at Maguire's new Opera
House in Virginia City."

Did James Stark return to California theatres or engage a
new troupe and continue his conquest of Silverland? He did
neither. Probably welcoming the dissolution of his company,
Stark cancelled the rest of his Washoe engagement. At last
he was free to answer another call. But when an eminently
successful actor gave up a paying profession to take up the
uncertainties of mining, he must either be ill or out of his
mind, insisted Sarah Stark. For the fever that had entered
Stark's blood his wife had no medicine; neither was her reasoning of any avail. In the end, Sarah and Jimmy Griffith
accompanied "Mr. Quartstruck" Stark to Esmeralda, where
Stark became as energetic a miner as he had been an actor.
In a short time he "had a quartz mill built and operating."
His mine looked promising. Mrs. Stark, however, was drawn
back to San Francisco and her stage career.

But Stark remained at Aurora. From this area he was
chosen a member of the first constitutional convention of
Nevada. And two years later the *Era* would report: "The
popular tragedian James Stark is deeply engaged in mining
operations at present and does not intend to resume the
histrionic profession." But the actor who had made a great
contribution to the early legitimate silver theatre had not
completely discarded "the buskin and the sword" though he
did not then know it.[8] As for Jimmy Griffith, he stayed with

---

[8] Unaware of Stark's theatrical seasons in Washoe, of Sarah's joining her husband
and playing there, and of Stark's venture into mining, the *San Francisco Theatre
Research*, vol. III, inadvertently had Stark "disappeared" those three years; although
the San Franciso *Call* of November 6, 1862, noticed "the familiar face of Mr.
James Stark, the eminent tragedian, on Montgomery Street again. He has just re-

Stark long enough to realize the precariousness of mining, then left to assist San Francisco theatricals.

6

During the summer Bartholomew's circus arrived as did Clark and La Font's Minstrels and Frank Hussey's Minstrels. The latter also suffered a rift in its ranks while at Virginia City. As a result Hussey's no longer had "Miss Jessie and her attractive extenuations," which probably proved "a great loss to it," but gained W. Stephenson.[9]

Clark & La Font's, having acquired Miss Jessie, took her as vocalist and danseuse over to entertain the soldiers at Fort Churchill and from there on around Washoe's theatre circuit, thereby missing the fire that broke out in Virginia City at three one morning. Hussey's saved their wardrobes, too, by being ensconced at Topliffe's since that "theatre and surrounding buildings mostly escaped destruction." But between C and D Streets about 150 people were "burned out." The Celestials were blamed; and a petition circulated to rid the city of them. But the fires were out now and there was variety enough in entertainment on the Comstock to divert practically everyone.

At Bartholomew's American Circus, "Wonder" and "Young America" were kneeling and counting, trying to uphold their billboard reputation as "beyond doubt the best trick ponies in the world," while riders, acrobats, and gymnasts sought to confirm their slightly less ambitious advertisement: "Best on the Pacific coast." Though Washoe children were supposed to "scream with delight at the antics of the celebrated ponies," Bartholomew's was a disappointment, especially the side shows, which, to even a sympathetic observer, were bilks:

turned from professional duties in Washoe." Actually Stark was in the Bay city from his mine to visit Sarah and purchase mining supplies.

[9] By October, Stephenson was at San Francisco's American Theatre with his old associates, Jimmy Griffith and Harry Brown. Later, while on tour, he would have the unpleasant task of informing a concerned public of a serious stage accident involving himself and other actors seen on the Washoe theatrical boards.

No. 1. — Large hog. Fat thing, well patronized.
No. 2. — A hen with three heads. Drew a great many people until
the other night; while the lecturer was discoursing as to
the wonderful freak of nature, one of the heads dropped
off. . .
No. 5. — A man swallowing a United States cutlass. It was rusty.
No. 8. — Engagement between the Merrimac and the Monitor.
Both bursted.

The "Last of a One-Horse Show . . . defunct and broken" was sold, but suddenly "turned up as an establishment" in northern California.

Then Joe Pentland arrived to keep his billboard promise to open at Carson. After Bartholomew's lavish puffs, with what could Pentland bark his Great World Circus? Perhaps Joe relied on the newspaper's brief but pointed: "Pentland's is making a successful tour through Nevada Territory." After enjoying a performance under the big top, the *Enterprise* reporters also insisted that Pentland does "not thrust on us mountain folks the mere skeleton of a show. There are no bauchle in the performance which inspires the spectacular with a feeling of mingled pity and shame for the failure. Every member of the company is master of his business and a succession of brilliant acts command unqualified applause from beginning to end."

The Queen of Comedy

1

In spite of the flood's devastation, 1862 was a good year entertainment-wise, the Washoites having been favored with legitimate dramas, farces, Dan De Quille's local comedies, and Shakespeare. After the dog fights at Dayton, the people had enjoyed "horse-races, baths, etc., the usual attractions for Sundays and other holidays" at Steamboat Springs, "a natural curiosity" puffing smoke and steam, which inspired a local Dutchman to say, "Drive on, Hans, we are not far from where ter Duyvel lives!"

One afternoon "Big Nick" cleared his Empire City saloon of furnishings and gave a children's party that included music, games, and then cake and ice cream — ice cream, "the best the market could afford." The children of Silverland also enjoyed picnics, parties, foot races, games, kit-flying, and circuses.

Preceding Pentland's Great World Circus by five days, arrived someone of definite theatrical note: a comedienne who the fall before had arrived on the West coast from a successful season at Laura Keene's theatre. As she had in New York, Mrs. W. H. Leighton "completely captivated her California audiences" and became an "instantaneous and tremendous hit," receiving such newspaper adulation as "the young, pretty, charming, smiling piquant siren, who sings like a nightingale and acts with an irresistible grace and *naivete*."

2

Whether the piquant siren entertained Genoa is unknown. However, on September 4, 1862, at the Carson City Theatre

64394

billed as the "Queen of Comedy," Mrs. W. H. Leighton, assisted by a full troupe, appeared in the three-act comedy-drama, *Pride of the Market,* and in the laughable farce, *Fool of the Family.* So taken were the Carsonites with Mrs. Leighton's gay and amusing presentations, Mrs. Perry's dancing, Mr. Woodhull's comic songs, and the troupe generally (which included also A. R. Phelps, Dave C. Anderson, C. L. Graves, A. Fischer, Yankee Locke, Mrs. G. E. Locke, and the former Washoe actor W. Stephenson), they demanded a repeat performance. Tickets were only a dollar. And four consecutive nights later "business was still good," the Carson Theatre nightly packed.

On September 6 the Queen of Comedy took what "was indeed a benefit . . . by even surpassing her usual frolicsome geniality and vivacity of humor. Indeed the whole company left no effort untried to please and delight the audience. . . Their engagement in this city has been a successful and pleasant one, and we hope to see them return at an early day. Wherever Mrs. Leighton appears, she is destined to please and draw crowded houses," predicted Carson City's *Silver Age.*

Not the least of those who ably assisted the comedienne was an attractive actress, who would please Nevadans for years — Mrs. H. A. Perry.[1] "Without possessing any striking ability as an actress," wrote a *Call* reviewer, "she is nevertheless industrious in study and careful in rendition." But a former theatrical critic for the same paper held a different opinion of the lady's worth. Prefacing his appraisal of principal stock actors on the West coast with, "We have no one to conciliate, none to please, none to punish, and with strict equality and justice we exhibit each name in its veritable

---

[1] Formerly Miss Agnes Land, the actress had married Harry A. Perry early the previous year, only to be widowed eleven months later. This unhappy circumstance caused sympathetic Tom Maguire to tender her a benefit at his San Francisco Theatre.

dramatic estimation." Then he wrote, "Mrs. Perry (nee Agnes Land), the leading juvenile actress is a young lady of great personal beauty, and the reigning favorite. . . With an acute perception and positive talent, she unites a finished and refined education, and is as much a delight and pride of the drawing-room as she is an ornament to the stage. She is preeminently distinguished in all the virtues and excellencies which adorn the female character." The Washoites were not blind to such charms. A. R. Phelps (Mrs. Leighton's light comedian) the *Call* critic thought "a very fair actor" though an "eccentric old man"; Dave C. Anderson "a good actor."

3

Glowing over their Carson City triumphs and anticipating new ones, the troupe entertained at Dayton on the seventh and noted the following item in the *Silver Age:* "The Leighton Troupe are doing a thriving business in Washoe." Next morning the company packed and traveled again, this time up Gold Cañon and over the grade into Virginia City, stopping at Number 49, 51, 53 C Street to fulfill an engagement for the Comstockers. Here at Topliffe's the star's husband (W. H. Leighton) took over the managerial post, appointed A. R. Phelps, stage manager, and G. L. Graves, promoter. A. Fischer was already leader of the orchestra.

Night after night the Comstockers crowding Topliffe's Theatre were as delighted as the Carsonites had been with the comedies presented. In fact, the people were so "loath to lose the laughing lady," they persuaded Leighton to extend his wife's stay another week so they might tender her a "Grand Complimentary Benefit." The date chosen was September 23, when Mrs. Leighton was featured in *All That Glitters Is Not Gold,*[2] a well-knit piece and a fitting choice

---

[2] William C. Miller, an unpublished manuscript, "An Historical Study of Theatrical Entertainment in Virginia City," p. 28, quoting a rare Topliffe Theatre program of Virginia City, September, 1862.

for presenting in a rugged mining town. As his contribution Woodhull sang a comic song called "The Windmill" and Mrs. Perry did a fancy dance. The evening concluded with one of the beneficiary's favorites, *Fool of the Family*, a farce the Washoites had enjoyed before and would again and again when the "Queen of Comedy" — so pleased with her first Silverland venture — returned the next year. The following night Mr. Leighton concluded the season with a "Magnificent Bill" for the benefit of the Virginia City guards. This benefit for a local organization made a "hit" with the Washoites. Theatrical companies generally assisted civic affairs; they found it the best advertisement possible.

4

About the time San Franciscans were "glad to learn that Mrs. Leighton and her troupe would shortly arrive from their interior tour," Washoe was opening a soap and candle factory, planning a gas company, and enjoying Joe Goldsmith's National Troupe of Glass Blowers in a novel and educational entertainment. Joe's glass blowers were artists, blowing, spinning, and working the molten glass "as if by magic" into flowers, baskets, wreaths, pens, gems, pins, and "a great variety of curious toys from the fragile material," all of which they gave to their fascinated visitors. Affording "such unqualified delight," the National Glass Blowers continued "a most successful tour" of Silverland's theatres.

The two Joes (Goldsmith and Pentland) had scarcely departed Washoe when the Panorama of Europe arrived and gave its first exhibition "at Gold Hill, Nevada Territory." Not as popular as the glass blowers, the Panorama, however, attracted fair audiences, mainly those of an educational inclination.

November-December 1862

River Boat Players

1

Although it was November the indomitable Chapman theatrical company arrived in Silverland. It was made up more than likely of father George, certainly also Mrs. George, her son Alonso,[1] Belle Chapman, William Hamilton, and of course Miss Caroline Chapman herself. Probably the Washoe veterans W. Stephenson, Harry Brown and Jimmy Griffiths were also in the cast.

For generations prior to their Nevada advent the Chapmans had appeared on the English stage, rumor insisting that a Chapman had been a member of Shakespeare's company. Certainly all the family knew Shakespeare — his plays, that is — but they were likewise prepared for a varied repertoire of tragedies, dramas, sensation plays, high-class comedies, extravaganzas, and farces, plus songs and dances in the form of solos, duets, or teams between the main acts. They were a resourceful family as many interesting stories illustrate. Harry Chapman, for example, in a tragic role also doubling as a musician, fell with his head and shoulder off stage and fiddled to his own dying.

It was probably 1827 when the patriarch William Chapman brought his family to America. Although two children remained in England, it was often difficult for the Chapman tribe to get parts in the same production or at the same theatre. In consequence, the Chapmans spread, some to

---

[1] Unhappily the Chapman troupe lost "a comedian of some merit" at Howard Flat the next February when Alonso Parks, step-son of George Chapman and known as Alonzo Chapman, died, leaving a wife and child.

perform, others to serve as theatre managers until the eldest
son was killed while riding to the theatre.[2] To keep the
family safely together, William Chapman conceived the idea
of the first showboat. Up the gangplank into the boat bearing
the sign "Theatre" came the Chapmans: father William, a
big smile on his face; Samuel's widow and son Harry; "Uncle
Billy" and wife Phoebe with Frank M. and soon Caroline
(named for her aunt "Our Caroline"); George (a good low
comedian); William Hamilton; and the youngest, known in
the West as "Our Caroline," the most versatile and famous.

Drifting along the Ohio and Mississippi Rivers, the Chapmans practiced their parts, loved and lived in the small house
forward and all over the boat, married, were born, died,
dropped a plank for a town and countryside to come aboard,
acted a surprising array of plays in the small hall with its
wooden benches and tallow candles, and fished — even between acts they fished, so legend related. A unique family of
Thespians, all but a few of whom would eventually play
Silverland.[3]

2

The George Chapman family, already with a large cast in
their growing numbers, were the first players to reach California in 1849. "Good old George" was admired and liked,
but it was Mrs. George Chapman, the invincible pioneer
actress — and, mother of 20 children — who first won Chapman fame for the entire group in the West, San Franciscans
showering her with benefit after benefit. In one of these
Alonzo was entrusted with a leading role, Belle had an
important part, and other children also assisted.

---

[2] But the "eldest son," Samuel, had married the sister of the famous actor,
Joseph Jefferson; so the Samuel Chapman line lived on in son Harry (already mentioned as playing his own dying dirge), who fathered two daughters, Blanche and
Ella Chapman, known to the theatrical world as "The Chapman Sisters" — the
same "Chapman Sisters" who one time entertained insistent highway robbers with
an impromptu song and dance program on a lonely mountain road in the West.

[3] Father William died before the Gold Rush and "Uncle Billy" passed away in
San Francisco in 1857.

PROMENADE BALL!!

TO BE GIVEN AT

OPHIR,

ON

Friday Evening, October 3d.

Invitation Committee.

OPHIR.	VIRGINIA CITY.
L. D. Young,	I. C. Bateman,
James Collins.	M. G. Hillyer,
FRANKTOWN.	George Hill.
F. A. Ent,	GOLD HILL.
Richard D. Sides.	F. A. Birge,
WASHOE CITY.	Edward Burke,
Peter Miller,	James McMarlin.
H. K. Tompkins,	SILVER CITY.
Charles Conger.	G. Koneman,
GALENA.	Mr. Benton.
A. K. Bonzy,	CARSON CITY.
Mr. Springer.	Fred White,
STEAMBOAT SPRINGS.	John D. Winters,
Joseph Ellis,	Charles W. Curry.
James Miller.	

FLOOR MANAGERS.

J. P. Foulks, Washoe City ; L. D. Young, Ophir ; Jos. Ellis, Steam boat ; R. D. Sides, Franktown.

sep27-td   D. S. EHLER, Proprietor.

EARLIEST EXTANT NEWSPAPER NOTICE OF A DANCE IN NEVADA, OCTOBER 3, 1862
From the Carson City *Daily Silver Age*, October 2, 1862. Courtesy, the Bancroft Library.

EARLIEST KNOWN PLAYBILL
FOR NEVADA, JUNE 1862
Courtesy, Nevada Historical Society.

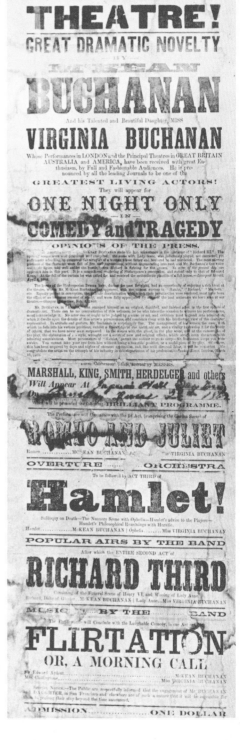

A HAND-WRITTEN INVITATION TO A
SOCIAL BALL AT GENOA, NEVADA TERRITORY, 1862
Courtesy, Nevada Historical Society.

By 1852 the rest of the Chapmans had arrived through the Golden Gate, later to wander interior-ward, playing in theatres, tents, saloons, and even on top of a huge tree stump. Silverland beckoned. It could not be otherwise. And the *Call* of late November informed its interested readers: "The Chapman Company were last heard from at Topliffe's Theatre, Virginia City." Where else did the company play? It is difficult to conceive their appearing only on the Comstock after crossing the Sierras. Undoubtedly they made the circuit followed recently by Mrs. Leighton, the circuses, and the glass blowers.

What the Chapman Company played on this first trip to Nevada is conjecture. There was scarcely a play from Shakespeare on, that they had not attempted. They may have repeated such productions, recently given in California, as *Beauty and the Beast* with Caroline in the role of Beauty, *She Stoops to Conquer*, *The Hunchback*, and perhaps *Box and Cox* with some of the cast in blackface. The possibilities are almost limitless. Rest assured the Chapmans spared no effort to please and so they returned again and yet again. (Of later presentations happily more information is available.) By December the Chapmans as well as all other troupes playing the legitimate theatre there departed Nevada Territory.

3

Before spring brought "flush times" (although "building was brisk" all winter) and imported entertainers, the people of Washoe filled in with home-variety diversion. "Since raising the flag on a 50-foot liberty pole," Aurora had prospered, the hills echoing with the mining blasts from such mines as the Wide West. Stages ran an extra every day now to accommodate the "rolled up, muffled up, long and short coated" newcomers pursuing "the almighty dollar." Also in pursuit was former tragedian James Stark, busy now with his sixty-stamp mill.

Over two hundred new houses were going up, but still "the tribulations of new arrivals lay in finding accommodations" in Aurora, where the streets were crowded with "horses, mules, and ox teams and pack trains loaded with all kinds of provisions, mining tools, and machinery," as well as liquor, playing cards, balls, and billiard tables for diversion in the more than forty saloons, where pretty women dealt the cards and "homely men raked in the dollars." [4] One wonders what had become of the Aurora Theatre (with its "scenery painted especially for it"), which had opened in March, and what troupes, if any, had played there. Did the Chapman Company, inured to the hardships of their profession, perhaps trek to Esmeralda and favor the people with a rare theatrical treat? Did the Aurora Theatre serve as the dancing academy, which was "in full operation with soireés every Friday night and plenty of votaries"?

Early in December to dedicate a "new and commodious military hall," Esmeralda Rifles "neatly and appropriately decorated" the hall with flags, emblems, "mirrors, paintings, the arms and accoutrements belonging to the company" and held a formal ball. Unlike later vigilante days, "all was carried on in good humor"; sixty ladies "in elegant dresses neatly trimmed in red, white and blue mingled as gracefully as sylphs in the mazy dance . . . to the excellent music furnished by the Aurora band." So pleased were the Rifles that the ball was "marred by no accident or indiscretion," they paraded through Aurora's streets, their brass band "discoursing sweet music among the silver laden hills."

On Christmas Eve two companies of Aurora firemen took charge of the dance, which turned out to be as jovial as their "handsome red flannel shirts," though a fire engine did not arrive as ordered and as a consequence several buildings

---

[4] Aurora also boasted two churches, one schoolhouse, several other public buildings and a newspaper, the *Aurora Times,* which began publication early in April of 1863.

burned during the week. Perhaps the Aurora Theatre likewise went up in smoke. Nevertheless, Stark's home town
danced through New Year's Eve in a "Grand Complimentary
Benefit by the Citizens of Aurora for Glen's Quadrille Band."

A new type of amusement arrived the last of December.
Many of Aurora's citizens paid a dollar each (fifty cents for
children) and crowded Preble and Devoe's Hall to enjoy
"the performance of a person calling himself the Wizard of
the East and the World-renowned Wizard and Ventriloquist"
in one of his "wonderful entertainments." [5]

4

Although all supplies in the Humboldt Mining District
were "higher than in Virginia," items of amusement were not
overlooked. Men could step up to the "polished mahogany"
and get liquid refreshments in most of the Humboldt camps.[6]
When the Bank Exchange at Star City held an "Inaugural
Ball," Humboldt City — not to be outdone — held another

---

[5] *Aurora Daily Times,* December 28, 1863 — a rare sheet — and the San Francisco *Daily Morning Call,* January 3, 1864.

[6] Its first mines discovered in May of 1860, the Humboldt Mining District laid
claim to having a "principal hotel" even though only "one house in the region"
had a floor. However, by the end of 1861 the papers recalled that the population
had reached 700, nearly half of whom lived in Humboldt City, "the most populous
point," surpassing Unionville, the new county seat on the other side of the mountain. "We have an assay office . . . also a furnace," H. B. Truett had written
the *Enterprise* in July of 1862. "Our little town is improving. Within the past
month many stores and dwellings with two hotels have been built and others are
in the process . . . making about 75."

The newspapers further recalled that on the evening of Independence Day the
"citizens of Star City turned out en masse" to enjoy the grand military ball sponsored by the Buena Vista Guards at Robinson's new building in Unionville, to
partake of the "superb supper" at Guthrie's Ohio House, and at dawn next day to
salute the Fourth with "loud-voiced anvils and guns." At Star a "programme at
the Grove" included the raising of the flag, a prayer by Father Lassetter, the
reading of the Declaration of Independence by O. R. Leonard, and orations by
citizens of Unionville and Star, a dinner, toasts, singing by the Glee Club, and
stirring music by the Buena Vista Guards.

The camp of Murphy enjoyed cricket matches. Down on their knees the Indians
watched the "desperate fight" of Mormon crickets and bet the four-bit pieces they
had acquired by gathering wild gooseberries and buffalo berries and selling them
to the white people.

that drew "representatives" from all the near-by towns. The music was good, the dancing enjoyable, and "nothing could exceed the sumptuous repast" — perhaps including "game from the wilderness — nor the avidity with which it was laid hold of."

"The Humboldt District, never so flourishing wore a bright face" since workmen in the Sheba had struck a rich ledge and construction on the Humboldt Canal and the tunnel above town had brought hundreds of men into Humboldt City, whose appearance, according to the *Humboldt Register,* showed "more signs of active business than any other town in the country." [7] Diversion was so welcome that even Superintendent White's lecture on the schools was largely attended although the morning had been upset when a lady practicing pistol shooting twice shot into a tentful of men. Yet Reaves and Usher spared "no pains or expense" to make evenings enjoyable at their scarcely completed 32-by-75-foot building with its thick adobe walls, plank floor, and tin roof.

The horse races on Buena Vista course and the foot races at Star caused "bushels of money" to change hands. The "Santa Clara, Nevada Territory, wedding of a gay and blooming widow" brought crowds to the couple's "new frame house" for a "happy party of cotillion and waltzes to a late hour," inspiring such lines in the *Humboldt Register* as:

> Life is a stream; man is a boat;
> Down its rough current he's destined to float;
> And woman's a cargo, so easily stored,
> That he's a great fool who doesn't take her on board.

---

[7] Ginaca had the contract for forty miles of Humboldt Canal — *Virginia Evening Bulletin,* October 22, 1863. Since they had "polled the second highest vote in the territory" at this time, the 1,238 voting citizens of the Humboldt-Unionville district considered their being "wholly deprived of the benefits of the United States mail facilities" as "a scandalous, outrageous injury." Ever since April, when Langton and Company had refused to carry the mails unless paid by the government, tons of mail intended for Humboldt had accumulated at Carson City.

But then, the *Register* gave newspaper space to coyotes, rattlesnakes — and a new hotel in Star.

Isaac Miller's "Grand Christmas Ball and Supper" seems to have warranted the eight dollars charged per ticket to open his "Splendid New Hotel." The holiday dance at Pryor's new hall in Humboldt City was also well attended. And the carrier for the *Register* announced that he would personally "call on his friends . . . New Year's morning with a handsome poetical Address."

Lamenting the lack of such legitimate fare as the Chapmans could have provided, Humboldt men enjoyed something of the theatrical during Christmas when for two weeks a troupe of "hurdy-gurdy artistes" gave the bachelor boys gay times while improving "their terpsichorean accomplishments."

Feet on the Comstock

1

During the bonanza year of 1863 the Comstock miners — struck with the "feet fever" — dug twenty million dollars worth of ore, which was to spread the fame of the Lode and influence the money systems of nations. Enjoying their "feet," the people danced; gave dinners; and skated, "ladies and the rest of mankind going out daily to engage in the sport." From six to ten "pleasure-seekers" stowed away within an ice boat "enjoyed themselves to the top of their bent, while jolly old Aeolus wafted them wheresoever they list." Some fun-seekers spent their "feet" at a shooting gallery and on "the horses." Others attended weddings, funerals — and a hanging. And most of the occasions — including the funerals and the hanging — required music. To answer this demand, local musicians organized commercial bands. Perhaps Mrs. Perry's stage dancing inspired the miners to attend night classes in dancing then being offered in nearly all the towns.[1]

However, on an evening late in January, Comstockers crowded La Plata Hall not to do "cancellation" or take dancing lessons, but to attend a concert, one that promised to be "on a scale of grandeur never before attempted on this side of the Sierras." [2] Maybe it was. Henry O'Keeffe, a San Francisco musician, arranged the vocal and musical entertainment

---

[1] Fox and Stauts opened dancing schools at Carey's new La Plata Hall in Virginia City and at Faulk's Concert Hall in Washoe City. McCluskey's Pioneer Quadrille Band advertised music for "Balls and Private Parties on the most reasonable terms." An "All Brass Band for Celebrations, Parades, Theatres, Funerals, etc.," also advertised.

[2] *Virginia Daily Union*, January 21, 1863.

assisted by such local musicians as Messrs. Bradish, Ball, Eells, Henry Franz, Griswold, Marsh, and Pardee, all of whom were members of the Virginia Glee Club. Certainly the concert was a success from the standpoint of attendance; for the Washoites always supported home-talent shows.

2

When Lincoln's "First of January Proclamation" (freeing certain slaves) arrived, the people observed it with a series of dances, the receipts, often in "feet," going to aid the sick and wounded soldiers of the War through the Sanitary Fund, a precursor of the Red Cross. Of the music supplied for the dance at Odd Fellows' Hall in Gold Hill, the *Enterprise* observed: "The excellence of the article was only equalled by the industry and the perseverance of the performers. We consider that the man who can fiddle all through one of those Virginia Reels without losing his grip can be depended upon in any kind of musical emergency."

The same paper considered the Sanitary Ball at La Plata Hall "a very marked success, proving beyond a shadow of a doubt the correctness of our theory that ladies never fail in undertakings of this kind." But in the Reel, "when the ladies were ordered to the center, two of them failed to make the connection. Their dresses were anchored under our boots," explained Sam Clemens. "Those two beautiful pink dresses let go amidships. . . We did not apologize, because our presence of mind happened to be absent at the very moment that we had the greatest need of it. But we beg permission to do so now." [3]

Supper this January evening was "served up" by the What Cheer House; and since couples were served first, Sam, a stag, felt slighted, though he explained:

We engaged a good many young ladies last Tuesday to go with us, but they all seemed to have got a little angry about some-

---

[3] Virginia City *Daily Territorial Enterprise*, January 10, 1863.

thing. . . They told us we had better go and invite a thousand girls to go to the ball. . . We stalked off to the Sanitary Ball alone without a virgin out of that whole litter. We may have done wrong but how could we help it? We couldn't stand the temperature of those parlors more than an hour at a time; it was cold enough to freeze out the heaviest stockholder on the Gould & Curry's books.

(No wonder Mr. Harris of Washoe City was doing a good business making sheet-iron stoves especially designed "for quick heating of parlors and sitting-rooms.") However, Sam "only ate a boiled ham and some pies," passing up a table of cakes decorated with patriotic mottoes in fancy icing.

Silver City, Dayton, Carson, and Genoa also held Sanitary Balls.[4] Washoe City delayed its "Patriotic Ball" until the last of January so as to hold it in a "more commodious building than its conflagrated predecessor." By this time the new Steamboat Springs Hotel had "risen from its ashes like a phoenix" and was again "on the full tide of successful experiment" with one of "the most splendid as well as the most joyous terpsichorean affair ever got up in the Washoe region. . . As a matter of course, the gentlemen were numerically preponderant, and were brave and all that sort of thing; but the ladies! Heaven bless the ladies! . . . There is no better spot in the Territory for a genuinely joy-inspiring pleasure party, than the Steamboat Springs,"[5] insisted the rather partial *Washoe Times*.

---

[4] The funds raised from all the Sanitary Balls were proudly forwarded to Virginia City's A. B. Paul, who sent them on to the Sanitary Commission in New York City. When the Washoites learned that their contributions had been placed to the credit of Nevada County, California, they were justly indignant. "This is one of the many blunders which are daily perpetrated at the expense of this Territory," sputtered the *Washoe Times*, "and all growing out of that stupid whim that gave it the name of 'Nevada.' Some of these fine days the 'State of Washoe' will sparkle among the stars of the American Flag and then our good deeds will be credited to the proper quarter."

[5] Other Washoites would echo the editor's words. Mark Twain, Joe Goodman, Dan De Quille, and others wrestling with illness and winter colds, enjoyed bathing and recuperating at Steamboat.

Como, a "rather pretty mining camp near Dayton," sent out elaborate, hand-written announcements, which named thirty-two committeemen, including Adolph Sutro (the famous Comstock tunnel builder), for their "pleasant affair," which "came off" at the large, three-story Cross Hotel. Not to be outdone by the civilians, the officers and men of Fort Churchill held a formal ball, splendid in patriotic and military coloring.

3

Not all the dances were well arranged or orderly. Mrs. Fanny Hazlett, a Washoe pioneer, recalled a dance she attended at Dayton. Trouble started; bowie knives gleamed; and the women fled from the hall through whatever opening was handy. One evening a father, seeking a barber to dress his daughter's hair so she might attend a dance, was killed by a chance shot. And while "a fancy dress ball was in full blast in Yreka," Dean shot Kirby, his saloonkeeper rival, over an incident that began merely as a prank involving cayenne pepper.[6]

When handsome Allen Milstead "paid the price" for murdering a man at Ragtown, the Washoites — even women from as far away as Genoa — gathered on the hills above Dayton to witness the event.[7] After the sheriff read the death warrant, Milstead mounted the scaffold; made a speech in a "clear voice without a tremor in it"; and "adjusted the knot . . .

---

[6] Saloonkeeper Dean, who was noted for playing pranks, sprinkled cayenne pepper on his competitor's dance floor thereby forcing the coughing dancers out of the ballroom. While waiting for the floor to be cleaned, some of the men wandered over to Dean's saloon — which was, of course, the intention of the joke. But Kirby did not consider it at all funny. He rushed across to Dean's place, called him several mouthfuls of vile names, then struck him over the head with a pistol. Shortly after midnight prankster Dean, soreheaded now and brooding over what he considered an unjust beating, stepped across to Kirby's establishment and emptied his six shooter into his competitor — *Washoe Times,* January 10, 1863.

[7] Virginia City *Daily Territorial Enterprise,* January 10, 1863. The *Enterprise* estimated 7000 were present, but Mrs. Hazlett thought 2000 people attended the hanging of Allen Milstead.

with as much nonchalance as if he were merely tying his cravat." A moment more — the drop fell. The "large concourse of citizens maintained profound silence throughout the solemn scene." Then to proper music and led by "the handsomely dressed Silver City Guards," everybody present escorted the body to the grave. Silverland could have enjoyed another hanging, but William Mayfield (found guilty of murdering Sheriff Blackburn) escaped from the new territorial prison in Carson as his guards, including Warden Abe Curry, played cards outside the cell although Governor Nye had sent an extra guard of 25 soldiers to prevent such an occurrence.[8]

When early in 1863 Roach traded off his common-law wife for $1800 and a yoke of oxen, Washoe was mildly concerned. But when he used the proceeds for a "done-in style wedding" by renting Doyle's Hall, hiring a band of musicians, buying champagne by the basket, ordering quantities of fruit cake, and laboriously writing hundreds of invitations, the hundreds responded. On the marriage night — dressed in a linen duster, carpet slippers, and a red necktie — Roach proudly brought his lady to the Doyle stage, where "with many flourishes" Judge Haydon "tied the knot."

Dancing then began "after the most approved style," pigeon wing being the favorite. Roach had failed, however, to plan how he would serve his refreshments. The champagne lay in the baskets on the floor of the stage; here too, the baker "plumped the cakes down still in the tins," but did include an oversized knife. Someone finally collected an assortment of glasses; so between dances the guests enjoyed a "hunk of cake and a glass of champagne" from the stage-buffet.[9]

Those who "attended the wants of the traveling public," such as the Central and the Collins Houses on the Ophir Grade, provided their patrons with "dancing and all its con-

[8] Forest Hill *Placer Weekly Courier,* March 22, 1862.

[9] Fanny G. Hazlett, "Historical Sketches and Reminiscences of Dayton, Nevada," *Nevada Historical Society Papers,* III, pp. 55-56.

comitants." In Virginia, Topliffe's Theatre, opened as a dance house on March 14 by "about a dozen German girls," was "crowded to suffocation" — the red-shirted men, the dancing girls in whirling skirts, and the milling crowds about the "gambling tables connected with the establishment" made everything look "like California in early times." An outside observer now noted "three things at Washoe: big mines, little mines, and whisky shops; in other words, Ophir holes, gopher holes, and loafer holes."

4

As spring advanced, the "feet fever" induced the *Enterprise* editor to predict, perhaps with tongue in cheek, that Washoe silver would "yet be measured and sold as oysters . . . by the bushel." Carried away by reports of unbelievable "finds" and the fact that tons of Comstock ore were actually being mined, another Washoe editor pronounced "the quartz lodes inexhaustible, and generations, a thousand years hence, will gather wealth from them." [10] Washoites heard "pay rock" and "value by the foot" so frequently they began facetiously to estimate all salable articles by lineal measure, including "bacon by the foot." Rhythmist Sam Booth gave the theme of the times in his

ABOUT "FEET"

Sad are the forms and of infinite names,
The diseases that rock these poor bodily frames —
Of fevers and phob as, rheumatics and agues,
That torment and worry, distract us, and plague us;
Disease of the heart, and disease of the head —
Diseases that seize and hold us in bed,
And now, the long list of disease to complete
Comes raging among us — disease of the "feet."

---

[10] To further aid the Washoe-minded, Bancroft's "Map of the Washoe Silver Region of Nevada Territory" had been made available. At the same time plans were taking shape for a Truckee and Washoe Valley Canal "to float timber from the well wooded regions around Lake Bigler" down the Truckee River — which, although many were "not aware of the fact," had its outlet in Lake Tahoe — to Washoe Valley and on to the ever-demanding mines of the Comstock.

Its victims, though free from all actual pain,
Are nervous, excited, and slightly insane;
And though the disease has its seat in the brains,
They fondly imagine it runs in the "veins";
They step as elastic, and stand as erect —
We discover no halting, as we might expect,
But they gather in groups, by the side of the street,
And question each other concerning their "feet."

On steamboat and railroad, in stage-coach and car,
It is the same subject wherever we are;
In the office, the workshop, the store and saloon,
It rings in our ears night, morning and noon.
We have "feet" when we breakfast, and "feet" when we dine;
"Feet" with our coffee, and "feet" with our wine,
And "feet" enter largely in all that we eat,
While many live wholly and *solely* on "feet."

Though scarcely four years old, Virginia, which now legally dropped "City" from its name, was "already a mining colossus of twenty to twenty-five thousand people bestriding lodes and tunnels and quartz mills with the proud self-satisfied air of an all conquering giant." But the city "in choice Chinese" was "too muchee uppee and too muchee downie." So were the roads. Yet over the "grand artery of travel," the Placerville road, five thousand teams drawing huge, cumbersome, freight wagons hauled "nearly a *ton a day* of gold and silver bullion" raising "such an infernal dust too thick to see following teams." No wonder to cross B or C Streets, pedestrians and buggies often waited half an hour for a break in the procession of quartz wagons, freight teams, ox carts, and stages.[11] All strata of society was experiencing the bonanza. Washoe already was asking Congress for a mint to coin its own money.

"Are you aware," a Bay correspondent wrote," of the airs

---

[11] Extracts from local papers indicate the frequency of runaways and accidents:
While the Pioneer stage was coming through at a rapid pace, a man, not listening to warning, was knocked down and injured.
A lady was knocked down crossing C Street and kicked by an ox. Her hoops prevented her being hurt. Some virtue in them after all.

your Washoe inhabitants assume when they come down here? We can tell that a man is from 'Silverland' the moment we see him, either swelling along Montgomery Street looking as if he designed buying the town, and planting it on the top of Mount Davidson; or else with a fast team raising the dust on the road to the 'Cliff House'; or in some manner showing that he doesn't care a continental 'whether school keeps or not.'" Those who felt rich in "feet" paid well for their wants. One man bestowed ten of his "feet" on a woman of ill fame. The stock reached $150,000 on the exchange, forcing the generous male to marry the woman, who in 1859 had sold apples on the streets of San Francisco.

Noting the bonanza times, the Nevada Indians wanted to be allowed again on the Comstock, having been excluded, it seems, since the 1860 Indian wars. The Peace Celebration arrived all too soon. Down Virginia streets came Paiutes and Shoshones riding ponies in single file and dressed in the skins of wild animals.

As a little girl recently arrived from Austin, Mrs. Isobel Field, stepdaughter of Robert Louis Stevenson, was deeply impressed; for the red men had pulled the animal heads down over their own so the wolf, bear, fox, coyote, and mountain lion seemed actually alive.[12] Many white people crowding the balconies and sidewalks, noting the small black eyes darting furtively in the wild beast masks, watched apprehensively as the primitive parade passed.

---

[12] In her autobiography, *This Life I've Loved,* Isobel Field described the Indian Peace Celebration. Research and correspondence with Mrs. Field indicate that the Indian celebration was held in Virginia City during 1863. (Emma Wixon, who would become America's prima donna Emma Nevada, must have been a baby in Austin at the time five-year-old Isobel was there.)

Oratorical Efforts

1

Through the oratorical efforts mainly of Chief Winnemucca, peace had been effected between red and white man in Washoe; hence Billy Birch, who three years before had been "driven back by the Red Men," arrived on the Lode with Sam Wells, Ben Cotton, and other black faced members of Tom Maguire's San Francisco Minstrels. From its introduction by Ned Bingham minstrelsy was popular in Washoe — enjoyed also by women and children on occasions. (When stranded in northern California, even Edwin Booth had turned minstrel.) For hours now the Comstockers chuckled at the performances of the San Francisco Minstrels, especially enjoying Billy's slow drawl and soft musical laugh. Birch was an end man with few equals.

At thirteen Billy had started his stage career in the East, making his debut in New York City in 1850. Then he traveled with the Christy Minstrels. Forming a partnership with Dick Slater and Sam Wells, Birch came to California, where he became affectionately known as "Brudder Bones." While on a trip to the East in 1856, he was shipwrecked, floated for days clinging to a piece of wreckage, and except for the Norwegian bark *Ellen* would have been lost to the theatre.

Attending a melodeon, no matter his position or worries, a man could be sure of sociability and his favorite drink in comfort. The bones, banjo, tambourine, Negro songs, and the dialogue of clever end men all joined in making minstrelsy a warm, genial entertainment, especially when Billy Birch came out and sang the nonsensical "Ri Fol Lol" or slanted "Few Days" to local conditions and tantalizingly drawled:

> Old P. T. Barnum had the rocks,
>   Few days, few days,
> But lost them all on wooden clocks,
>   I'm going home.
> He bragged about his wit too soon,
>   A few days, a few days,
> For now he hasn't a picayune,
>   I'm going home.
>
> The Senate and Assembly sit
>   A few days, few days,
> And when the Members lazy get
>   They're going home.
> Now when the session fairly stops,
>   A few days, few days,
> 'Twill break up all the liquor shops
>   I'm going home.

Then the basso profundo, Sam Wells, would have Comstockers "holding their sides" while he sang the laughable "See, Sir, See" from *Sonnambula* or "Rocked in the Cradle of the Deep," which Sam did "to perfection," as well as a ballad called

> JOE BOWERS
> My name it is Joe Bowers,
> I've got a brother Ike;
> I come from Old Missouri,
> Yes, all the way from Pike.
> I'll tell you how I came here,
> And how I came to roam,
> And leave my good old mammy,
> So far away from home.[1]

---

[1] Samuel A. Wells is generally credited with writing the words to "Joe Bowers" and Charles D. Abbott, a violinist (also with the San Francisco Minstrels), with composing the music.

Between the songs, jigs, walk around, burlesques, and dialogues, Sam read such conundrums composed and handed up from the audience as:

> Why are the female portion of this community like laundresses? — Because they are Wash (oe)er women.

Sometimes prizes were given the best original conundrums; sometimes the prize went for the "worst." One is not surprised to learn that the minstrels stayed for nearly a month in Washoe reaping "golden opinions" in spite of the bursts of patriotic excitement and other competition.[2]

2

Among the first women to make Washoe home were the talented Mrs. W. K. Cutler and the pioneer educator Miss Hannah Clapp, who, history notes, built the fence about Nevada's capitol and founded Carson City's Sierra Seminary with which Mrs. Cutler was also associated. The maintenance of schools was more of a private than a public concern at first. (Virginia counted only 17 pupils in 1862, but the next year had 360! Gold Hill had 40 enrolled in a new building.) To replenish the funds of the Seminary, Mrs. Cutler periodically took to the stage to entertain the Washoites.

By June she reached the Comstock, her first appearances at the new courthouse in Virginia were highly flattering, but soon entertainment from California reached the Lode. To climax Mrs. Cutler's season and to show their appreciation, the people gave her a "Complimentary Testimonial" on July 6. Because of the lively entertainment going on elsewhere, only "a fair audience assembled" to hear Mrs. Cutler's variety

---

[2] "Richmond captured!" shouted the Washoites and engaged in "demonstrations of joy," building bonfires, ringing bells, blowing mill whistles, and running up the flag "on nearly every housetop." At night brass bands played in the streets. But the celebration was premature; the news only rumor. So the Washoites returned to the minstrels, the dances, the saloons, and to Mrs. Cutler.

program, which the newspapers published in full. Having used her voice for weeks, "the lady was laboring under a slight hoarseness," but the program was enjoyed, a *Bulletin* reporter insisting that "the rendition of the two request numbers, 'The Bells' and 'Bonnie Nannie' especially fine."

After addresses by Superintendent Collins and the ordeal of public examinations, the school children presented "delightful programs of concerts, readings, etc.," the proceeds going to pay for "the uniforms and muskets of the Virginia Cadets, a company of boy-soldiers," who had so "creditably acquitted themselves in their drill on the Fourth." (Any balance would be applied to the purchase of a melodeon for the school.) Freed at last from educational fetters, the children scampered up Mount Davidson and gave their attention to "kite-flying, the first of such sports in Nevada."

3

Just as the Washoites had applauded the oratorical efforts of the Reverend Mr. Rising at St. Paul's Church and of Professor Pinkham to raise money for the Baptist building, so now they crowded into Maguire's new Opera House Sunday after Sunday to hear the Reverend O. W. Briggs, "late a Chaplain in General Grant's army," deliver his "eloquent sermons." Washoe was not wholly irreligious. "Whoever thinks this is a wild and uncivilized country," wrote a local reporter, "should pay us a visit some Sunday and see the immense throng of men, women, and children on their way to church."

Needing more money for their church, the Catholics built a large pavilion, held a colorful fair, then used the floor for summer evening dances, "where our young folks enjoyed themselves amazingly." The Masonic Order lent their hall in Virginia to the Hebrews, who on Jewish New Year and the Day of Atonement considered it their synagogue. Aspiring young men looked with such longing on the verbal powers of Briggs, Stark, Pope, Stewart, and others that they organized the Library Debating Society, which by 1863 became the Silver Star Lyceum.[3]

4

Back to Nevada now came another orator, the tragedian McKean Buchanan, with an alert eye on the 1863 mining boom. Disregarding his former unprofitable Silverland experience, Buchanan closed his Sacramento engagement in April, piled his props, wardrobes, and company into stages, and again climbed the Sierras. By May 10 "Buck" and his troupe arrived in the "mining capital of Nevada."

"Our first performance was given in a hall, the name of which I forget," wrote Walter Leman in his *Memories of an Old Actor*. This was probably Carey's La Plata Hall, located at 15 South B Street; but after the San Francisco Minstrels left the Lode, Buchanan moved his troupe to Topliffe's Theatre. A Virginia correspondent writing on May 14 told his readers: "Our amusements at present are Colonel Wood's Great American Exhibition and McKean Buchanan's troupe of theatricals. The latter is more successful than was his first visit to the territory having brought with him a pretty respectable troupe and two performers at least — Mr. and Mrs. Chas. Pope — that rank as stars."

Charles Pope had played in such heavy roles as Othello opposite Edwin Booth's Iago at the Old Bowery in New York, where Mrs. Pope also had played in Laura Keene's well-known company. In 1861 the attractive Virginia Cunningham Howard had married Charles Pope and both were persuaded by Julia Hayne to come to California. Washoe would claim the Popes; and Charley, like Jim Stark, would succumb also

---

[3] Meetings of the Silver Star Lyceum were given special notices by newspaper reporters, many of whom were members. Saturday meetings (open to the public) were for hurling wordage about on such subjects as "*Resolved*, That the Pulpit affords a greater field of eloquence than the Bar" and ". . . Universal Suffrage is Detrimental to True Freedom."

to the lure of the mines. Virginia Howard, too, would be associated with the theatre, the social life, and the mines of Washoe for years.

The actor-manager McKean Buchanan was himself an interesting, dynamic personality; son of Purser Buchanan, U.S. Navy; grandson of Thomas McKean, one of the signers of the Declaration of Independence; and second cousin of the then recent president, James Buchanan. Educated for the Navy, "Buck" served three years as a midshipman, then entered the mercantile business in New Orleans, but nine years later abandoned it for his stage debut, "a decided success" as Hamlet — perhaps the most difficult role of the drama. Buchanan soon appeared in the principal cities of the United States and abroad, giving London 126 nights of commendable Shakespearean characters.[4]

"We had powerful rivals in the minstrels and hurdy-gurdy establishments," Leman now further recalled. "But a fair patronage was secured" in wild, restless Virginia City where men with angry antagonism (for it was the time of civil war) met together, each one with a pistol in his pocket." One evening "up through the floor came a pistol bullet," just grazing Leman's ear and "buried itself in the ceiling." To pioneer theatricals such unnerving experiences were not unusual as Stark, Buchanan, Billy Sheppard (the minstrel who had been forced to kill a Virginia man in self-defense), Leman, and others could testify.

Walter Leman was a reserved and generous gentleman in private life; on the stage a player of old men's parts, which he did, however, with a sameness that kept him from stardom. Leman became attracted to Boston's Tremont Theatre as a call boy. His first stage appearance was there as a member of a crowd in the *Taming of the Shrew*. By 1854 he was in Cal-

---

[4] *Ballou's Pictorial Drawing-Room Companion*, February 6, 1858. Less than eight years later the tragedian was stricken with paralysis and died at Denver, Colorado, on April 16, 1872.

ifornia being billed with James Stark, McKean Buchanan, Frank Mayo, the Popes, Julia Dean Hayne, and others who would eventually play Silverland. And Leman would remain in the West well-liked and respected until his death nearly forty years later.

What types of entertainment Buchanan and his company served during their 1863 Silverland season is conjecture. No doubt Shakespeare and other dramas interlarded with comedy and specialty numbers such as they had recently given at Sacramento, since all the troupe were seasoned actors who soon would be helping dedicate an Opera House in the Nevada desert.

An Opera House for the Desert

1

Shortly after Buchanan and his company had returned to the Lode, the newspapers finally let Washoe and California know that preparations were being made to assure theatricals for coming seasons:

> A NEW THEATRE GOING UP
>
> The early pioneers of '49, '50 and '51 are re-echoed in the so-called Washoe, and our old friend Thomas Maguire, Esq., the indefatigable pioneer of the theatres in California, has commenced the erection of a new Temple of the Muses for the recreation of the free-hearted and liberal mining population, and no doubt, he will find a rich harvest and a well-deserved reward for his energy in coming amongst us for the purpose of building a theatre. The site is on D Street, in the very heart of the city. He can't miss . .

Knowing the ephemeral quality of mining towns, millionaire Maguire cautiously advanced the funds, but Johnny Burns was to serve as agent and pay from his share of the profits until the agent's contributions equaled the money Maguire originally put into the business. According to the contract both men were to be "equal partners in the property, and entitled to an equal division of the profits."

Perhaps Maguire and Burns reasoned that Virginia had enough competition in (1) the Melodeon on C Street; (2) the Howard Theatre on Howard Street — if indeed it were still in existence; (3) Topliffe's Theatre on C Street; (4) E. W. Carey's La Platte Hall at 15 South B Street, a building designed for dancing, concerts, and theatricals; (5) also on B

Street a new courthouse, its District Court Room available for "high class entertainment"; (6) plus a hall under construction; (7) another melodeon, possibly two; (8) along with a handful or more of variety, hurdy-gurdy, and two-bit houses; and (9) an entire gamut of saloons.

Another playhouse more might do, especially since Tom Maguire planned to build Washoe a theatre of which it could be proud, one that even would rival his own in San Francisco. Certainly a business venture of so influential a San Franciscan should have rated newspaper attention in theatrical circles and elsewhere. Neither seems to have been the case. Nevertheless, sometime during 1862 without any fanfare Maguire and Burns agreed on a partnership arrangement for the purpose of "carrying on the business of a theatre, and giving theatrical entertainments, and to keep a refreshment saloon" in the principal city of the Comstock.[1]

Handsome, immaculate, suave, and possessing a flair of showmanship of the gambler and saloonkeeper that he had been, Thomas Maguire was at the vertex of his power in 1863. He commanded nearly as much interest as his new Washoe Opera House; for this engaging giant would dominate theatricals in Washoe for nearly a quarter century, his finger in many another Washoe amusement-pie as well. As a young man Tom Maguire in New York drove a cab, maintaining his stand near the old Park Theatre. There his fights with the rowdies developed in him a daring and a willingness to flirt with fate that was to carry him into the West and on toward the close his life — but not quite to the end. After Lucky Baldwin withdrew financial aid from the Baldwin Academy and Maguire's gambling attempts failed, the place closed in 1877; and so ended Maguire's theatrical management.[2]

---

[1] Maguire vs. Burns, Judicial Records, Register number 2048, Judgment number 1496, p. 305. The architect and builder of Maguire's Virginia City Opera House was R. Stackhouse; the "scenery, painting, etc.," was done by Torning & Co.; upholstery by James Howard; "plastering, etc.," McIntosh & Co.; and the gas fixtures by Day & Co.

With the fabulous Gold Rush, Maguire had arrived in San Francisco and had built his first theatre, the "magnificent" Jenny Lind, above his saloon, as was the usual arrangement then. To open the theatre he engaged the tragedian James Stark, who brought to the Bay region the first classical productions of Shakespeare and English comedy. Although fire after fire consumed Maguire's theatres and dull times came, always the "indomitable Napoleon" not only schemed a way out, but enlarged his domain until he was controlling the theatres of San Francisco, Sacramento, and those of the mining interior. He booked stars from Europe, Australia, and the East to play his string of theatres, not neglecting his new Virginia City venture on D Street. Although few restrictions seemed imposed upon the impetuous Washoites, definite rules of conduct posted in the Green Room were enforced upon Maguire's theatrical people at the new Opera House.[3]

2

And what an Opera House! The newspapers devoted columns to describing it; and Comstock's new Virginia *Evening Bulletin* lauded:

This theatre, which can seat 1600 comfortably, is 18 inches wider and a foot longer than the Opera House in San Francisco and reflects the highest credit upon the mechanics and artists who had its erection in charge. To say that it is a first class establishment would convey but a faint idea of its magnificence. . . The new Opera House was completed and thrown open to the public on the evening of the 2d of July; and from that time every performance given therein has been witnessed by immense audiences.

---

[2] Though Maguire probably made a million dollars in the theatre business, he died in poverty, New Yorkers remembering his tiresome accounts of his golden days as he gradually drifted into obscurity. Finally, "like so many others of the clan, he died in destitution."

[3] The Green Room — so called because the first "retiring room" in Covent Garden Theatre was in green — was a reception room, where actors waited until called upon the stage. All actors knew the risk of over-indulging in intoxicants (penalty, a week's salary or discharge) or addressing an audience without permission (penalty, five dollars). Neither was an actor to make the stage wait, use his own langauge or swear in his part, refuse to wear a prescribed costume, copy parts of a play without permission, or use a book or other assistance while on the stage.

With a 50-foot front on D Street and running 114 feet back into the sagebrush-covered hill — an incongruous contrast of elegance and primitiveness — the $30,000 edifice boasted a stage (35 by 50 feet) comparable with those of the largest theatres. Seating was such that Washoe audiences had full view of the stage from any part of the house; and the four private boxes, which Adolph Sutro, Mrs. Sandy Bowers, John Mackay, and other wealthy Comstockers would on occasion occupy, were "all beautifully arranged and exquisitely finished." In short, "the long desired luxury of a first class theatre" was a reality in "the finest style imaginable."

With his usual foresight Maguire had equipped the building with both gas fixtures and chandeliers. Though oil served at first, Comstock-manufactured gas was soon used in the theatre, in the "neat cigar stand" attached to the saloon on the Union side, and in the two "fine saloons," one of which was chosen now for a "Great Billiard Match" between Washoe's champion, A. M. Jamison, and New York's "great billiard player, Goldthwaite." [4]

---

[4] Thrilled that the "village of Virginia" had been chosen for the championship game to be played at Maguire's new theatre-saloon, the Washoites made bets from $1000 to $5000. But Virginia sports writers praised Jamison's skills so highly, Goldthwaite's backers became frightened, persuaded him to use the name of Wilson, go to Virginia and study Jamison's techniques. When the Comstockers became suspicious, they asked embarrassing questions. Goldthwaite admitted being in Virginia three days. Finally the lovers of billiards "patched up their differences," brought a new table to Topliffe's Theatre, and sold seats for $2.50 each. Goldthwaite and George Phelan, "the celebrated player of San Francisco," became the guests of Maguire's saloonkeeper, Ralph Benjamin, also a fine billiard player. But the friends of Jamison, still considering the affair irregular, called off the "great carom match."

Nevertheless, the attendant excitement inspired the scheduling of contests in Austin, Aurora, Washoe City, Carson, and Dayton. And by Thanksgiving Messrs. Benjamin and Jamison, still acclaimed "the great billiard players," would be giving matched games of pool for $200 a side. Jamison was usually winner. But the frigid weather and the high price of stove wood ($22 a cord) forced Tom Maguire to close the Billiard Saloon over his theatre and "sell at auction the fine tables and other expensive fixtures."

3

What troupe would open the "elegantly arranged dwelling of Thespis"? Not the Westwood players this time. But another group of pioneer theatre people, who were even then playing at Topliffe's Theatre and watching Maguire's playhouse grow from ground breaking. This company under McKean Buchanan, including Virginia Howard Pope, Charles Pope, Walter Leman, and others, Maguire now engaged; and to this nucleus added W. C. Forbes, Mr. Bowes, Mr. Livingston, Fred Franks, and the well-known Jimmy Griffith. But these were not all. Over the Sierras, where Hank Monk had let out the lines of his six-in-hand, swayed the stage coach bringing leading lady Julia Dean Hayne, Frank Mayo (whom Maguire had "detailed to support Mrs. Hayne"), William O'Neil, Mrs. H. A. Perry, and Junius B. Booth, Jr. (brother of Edwin and John Wilkes Booth).

The star of stars for the historic Washoe occasion had received a more brilliant welcome than any other actress in San Francisco, where for thirty continuous nights — the longest consecutive run on the West coast — she had appeared at the Metropolitan Theatre. Her stage heroine was the most acceptable one of the time. "As an actress, her merits are considerable, her conception of character is quick and correct; her development of it always marked by intelligence, discrimination, and good taste. She always dresses her part with singular propriety. In private life she is much beloved on account of her exceedingly amiable character." Thus Comstock newspapers introduced lovely Julia Dean Hayne to her new public.

Of the great theatrical family of Drakes, Julia Dean (1830-1868) had made a hit at fifteen on the New York Bowery stage as Julia in *The Hunchback*. After her marriage to Dr. Hayne, she came to California, conquered the state, went to New York with her western earnings of $20,000, and returned as leading lady of a new dramatic troupe under the management of Charles Tibbett (who also would soon enter the amusement world in Washoe). "When I was out with Julia Dean," recalled Walter Leman, "it was a rare thing to play anywhere, even in the roughest mining camp, to less than three hundred dollars a night and the audiences were as appreciative, perhaps more so, than in places that boasted more refinement."

4

Since ten o'clock that morning of July 2 till four in the afternoon, the Washoites pushed up to the ticket office window; bought private boxes for $5 and $10, dress circle and orchestra tickets for $1.50, and seats in the parquette for $1; then, dressed in their most fashionable attire, at seven found their seats in the new theatre. Perhaps with male escort, Julia Bulette, Comstock's best-known "fair frail one," also sought admittance. (Her small white house was also on D Street just down from the Opera House.) In spite of legend, Jule probably was refused entrance; for — as the Gold Hill *Evening News* later related — she was refused admittance on January 19, 1867. Why not, then, at the opening?

Interesting also is the over-theatrical rumor that an impromptu duel took place in front of the Opera House; or that shots were exchanged inside the crowded theatre. Since Leman and others present, who wrote at some length describing the opening night, fail to mention any gun play, it seems unlikely that such incidents actually took place. The dedication did.

Having struggled with and completed the ode of dedication, Leman handed it to Julia Hayne, who stepped before the footlights and gazed out over a sea of faces such as never before had assembled in Virginia. "There was scarcely space to move throughout the theatre, it was so densely filled. Large as was the audience, its magnitude was surpassed by its beauty and manliness." An expectant hush greeted Julia

Hayne's appearance. Then rounds of applause rolled through the theatre. Mrs. Hayne smiled and began to read Leman's poem:

Where the Sierra's rugged mountains show
Their peaks aloft — amid the drifted snow,
Skirting the vale where Carson's placid stream
Flows onward to the desert — where the gleam
Of God's own sunlight shines in fervid power
On rocks of gold, and hills of glittering ore;
Where thunder-smitten mountains lift on high
Their rifted battlements against the sky,
In this fresh clime, a youthful empire springs
　　To life and vigor upon freedom's wings,
Nevada! — soon her starry gem to set
Upon our Union's glittering Coronet.

❋　　❋　　❋

And here is reared a rich and gorgeous dome
Of taste, the temple and the Muse's home,
And here, obedient to Thespian laws,
We stand to-night to plead with you our cause.

Julia Hayne had scarcely begun the address when the Washoe Zephyrs rained gravel stones against the building. The star controlled herself and went on, but she was noticeably affected, and "there was considerable agitation visible in the fairer portion of the audience" also. Whether fact or legend, the tinkle of a small hand bell — now in the Nevada Historical Society — signaled the rising of the curtain with its uncompleted "fine view of Lake Bigler." The stage came into view and on it an evening of make-believe began. Lytton's comedy of *Money; or, The Poor Scholar* was undoubtedly an appropriate choice.

By the time Alfred Evelyn, the poor but worthy scholar, had received his legacy, "having known privation, may better employ wealth," the wind had somewhat subsided, and Alfred and Clara moved on through a maze of complications to the ironic "Now I am rich, what value in the lines! How the wit brightens — how the sense refines." What if the play was rather insipid? The talents of Julia Hayne, Frank Mayo, Mrs. Perry, and others of the "Great Star Company" could halo any presentation. And reporters afterwards, in praising the cast at the Opera House, finally resorted to one sentence: "Of the company who are at present performing there we deem it superfluous to speak, . . . their well known talent being a matter with which our readers are already too well acquainted." [5]

Though delighted with the program that Thursday evening, Virginia first-nighters could not easily forget the " 'Washoe Zephyr,' sweeping up the cañon that 'rained' the stony artillery upon the rear of the new building, which creaked in the tempest like a ship at sea." "I thought for a moment that the opening and closing of 'Maguire's New Opera House' would occur on the same evening," Walter Leman recalled long afterward. "But it was reserved for the *usual* fate, which befell it years after; it went up in a cloud of fire, and took a good portion of the city along with it."

---

[5] The *Enterprise* writer added the general observation of the audience: "Well, we'll just bet, that if there's a marriageable actress in the company with winning graces and matrimonial inclination, she never goes over the mountains unwedded."

Bonanza Theatre

1

Showing no respect for the opening of the Opera House, the Washoe Zephyrs caught up a donkey — his "neck outstretched . . . shrieking in the most despairing tones" as he was "carried over the town." Some say an old gander was lost in the storm. "This may be so," conceded Dan De Quille, "but most folks along the Comstock cling to the donkey and sneer at the gander." The Washoites would have "roofed in the towns to keep out the wind," but lumber was expensive and "half you get is just what it's *cracked up* to be and the other half is *knot.*"

But Maguire's Opera House was to withstand more than windstorms; and its capacity and strength was fully tested during the exercises of the Fourth of July. Before sunrise two hundred "muscle men" climbed Washington Peak, put up a new pole, ran up the flag, and saluted it with Fremont's 12-pound howitzer (No wonder Washoites were indignant ten days later when some "miscreant cut the halyards and stole the flag").

By ten o'clock the streets of Virginia were crowded with people to witness the parade, which included the officers from Fort Churchill mounted on "gaily caparisoned steeds and glittering with buttons and shoulder-straps"; the Virginia and the Silver City Guards, "both well drilled and fine looking bodies of men"; Virginia Engine No. 1 in neat uniforms of red shirts, black pantaloons, and fire caps, followed by their fire engine "handsomely decorated with wreaths of real and artificial flowers"; Young American Engine Company No. 2,

"fairly excelling themselves" by the snap in their marching;
Hook and Ladder Company; and the Virginia Cadets, a
squad of youngsters, who "fairly stole the parade with their
youthful excellence," wearing soldier caps, stripes on their
pants, and "sons of guns" on their shoulders. The Sons of
Temperance walked by.

Drawn by six horses a large ship "rigged with about 40
pretty, little girls, dressed in white and crowned and gar-
landed with wreaths," moved past, each little lady waving a
flag on which was inscribed the name of a state or territory.
But the simile was "carried out more correctly than the
projectors anticipated; for up on B Street the ship ran ashore
and the cotton states were nearly precipitated into the dust
of humiliation, which their prototypes must soon roll in."
The fire boys, "always willing to shelter beauty in distress,
found room for the shipwrecked girls between their engine
ropes."

Carriages bearing the dignitaries of the day brought up the
rear of the half-mile-long parade. However, long before the
parade reached the three-day-old Opera House, the Washoites
had packed the theatre, and hundreds more, unable to gain
admittance, crowded the entrance, overflowed, and filled D
Street between Union and Taylor.

2

Perhaps it was well Nevadans did not yet know of the
Union victories of Gettysburg and Vicksburg or in their exu-
berance they might have demolished the new theatre. As it
was, the Opera House fairly creaked with human weight as
Judge Morgan made "a few appropriate remarks," a chaplain
prayed, the band played "Hail Columbia," and W. E. Mell-
ville read with "excellent elocution" that "immortal docu-
ment, the Declaration of Independence."

Frank Mayo gave a "magnificent rendition of 'Washoe'"
(composed expressly for the occasion by "Poet of the Day"

THOMAS MAGUIRE
This theatrical Napoleon, suave and handsome, engaged world-famous actors and actresses to play his theatres in Nevada and California.
Courtesy, the Bancroft Library.

D STREET, VIRGINIA CITY
About 1865, looking north. Second building on the right is Maguire's Opera House.
Courtesy, the Bancroft Library.

MAGUIRE'S OPERA HOUSE, VIRGINIA CITY

The two-story wooden building at left center, with sign on the left side and billboard in front. A view from the International Hotel. Courtesy Harold and Lucile Weight and Charles Yale.

Joe T. Goodman) in "a splendid baritone voice, and entered into the spirit of the poem in a manner which carried the audience by storm":

WASHOE

The mighty tide of Empire dashed
  Upon a continent's bold strand,
And rolling back its billows washed
  And fertilized a desert land.

They came, the founders of a State,
  The men with spirits bold and free,
Who snatched the magic wand of Fate
  And shaped their own high destiny.

They smote with it the barren rock —
  A silver stream was disentombed;
A mountain sank beneath the shock.
  The arid valleys rose and bloomed.

In cañons, deserts, plains and glades,
  On mountains towering to the skies,
The broad foundations have been laid
  On which our noble State shall rise.

Mark Twain admitted Mayo read Joe's poem in a masterly manner "as was amply attested by the tremendous applause with which it was received." Then Clemens grinned across at his editor-in-chief, "Had I dreamed of such an enthusiastic reception as that, I would have dashed off a dusty old poem myself for the occasion."

"My Country 'Tis of Thee" sang the Glee Club while the shipwrecked girls waved their flags. Charles Pope read Washington's Farewell Address, "though not quite loud enough." After "The Star Spangled Banner," Thomas Fitch came forward amid applause. "Ladies and Gentlemen: . . . We are standing far above the level of two oceans, which beat upon either shore of a mighty republic," began the silver-tongued orator. ". . . The progress of our country was not altogether marred or unmolested. There was a ledge of treason running through this mountain of shining ore. It cropped out in 1770 and developed Benedict Arnold. It cropped out in 1803 and produced Aaron Burr. It cropped out in 1861 and gave us Jeff Davis. (Laughter and applause!) There was a Washington, Jefferson, and a Jackson, to deal with the first three traitors . . . only a Buchanan to deal with the latter."

Fitch sat down to "thundering applause." But the audience rose "and with a mighty roar like the rushing of many waters, rang out the old Saxon shout which speaks of victory." The band blared "Yankee Doodle" and the children sang "John Brown's Body" while the crowds unpacked themselves and left the Opera House. At dusk a committee set off $2000-worth of fireworks from "Federal Hill" and climaxed the "Pyrotechnical display" by a "Pillar of State with an American eagle on its summit."

Then the celebrators danced in Lynch's new building, some returned to Maguire's to witness the Great Star Company, a few went to bed, many more crowded the saloons to "keep up the Fourth in less creditable ways." Only one "shooting scrape" marred the occasion. "It was the greatest day Virginia ever saw," concluded Sam Clemens; and next evening wrote further:

HOME AGAIN

Editors Call: — After an absence of two months, I stand in the midst of my native sagebrush once more; and in the midst of bustle and activity, and turmoil and confusion, to which lunch time in the tower of Babel was foolishness. B and C Streets swarm with men. . . O, for the solitude of Montgomery Street again! Everybody is building . . . the number of houses has been fearfully increased. Some portions of the town have grown clear out of my recollection. . . Maguire has erected a spacious and beautiful theatre on D Street, exactly after the pattern of the Opera House in San Francisco, and it is nightly crowded with admirers of Mr. Mayo, Mrs. Hayne, and other "theatricides" whose names are familiar to Californians. . .

3

Maguire's Opera House continued to be the major attraction. A theatrical bill in the *Bulletin* announced:

MAGUIRE'S OPERA HOUSE

D street	between Union and Taylor

T. Maguire	Proprietor
Stage Manager	McKean Buchanan
Treasurer	Sam E. Wetherill

Continued Success of
Mrs. Julia Dean Hayne
Mr. Wm. O'Neil
And the Great Star Company

Monday Evening	July 6th, 1863

Will be performed the Comedy of
She Would and He Wouldn't!

The Marchioness	Mrs. Julia Dean Hayne
Count Rafael di Villani	J. B. Booth

To Conclude with the Irish farce
Barney the Baron!

Barney	Mr. O'Neil
Edith	Mrs. H. Perry

Mrs. Hayne seems to have been a most acceptable Marchioness. Pretty Mrs. H. A. Perry, who had first appeared in Washoe the summer before with Mrs. Leighton's troupe, and the popular Irish comedian William O'Neil in the hilarious final piece "brought down the house." That same Monday evening, however, the teacher-entertainer Mrs. W. K. Cutler was taking her benefit at the courthouse. The Maguire players drew a "large and brilliant audience"; the rather hoarse Mrs. Cutler a more duty-bound "fair" one.

The headlines "Battle of Gettysburg 'Glorious News!' The Enemy in Full Retreat from Pennsylvania," flung across the *Enterprise* set off a flare of celebrating. At the afternoon races

Tom Maguire's favorite trotter, "Bounce," came in first. At Tom's Opera House the sensation drama of *The Marble Heart* was "handsomely played." The one act farce by the Earl of Glengall, *The Irish Tutor; or, New Lights,* concluded the evening's program. However, Frank Mayo seems to have come in "first" theatrically as the following praise testified:

> *Frank Mayo.* — This gentleman, now performing some of the leading and most difficult characters at Maguire's . . . is fast rising to great eminence in his profession. As a reader he has few superiors, and as a correct and dignified delineator of the parts he assumes, he certainly occupies a prominent position in the theatrical world. . . The mere mention that Mayo is to sustain a certain character, no matter how difficult, is sufficient to fill the house . . . and bids fair to add new laurels to his already richly decked wreath of fame.[1]

Next night brought out "the exciting drama of *Retribution; or, A Husband's Vengeance.*" This time the critic praised Mrs. Hayne: "Clarise de Beaupre is one of those characters in which Mrs. Hayne excels herself. Whenever the finer and better feelings of the woman are called into play she shows herself invariably to advantage, and in this character she had full scope to display all these qualities." The reporter also conceded that Mr. Mayo as Oscar de Beaupre and J. B. Booth "sustained their respective characters with unusual credit to themselves." O'Neil took the role of Paddy Miles in the farcical afterpiece of *Limerick Boy.*

Victor Hugo's romantic drama of *Ruy Blas* was presented on July 9 with Frank Mayo and Julia Hayne as the hero and heroine while Booth appeared as Don Caesar de Bazan. And Billy O'Neil repeated his favorite character of Paddy Miles in the popular *Limerick Boy.* But the theatre was not as well attended as on former nights, and the *Bulletin* felt compelled to remind Comstockers, "When we had no comfortable place of amusement here, there was a general growl and a unan-

---

[1] *Virginia Evening Bulletin,* July 8, 1863.

imous wish that somebody would build a good theatre. Now we have a first class place of amusement. . . Turn out, gentlemen, with your families and sustain the endeavors of the proprietors of the Opera House."

The weather was so hot local reporters insisted the spirits of recently departed, not-so-good Washoites had to return "to get their blankets, finding their new quarters so much colder than their whilom earthly homes." But despite the weather, and as if heeding the *Bulletin's* advice, "a fashionable audience" next evening filled the theatre. *Romance of a Poor Young Man* was the play. The Comstockers especially enjoyed the "splendidly rendered" fourth act containing the "jumping scene," where "the hero (Mayo) jumps off a tower, in which he is accidentally locked up in order to avoid compromising the lady he is escorting (Mrs. Hayne), and with whom he was in love." In the afterpiece Billy O'Neil as *The Happy Man* "brought down the house."

The week end brought varied attractions. The "Hayne Company at Maguire's Opera House" served a repeat performance of *A Husband's Vengeance;* the rollicking *Tom and Jerry; or, Life in London,* a play new to Washoe and particularly appealing since Captain Harry Lazarus and Young Haley, both well known in sporting circles, gave "an exhibition of the manly art" in a sparring encounter. *Oliver Twist* played both Saturday and Sunday evenings. On Sunday afternoon the Opera House was given over to a benefit program for the Sanitary Fund.

4

Some plays were popular enough to be repeated. For *East Lynne* this procedure became almost habit. Written in 1861 by the English playwright Mrs. Henry Wood, *East Lynne; or, The Elopement* soon became one of the most popular melodramas ever put onto paper, attracting "fashionable and overflowing audiences in every theatre in which it was performed." "Never darken my door again!' became a household expres-

sion repeated more times than a line from any other melo-
drama.

Tuesday evening, July 14, 1863, was the opening performance of this sentimental piece in Washoe. "Most of our readers
are doubtless acquainted with the thrilling merits of the
novel from which this drama has been taken," wrote the
Bulletin; then, assuming they were not, proceeded to give the
story of the play:

> The scene is laid in England, and the plot runs thus: Lady Isabel
> (Julia Dean Hayne), a young girl of noble birth, is married to
> Archibald Carlysle (Frank Mayo), a young gentleman of respect-
> able connections; a son is born to them and for a time all is
> happiness and prosperity. Subsequently a miscreant, Captain Levi-
> son (J. B. Booth), becomes acquainted with the Lady Isabel, and
> after using all the villainous means at his command succeeds in
> alienating her from her husband. She elopes with Levison and
> remains with him for the space of about six years, during which
> time she becomes the mother of two children. At the expiration of
> this period, Captain Levison becomes tired of his victim and
> deserts her. With a broken heart, she returns to her former home.
> Here she remains *incog.,* her changed and dejected appearance
> rendering her unknown even to her husband. In this position she
> remains for the space of six months, when the boy — the legitimate
> result of her marriage — dies, and over his death-bed the recogni-
> tion between herself and her husband takes place. Shortly after
> this she herself dies of a broken heart, and the curtain drops upon
> the bereaved and injured husband.

A one-word act by act synopsis of this lachrymose, woman-
must-pay heart throb could as well have been:

Act 1 — Mated
Act 2 — Tempted
Act 3 — Exiled
Act 4 — Remorse
Act 5 — Death

"Few can witness any of the scenes without being affected
to tears; and we have no doubt that there will be many a
moist eye and throbbing heart at the Opera House to-night,"

predicted the *Bulletin;* and followed next day with an item:

JACK PERRY IN TEARS. — It was currently reported   .   .   .   that our worthy City Marshall actually shed tears during the performance of *East Lynne* at the Opera House. Who says the play is not affecting?

Not all Washoe theatrical reviewers rated *East Lynne* in the four-star class. Jack Perry's less emotional friend Sam Clemens wrote the *Call* in this vein:

On Tuesday evening that sickest of all sentimental dramas, "East Lynne," will be turned loose upon us at the Opera House. It used to afford me much solid comfort to see those San Franciscans whine and shuffle and slobber all over themselves at Maguire's Theatre, when the comsumptive "William" was in the act of "handing in his checks," as it were, according to the regular programme of "East Lynne" — and now I am to enjoy a season of happiness again, I suppose. If the tears flow as freely here as I count upon, water privileges will be cheap in Virginia next week. However, Mrs. Julia Dean Hayne don't "take on" in the piece like Miss Sophia Edwin; wherefore she fails to pump an audience dry, like the latter.

On each repetition of *East Lynne* the audiences exceeded "the previous ones." Except for Wednesday (July 15) when another benefit was given for the Sanitary Fund, the lachrymose drama ran from Tuesday through Saturday.[2]

---

[2] A few incidents connected with the producing of *East Lynne* are perhaps interesting enough to pass on. As Maguire and Burns owned the Opera House, they each had a saloon in the entrance. One afternoon the "boys of Johnny Burns' Branch had a good time to themselves." Procuring the handcuffs used in *East Lynne,* they got them onto the wrists of a well-known barkeeper. Somehow the springs snapped shut and the pranksters "without the key belonging to the bracelets" rushed about Virginia in search of the Opera House manager or some male member of the troupe. After three hours the pranksters managed to release the barkeeper, who — cognizant of Washoe humor and its power — "went down to his own saloon and treated the crowd, considering the affair a good joke," but thereby keeping the jolly-makers at his establishment most of the drinking evening.

When dressed in hoops and finery, Washoites liked riding to social functions, particularly to see *East Lynne* at the theatre. Hence, to "accommodate the ladies and their escorts   .   .   .   with splendid Saddle Horses and Buggy Teams" a Fashion Stable now wedged itself into the space "opposite Maguire's Opera House."

5

Virginia was not alone in enjoying the legitimate theatre. As early as May the *Era* had told its readers that "the Leighton Troupe is sloshing around through the interior. *The Fool of the Family* seems to be the *Object of Interest* largely predominating" with "that instantaneous and tremendous hit, Mrs. W. H. Leighton."

Shortly afterwards the Leightons sloshed into Silverland. (Charles Tibbetts also crossed the Sierras. He had been arrested for assault and battery of actor Harry Courtaine, who also would soon be in Washoe.)[3] By July 11 the *Washoe Times* was announcing:

> The Leighton Troupe, comprising some of the best talent of the San Francisco boards, is again in our town for a brief season. The entertainment last night was "Ten Nights in a Bar Room," an ingenuously constructed and effective drama, in which sin and sentiment, pathos and petulancy, fun and philosophy, stirring mirth and stern morality are mixed in delightful proportions.

Yankee Locke, for whom *Ten Nights* had been written, shone out "in all the glory of a New England whimsicality as Samuel Switchell, sustained by that incarnation of fun, Mrs. W. H. Leighton, and by such decided artists as A. R. Phelps, E. T. Thayer, L. F. Browne, J. H. Ruby, O. Wilson, Mrs. G. E. Locke, and Misses Parks and Leslie."

Washoe City theatre-goers next enjoyed *Fool of the Family*, in which Mrs. Leighton could create "a smile under the ribs of death." With Mr. Leighton as lessee and manager of

---

[3] Three months after his trouble with Harry Courtaine, Tibbetts quit managing the legitimate stage and went over to the "quadrapeds and their bespangled riders" of John Wilson's circus. Then he took a job as timekeeper with the Gould and Curry Company on the Comstock. "From Momus to Mammon! How true it is that all the world's a stage and that one man in his time plays many parts," philosophized the San Francisco *Mercury*. "Instead of summoning kings and queens to their mimic thrones upon the stage, Tibbetts is now calling the humble laborer to the scene of his daily toil. Instead of the 'voluptuous swell' of a Metropolitan orchestra, the ringing of the pick and shovel is the only music that greets his ears! We admire Tibbetts' pluck, and can assure him that this evidence of his industry has raised him in our estimation at least a 'foot.'"

Faulk's Concert Hall, A. R. Phelps as stage manager, and the price of admission at a dollar only, no wonder the *Washoe Times* asserted: "The theatre will run tonight and tomorrow night . . . with new and varied bills of fare. Now is the time for our people who wish to enjoy the delights of genuine stage-playing." And enjoy it the people surely did.[4]

The Comstockers also enjoyed the "delights of genuine stage-playing" again in *East Lynne* and *Ireland as It Was* with Mrs. Hayne as Judy O'Trot assisted by "the strongest cast ever given this piece on the Pacific slope." Mlle. Lamoureux's Medley Dance was "warmly applauded." And "deliberate with fun," the afterpiece of *The Happy Man* kept the house "in a roar of laughter."

Enroute to Maguire's Opera House those early days of July, Comstockers noted workmen carrying lumber up to the second floor of Rice and Livermore's store, leased by W. H. Leighton. Here carpenters were building a "comfortably and elegantly fitted-up," second-floor playhouse, which was given the pretentious title, the Temple of Comedy.

Fresh from such Silverland theatrical conquests as Carson, Genoa, Dayton, and Washoe City, the comedy-variety playing Leighton troupe were eager to open the new Temple of Comedy. On Monday evening (July 20) Manager Leighton, assisted by A. R. Phelps, welcomed the Lode public with a sure-hit program, starring Mrs. Leighton in three of her most popular characters: Sally Scraggs in *Sketches in India*, Betty Saunders in "the invincible farce" of *Fool of the Family*, and

---

[4] Interested in what flavored of grease paint, the Washoites, perusing their newspapers, were delighted when they found an anecdote related by the actor Saul Smith: During the farce of the *Lovers' Quarrel*, the landlord was in the habit of witnessing the performance behind the scenes because, belonging to the church, he did not want to be seen out front. When Carlos was making a present of his watch, purse, etc., to the stage Jacinta, Saul Smith, playing Sancho, advised Carlos to save something to pay his board. At this moment the religious landlord, carried quite away by the play, popped his head on stage and said, "Mr. Smith, don't mind your board, go on with the play just as you would — if you haven't the money at the end of the week, I will wait." At this the audience gave such applause, the landlord "backed out, overwhelmed with his reception."

Angelica in the Yankee farce entitled *A Wife for a Day.* Local newspapers carried advertisements of the program listing the plays and the important members of each cast.

Calling Mrs. Leighton the "bright particular Star, the Queen of Comedy and Song," and praising Misses Taylor and Parks, Mesdames Locke and Leslie, and others of the troupe, the *Bulletin* predicted: "Mrs. Leighton will . . . be greeted with an overflowing house as she has warm friends among us who are ever ready to testify to her rare qualities as an actress by their presence." Although the "great sensation drama," *The Woman in White,* was put on at Maguire's "in the best possible manner" and the graveyard scene had "never been surpassed in any of the older cities," still it was *the* night for the Temple — its opening. Fulfilling the *Bulletin's* prediction, the place was "crowded to suffocation . . . despite the extraordinary attractions elsewhere." In fact, the tops of adjoining buildings were crowded with first-nighters, who, unable to gain admittance, were "bent upon seeing as much of the performance as possible through the open windows." Certainly this was flattering to the "merry Mrs. Leighton," who, according to the *Era,* was "shaking the sides of the Nevadans."

6

Because the Opera House troupe played to some vacant seats the Monday night of the Temple of Comedy's opening, *The Woman in White* was repeated on Tuesday while at the Temple Mrs. Leighton, Yankee Locke, and the company gave the temperance drama, *Ten Nights in a Bar Room,* and followed it with the farce, *An Object of Interest.*

Wednesday night though Mrs. Leighton "did her best to please," the Temple of Comedy suffered vacant seats. The reason? Hook and Ladder Company was having a benefit at Maguire's, where the friends of the fire company "turned out in such force . . . many persons were unable to obtain even standing room in the spacious building" to witness

Brougham's drama of *Romance and Reality*. The benefit was
a success, Comstock Chinese even contributing $61. The
evening was a success too for little Lotta Crabtree. Having
arrived with Maguire and a new troupe of minstrels, Lotta
volunteered her services and "this popular favorite was the
recipient during the evening of a perfect shower of gold and
silver coin, thrown to her on the stage by our ever-liberal
citizens."

"Virginia is the only place, save San Francisco . . .
able to support two theatrical companies at a time," observed
the *Alta California*. But a packed house at one theatre usually
meant a slim audience at the other. For example, the "thrilling
scenes and magnificent effects of *Alice the Forsaken*" and the
ever-popular *Limerick Boy* did not bring out as large an
audience "as the merits of the pieces and the efforts of the
actors deserved."

To remedy the problem of vacant seats, Tom Maguire used
the simple expedient of dividing audiences. Seemingly in
competition with himself, Maguire planned to open yet another theatre, weather the further lull this would cause and,
when the competing house closed, take over the field. Topliffe's Theatre was dark so he and Johnny Burns leased it.
Then while Burns refitted the place, Maguire recrossed the
Sierras. Maguire's minstrels in San Francisco welcomed the
chance to return to Washoe.

The rejuvenated Topliffe's was ready, its new name in
evidence. As business manager for the new Virginia Melodeon, Maguire chose W. H. Smith; as stage manager, the
talking Negro minstrel Walter Bray; and as director of music,
F. H. Oldfield. Prices of admission were less than at either
the Opera House or the Temple of Comedy. Front seats were
a dollar, back seats 50 cents, and gallery gods could get in
for the least coin in Washoe, "two bits." There were box
seats also, a few, at three dollars each.

Theatrically July 23 was a big day for Virginia City as

three main theatres were in operation that night when Maguire and Burns opened the doors of their new Virginia Melodeon. No wonder the Opera House, presenting *Alice the Forsaken,* and the Temple of Comedy, even with such a triple bill as *Our Female American Cousin, Sketches in India,* and *Raising the Wind,* as well as lesser houses, counted vacant seats that first night of Negro minstrelsy.

Competitive amusement houses would know decreasing audiences on the following nights also. In the end the Minstrels would win against the field, especially when the troupe included such "first class talent" as Lotta Crabtree, Carrie Howard, Walter Bray, Jake Wallace, Ned Hamilton, W. H. Smith, Miss Sager, Mlle Lamoureux, J. H. O'Neil, Pete Sterling, W. D. Corrister, and F. H. Oldfield, all of whom conspired to give such "inimitable performances" the Virginia Melodeon was "crowded to its utmost capacity." No wonder *Alice the Forsaken* had to be repeated at the Opera House "in order to give all our citizens an opportunity to witness it."

No one seems to have championed Mrs. Leighton on her slim crowd, even when the management of the Temple of Comedy announced that Friday would be the comedienne's benefit and "last night but two." *Our Female American Cousin, The Widow's Victim,* and *Fool of the Family* made up the program for the benefit night, but the Minstrels at the Virginia Melodeon gathered in the lion's share of the evening's amusement business. Even at reduced prices on the two remaining nights when *The Rough Diamond, A Kiss in the Dark, The Pleasant Neighbor,* and a variety show made up the bills, Mrs. Leighton, Yankee Locke, and the troupe played to many empty seats.

Though far from lucrative, a benefit had been accorded the "Queen of Comedy and Song." It was time also for Julia Hayne's benefit at the Opera House, for Frank Mayo's, Mrs. Perry's, and others. A word about benefits seems in order.

July-August 1863

Stars and Benefits

1

The management in giving theatrical benefits paid the expenses of the production and turned over the receipts of the box office to the actor. Often business men and other admirers tendered a benefit to a favorite, who arranged his own program. The liberality of the Washoites during benefits made the *Bulletin* reporter and others "proud of our residence in their midst." Mrs. Cutler received full houses to champion the cause of education; youthful cadets got new uniforms; and fire companies bought new engines. Sandwiched between two performances of *Oliver Twist,* the Opera House also aided the Sanitary Fund.

But the Sunday afternoon program for the Fund was only a preview of the one put on during the middle of July when the Opera House troupe and "a host of talent volunteered," including Mr. and Mrs. Pope, who "were frequently applauded in the witty *Flirtation; or, A Morning Call.*" After the farce of *A Rough Diamond,* Billy O'Neil came on in *Barney the Baron.* Later Leman announced the surrender of Port Hudson [1] to thundering applause; then he and Mayo recited patriotic addresses. "The friends of our sick and wounded soldiers," wrote the *Bulletin,* "certainly realized their most sanguine expectations, . . . adding more than $3000 to the amounts already contributed."

Next evening the Popes were themselves tendered a benefit at the courthouse, where, according to the *Golden Era,* they

---

[1] With the advent of the telegraph Maguire's managers started the practice of having late news announced from the Opera House stage.

had been "bestowing their united favors upon Virginia City in a course of dramatic readings," popular even in the face of Opera House attractions. Between numbers two local musicians, Messrs. Kube and Hickman, performed on the piano and the violin. The esteem with which the Popes were held is shown by the lengthy list of prominent Washoites who signed the published correspondence legalizing the benefit.[2]

Even with *East Lynne* on the Opera House boards and tickets to the Pope benefit at two dollars, the courthouse "presented quite an array of beauty and fashion" to hear the selections from Shakespeare's *Much Ado About Nothing*, scenes from *Ingomar, the Barbarian,* and ballads such as "No One to Love," "Babie Belle," and "Whisper What Thou Feelest" — all sung by Virginia Pope. Charles received acclaim for a humorous selection, for Poe's "The Raven," "The Charge of the Light Brigade," and the "Elegy Written in a Country Churchyard." A "decided success, the recitations and songs were repeatedly applauded" and the "instrumental portions of the music were gems in themselves." Virginia recited Drake's patriotic and stirring "Address to the Flag." Though only two actors held the stage at any time, the Popes gave their programs with such professional poise and finish, the evening was complete and satisfying.

2

Less than a month from their benefit night the Popes were shocked to learn that Virginia's former husband (Cunningham), long believed dead, was living in Australia. Immediately the Popes took legal action, the Civil Probate Court of Nevada Territory annulling their marriage. And Charles, to save Virginia further embarrassment, departed for the East and was soon playing a star engagement in New York. Virginia quietly started divorce proceedings against Cunningham, but an unnamed person unfortunately bought space in the *Enterprise* and attempted to analyze the "past life and

[2] *Virginia Evening Bulletin,* July 16, 1863.

character of Virginia Howard." Coast and local papers took up the torch for the actress, saying "Virginia Howard (Mrs. Pope that was) is a lady of irreproachable character as those who know her can testify." Then followed a series of public correspondence, which hinted at friction between McKean Buchanan and Mrs. Pope's attorney. However, hotheaded Buchanan publicly apologized and the "anticipated difficulty" was "amicably settled." Mrs. Pope resumed her maiden name of Virginia Howard and stayed on in Washoe, "highly esteemed and respected."

Charles Pope did not remain long in the East. Though "one of the best all around actors of his time," he quit the stage for the mining boom on the Reese River. But the fates frowned sooner on his venture away from the footlights than they did upon James Stark. By winter Pope and Virginia Howard were both engaged by Buchanan to star at the Metropolitan in San Francisco.

A "famous company" of Glass Blowers now favored Silverland with a series of interesting and so-unusual demonstrations they attracted curious crowds for several days. Then the Glass Blowers gave way to Martin the Wizard. "This wonderful genius in the thaumaturgic art surprised us all by his dazzling miracles," wrote the *Washoe Times* of Martin's appearance in Washoe City. "Martin Luther made the devil scamper by throwing an inkstand at the old villain's head, but Martin the Wizard puts him in the bowl of a tobacco pipe and *puffs* him."

"Hot! Whew!!" complained the papers. And the Virginia Ice Company even at two cents a pound could hardly supply the saloons, where — to quote Sam Clemens — "all kinds of stimulating iced beverages were 'yelped down,' as our devil says, with an avidity 'corresponding with the unmoist state of the human esophagus.'" In spite of the heat, Wilson's big circus tent, pitched by turns in the various Washoe towns, filled and refilled with enthusiastic miners and their eager offspring. All the tricks and oddities that could be crowded into an abbreviated circus were there. And the Comstockers relished them all, including the benefit performance that Wilson gave for Young America Engine.

3

Benefits were in order again at the Opera House, too. For her benefit on July 24 Mrs. Hayne chose the romantic tragedy of *Griseldis,* the "fair beneficiary" taking the part of Griseldis to Frank Mayo's Percival. As predicted, the Opera House fairly groaned "under the weight of the immense audience," who were so pleased with the excellence of the performance, they called loudly for Mrs. Hayne. "Led to the footlights by Mr. Mayo," the lovely leading lady expressed in a neat little speech "her heartfelt thanks for the liberal manner in which our citizens had responded to her call."

Later she recited "A Fireman's Address" for them. Billy O'Neil sang and danced. And the evening closed with the petite comedy — given for the first time in Nevada — *Faint Heart Never Won Fair Lady* with Mrs. Hayne as the Duchess and Mr. Mayo as Ruy Gomez. "The benefit was an occasion," the reviewer insisted, "of which the lady will long have cause to be proud."

Ten days later "the elegant actress and accomplished lady" was reading:

> Dear Julia Dean Hayne — Madam: Remembering that your sojourn among us is about drawing to a close, and desiring to express our appreciation of your efforts to please, a few of your many admirers beg leave to tender you a Complimentary Benefit . . .

Then followed a listing of more than three dozen names of influential Washoites. It would be redundant to say that Mrs. Hayne was pleased with the compliment. In her published reply she set the date for August 7, her "last appearance," and added, "It shall be my care to provide an entertainment worthy of the occasion."

JULIA DEAN HAYNE

"Elegant and accomplished" actress,
star of the troupe that opened
Maguire's handsome Opera House in
Virginia City.
Courtesy, the Huntington Library.

FRANK MAYO

Handsome and able leading man, who
played opposite Julia Dean Hayne
at Maguire's Opera House in 1863.
Urged by Comstockers to attempt
Hamlet, he won the admiration and
affection of the Nevadans.
Courtesy, de Young Memorial Museum.

VIRGINIA HOWARD

This pioneer actress so pleased
Washoites, she held the theatrical
boards longer than any other actress
of Nevada's Civil War period.
From a contemporary woodcut.

Earliest extant published theatrical bills for Virginia City as appearing in *The Virginia Evening Bulletin*, July 6, 1863.
Courtesy, University of Nevada.

The bell that rang up the first curtain at Maguire's Opera House, Virginia City.
Courtesy, Nevada Historical Society.

Complimentary Testimonial

.. TO ..

MRS. W. K. CUTLER,

By the Citizens of Virginia.

This (Monday) Evening......July 6th,

AT THE COURT HOUSE

PART I.

1. Song of the Swiss Shepherdess..........Abt
2. Song—Land of my Childhood..........Keller
3. Song—Katie Strong..............Wallace
4. Reading—Excelsior ....Longfellow
5. Reading—The Bells (by request).....E. A. Poe
6. Reading—Horatius,..............Macaulay

PART II.

1. Song—The Maid of Judah ....Kucken
2. Song—The Last Rose of Summer......Moore
3. Ballad—Auld Robin Gray............Scotch
4. Reading—The Falls of Lodore.......Southey
5. Reading—The Unhappy Lot of Mr.
              Knott ....Lowell
6. Song—Bonnie Nannie (by request)....Scotch

Admission.................$1 50 each.
To commence at 8¼ o'clock P. M.
jy6 1t

Summit Gold and Silver Mining Company.—A meeting of the shareholders of the above Company will be held July 10th, at seven o'clock P. M., at the Medao Building for the purpose of a reorganization of said company.
JOHN McCARTY,
JOHN STERRET,
GROVE ADAMS,
G. A. HUDSON,
A. C. WIGHTMAN,
J. F. ATWILL,
jy6 td   And others.

MAGUIRE'S OPERA HOUSE,
D street...........between Union and Taylor.

T. MAGUIRE........................Proprietor
Stage Manager..................McKean Buchanan
Treasurer...................Sam. E. Wetherill

Continued Success of

Mrs. Julia Dean Hayne

MR. WM. O'NIEL,

AND THE GREAT STAR COMPANY.

Monday Evening.......July 6th, 1863,
Will be performed the Comedy of
She Would and He Wouldn't!
The Marchioness.........Mrs. Julia Dean Hayne.
Count Rafael di Villani............J. B. Booth.

To conclude with the Irish farce
Barney the Baron!

Barney......................Mr. O'Neil.
Edith.....................Mrs. H. Perry.

Box office open to 10 A. M. to 4 P. M.
Dress Circle and Orchestra, $1 50; Parquette, $1; Private Boxes, $5 to $10.   jy6 tf

SAMUEL LANGHORNE CLEMENS
At the time he became Territorial Nevada's reporter
Mark Twain, and speaker of the Third House.
From a rare photograph; courtesy, Yale University Library.

AURORA, ESMERALDA DISTRICT
Courtesy, the Bancroft Library.

1. Court House and Herald Office.
2. New Real del Monte Hoisting Works.
3. Last Chance Hill.

4. Middle Hill.
5. Mt. Hicks.
6. Silver Hill.

While Mrs. Hayne was making another romantic tragedy "worthy" for the August occasion, Mrs. W. H. Leighton was being honored at the Temple of Comedy, that being her "last night but two." Though the laughing lady — as previously noted — performed with her usual éclat, the theatre was far from crowded. In view of the reduced patronage Manager Leighton cut reserved seat prices from $1.50 to $1.00 and sold seats for "all other parts of the house" at 50 cents for the remaining two nights including the variety program, scheduled for the closing night on July 26. Thus the Temple of Comedy had a short but lively season with Mrs. Leighton *"au fait* in all the characters she assumed" while Messrs. Yankee Locke, A. R. Phelps, and Thayer and Mesdames Parks and Leslie "lent their usual valuable aid."

Friday and Saturday (July 24-25) were of theatrical note. Those evenings Virginia could boast four theatres dispensing amusement for the varied tastes of the Comstockers: the Opera House, of course, catered to those who desired drama with *Idiot of the Mountains* and *Jack Sheppard; or, The House Breaker of the Last Century;* the Temple of Comedy served light legitimate drama and farces in *The Rough Diamond, A Kiss in the Dark,* and *The Pleasant Neighbor;* the Virginia Melodeon obliged those who preferred Negro minstrelsy; and the Great Republic Melodeon in a basement at B and Taylor dished up a variety program not intended for chaste listeners.

4

The management of Maguire's Opera House set July 27 as the benefit night of its leading actor, Frank Mayo, "one of the most promising young tragedians of the present day," wrote a theatrical critic, who continued:

The rapid rise of Mr. Mayo from obscurity and penury, by the simple efforts of his genius, to the highest walks of dramatic fame, the natural aptitude which he exhibits for catching the most striking features of the most difficult characters, as it were by intuition, his youth, his social qualities, and in fact his *tout ensemble* of everything constituting an actor of the highest order, entitle him to more than a passing notice. This, we believe, is his first exit from California in a professional character, where but a few years since he was but an unnoticed youth in the streets of San Francisco. Having accidentally, in the course of his boyish strollings, on one occasion gained access to a theatre, he at once became enraptured by the art, and applied for employment. In his very first appearance, he is said to have carried off the palm of success, an occurrence, which we believe, cannot be cited in support of the career of even the most eminent of the devotees of the stage. The people of this city have been entertained by this talented actor for some weeks, and have enjoyed the opportunity of seeing for themselves that although Mr. Mayo came among them preceded by considerable fame, yet he has far outstripped all preconceived expectations of his ability.[3]

Lavish praise. Yet this portrayal of Frank Mayo was not unwarranted. For more than thirty years he would take rank with the finest actors of the country as leading man in some of the best stock companies. He would win great fame by his creation of the character of Davy Crockett, with which he later came to be identified. It was while in Washoe, however, that Frank Mayo was given the opportunity and encouragement to launch into a larger field of acting. R. W. Daggett, Joe Goodman, Tom Fitch, Henry Edgerton, and some 250 other Virginia men wrote Mayo "a public card" requesting that he favor his admirers "by representing the character of Hamlet, prince of Denmark, in the tragedy of the same name."

The proposal startled Mayo. He knew that Comstock audiences generally were so familiar with the play that nearly

---

[3] When Edwin Forrest planned coming to California, the *Golden Era* informed him: "Our critics will make you sing a lively tune. They will soon let you know that your great reputation cannot protect you on this coast. You have passed muster in New York, but they will show you up here. . . They will set up Frank Mayo for your model as soon as you get here, and they will say you don't play up to him, whether you do or not. And then they will decide that you are a 'bilk.' That is the grand climax of all criticism. . ."

the complete text and action of the actor would be anticipated
with "preconceived ideas of correctness." Understandably,
Mayo hesitated; then replied:

> Gentlemen: . . . I think a greater compliment under the
> circumstances could not be paid to anyone. I . . . fear you
> entertain an exaggerated sense of my talents, but the implicit
> confidence so candidly expressed determines me to attempt that
> which I readily admit I would hardly dare venture upon without
> such encouragement.

Maguire's Opera House (postponed from its eventual fate
by the prompt action that morning of citizens with buckets
of water on a pile of burning shavings underneath the theatre)
seemed almost to bulge with the "large and appreciative
audience" that Monday of Mayo's two benefits combined into
one evening of Shakespeare's melancholy prince. "Occasionally he marred the text by accidental omissions, and now and
then tripped lightly over some of the hackneyed 'points' that
older actors dwell upon," declared a Comstock reviewer, "but,
taken as a whole, its excellences far outweighed the faults.
The scene with the Ghost was very impressive, and the closet
scene with his mother was a powerful piece of acting and
elicited hearty applause." The critics did not overlook the fact
that Mayo in his "rendition of the difficult character" had
excellent support from other members of the company. For
one, McKean Buchanan, submerged his natural desires and
gave "invaluable aid as the Ghost."

Mr. Clifton was a "very correct" Horatio and Mr. Leman
did Polonius with good accent and discretion. Mrs. Hayne's
Ophelia was "very artistically performed, but we should
prefer to hear her sing the text where it is so set down."
Having gone this far the critic felt compelled to complete
his review. "The scene in the graveyard was not tedious, and
Hamlet and Laertes mouthed and ranted as moderately as
the author himself, perhaps, could have desired. The last

scene was not so thrilling as Macready was wont to make it, and his Majesty the King was badly killed."

All in all, the audience were pleased and sympathetic. They called Mayo before the curtain, encouraging him with generous rounds of applause. And he thanked them "feel-ingly" and "cried mercy for his faults." Concluded the *Bulletin* reviewer:

> Mr. Mayo will play "Hamlet" better hereafter . . . though his friends feel proud of his first effort in that really difficult *role*.

Having closed the Temple of Comedy the evening pre-vious, Mrs. Leighton had volunteered for Mr. Mayo's benefit to do her favorite character of Betty Saunders in *The Fool of the Family* through which the laughing lady succeeded in lifting "doom from the minds of the audience by her comic good humor." Everybody went home smiling from Mayo's bumper benefit.

5

Next day the managers of the Opera House announced: "For the last time the affecting drama of *East Lynne* will be performed." On July 29 the Opera House troupers presented *Lady Audley's Secret*, and the next night *Camille*, in which Mrs. Hayne sustained "her great character of the heroine" and Mr. Mayo that of Armand Duval.

The last evening of July went to the benefit of Junius Brutus Booth, a handsome, athletic actor, in the prime of his life and at the height of his career. Booth had been identified with the California stage since its inception, having — as the *Bulletin* declared — "together with his renowned brother Edwin, played in San Francisco before it could be called even a town." Never so famous as his eminent father after whom he was named, or his brother Edwin whom he greatly assisted, or yet so notorious as his brother John Wilkes soon became, "June" Booth forged for himself a positive niche in the West.

Even when minstrelsy came near taking over the California theatrical world, Booth's popularity survived.

Aping a San Francisco benefit of seven years previous, Booth chose again *The Three Guardsmen,* a romantic drama expertly handled now by one of the most forceful casts of the theatre:

Anne, of Austria	Julia Dean Hayne
Constance	Mrs. Perry
Lady De Winter	Mrs. Forbes
D'Artagnan	J. B. Booth
Athos	Frank Mayo
Porthos	McKean Buchanan
Boniface	Wm. O'Neil
Richelieu	W. M. Leman [4]

Despite the large audience, the excellence of the cast, and the fine performance of Mr. Booth, the *Bulletin* could not lull its disappointment: "We would have rather seen him perform his celebrated character of Iago in the tragedy of 'Othello' — decidedly the best character we have ever seen him delineate and one in which he stands unrivaled."

The Washoites evidenced as much, if not more, interest in the Fitch-Goodman duel (involving two Comstock editors), than they did in theatrical make-believe on August first. Nevertheless, seats were filled that Saturday night for three plays: *A Glance at New York, The Rough Diamond,* and *The Irish Diamond,* in which Yankee Locke made his first appearance at the Opera House.

6

In the cast of the Washoe premier of *The Three Guardsmen* for Booth's benefit a few nights before, was a young actress of talent and beauty, who would one day hold an important place in Booth's private life. Now as the wife of the creditable actor H. A. Perry she was considered so valu-

---

[4] *Virginia Evening Bulletin,* July 30, 1863.

able a member of the theatrical profession as to rate a benefit, for which she chose the beautiful comedy of *Masks and Faces; or, Before and Behind the Curtain,* a dramatization of Charles Reade's popular novel, *Peg Woffington.*

Ernest Vane, a country gentleman, came into London and fell in love with a popular actress, Peg Woffington (Mrs. Hayne). Vane was a poet with a habit of blushing, a novelty that pleased the actress. Everything was "going on swimmingly" until Vane gave a house party at which his wife Mabel Vane (Mrs. Perry), suddenly appeared. Peg abruptly concluded that men "who write poetry and blush are not to be relied on." Mrs. Vane learned the "true state of things through Sir Charles Pomander" (Buchanan), who had designs himself on the beautiful Mrs. Vane.

Triplet, a poor artist, whom Peg had befriended, attempted to show his gratitude by painting the actress "with the beatific attributes of an angel." The "grand point" of the piece was made when friends viewed her "portrait," which was Peg herself, "she having posted herself there previously . . . through a hole, which she cut in the canvas." At their leisure the friends found all manner of fault with the supposed painting until Peg stepped from behind the canvas and confronted them with the face they had been "branding as a lamentably bad imitation of itself."

In the end, of course Mabel Vane retrieved her husband; Triplet had a measure of success; and everyone was happy, except perhaps Peg, now without a poet, blushing or otherwise. In viewing *Masks and Faces,* a Virginia critic thought the "the talented and amiable" beneficiary creditable, and Mrs. Hayne, faultless, as was Buchanan. Although the Minstrels had departed for Carson, Mrs. Perry's benefit brought only a "tolerable house." Nevertheless, the actress gave a pleasing dance and then, typical of her joyous youth and vitality, as Susan to Billy O'Neil's Larry, launched into the Irish farce, *More Blunders than One.*[5]

Il Trovatore was "creditably performed" at the Opera House on August 4. The next evening the troupe presented *The Rag-Picker of Paris* in competition to Mr. Millington's recherché soirée. The papers do not say what performance was given on the sixth, but they mention that the new Methodist Church was "beginning to take shape"; that another incendiary fire was averted at Topliffe's Theatre; and that some admirers were preparing a silver brick as a surprise for Mrs. Hayne, but "Mark Twain, the incorrigible newsmonger, spoiled the affair by 'blowing' about it."

For more than a month Mrs. Hayne and Frank Mayo had successfully played the Washoe boards. Their last appearance on August 7 was for Mrs. Hayne the benefit requested by leading citizens, who now crowded the Opera House "to excess" to enjoy Mrs. Hayne's Juliet opposite the Romeo of Frank Mayo. Although Mark Twain may have spoiled the silver brick as a surprise, the "argentiferous product" was presented the star so that she might "keep bright in remembrance dear the recollection of her visit, and the material as well as spiritual appreciation in which she is held in this community, both as a lady of great virtue and an actress of consummate skill." To the silver bar Mrs. Hayne responded "most feelingly." O'Neil sang "When This Cruel War is Over." La Petite Amelia sang a ballad and received a "silver shower of quarters and halves." Mrs. Hayne came on again as Margery in *The Rough Diamond,* which she played "with a spirit and vim increased, probably by the previous receipt of the silver brick."

Weighed down with her polished brick and good wishes, Julia Hayne and Frank Mayo left by stage on the ninth for

[5] For Agnes Land Perry many things — such as the death of her actor-husband, Harry A. Perry — would happen between that August, 1863, benefit night and a day four years hence, when the "classic Booth head and flashing black eyes of Junius Booth would so affect her heart that in private life she became Mrs. J. B. Booth."

San Francisco. The departing stars were not easily forgotten however. The *Bulletin* consoled with: "Miss Annette Ince, a bewitching young tragedienne, . . . shortly will appear at our theatre in some of her celebrated characters."

7

Neither did the Washoites forget a song sung at Mrs. Hayne's benefit, at Mrs. Perry's benefit, at orchestra leader Hubert Schreiner's benefit, and on many programs between benefits. It was a hit song of the War Between the States, so popular that both Yankees and Confederates sang it. "Not bad when you get the whole of it with a strong chorus," J. Ross Browne maintained on his trip to Washoe, but a little could be too much as he explained: "The driver, by whose side I had the honor to sit, had evidently cultivated his voice for singing; but unfortunately he knew but one song — and of that he remembered but the title line . . . which he sang straight ahead for three hours, commencing at the top of the grade and ending only when relieved by a new driver." Let it be hoped Browne's new driver knew more of the song:

WHEN THIS CRUEL WAR IS OVER

Dearest love, do you remember
　　When we last did meet,
How you told me that you loved me,
　　Kneeling at my feet?
O how proud you stood before me
　　In your suit of blue,
When you vowed to me and country
　　Ever to be true.

If amid the din of battle
　　Nobly you should fall,
Far away from those who love you,
　　None to hear your call,
Who would whisper words of comfort,
　　Who would soothe your pain?
Ah, the many cruel fancies
　　Ever in my brain!

But our country called you, darling —
   Angels cheer your way;
While our nation's sons are fighting,
   We can only pray.
Nobly strike for God and Union,
   Let all nations see
How we love our starry banner,
   Emblem of the free!

Mr. Heuman, a Virginia musician, arranged the music into a quickstep, which soon became one of the most popular marches of Northern military companies. Seemingly unable to endure hearing the piece again, Mr. Evans, a Virginia pianist, composed a response: "Yes, I Wish This War Was Over." Mr. Evans' composition was but one of many such set to the tune of the then hit song. Some arrangements pointed out political and social corruptions and abuses of the times.[6]

---

[6] Unionville *Humboldt Register*, March 19, 1864.

Mark Twain
Incorrigible Newsmonger

1

Prematurely "blowing" about Mrs. Hayne's benefit brick-surprise provoked only a mild explosion compared with some of the atomic blasts set off by Mark Twain's writings. The "incorrigible newsmonger" was not alone in this ability. Under a caption "Talent for Discount" the *Bulletin* complained that Virginia was "nearly overrun . . . with editors, artists, and scientific men." But the man whose name would eventually outrank all of the nation's leading newspaper men then in Washoe, was a newcomer, an unknown, except that his brother was territorial secretary of Nevada.

After a very short time in the Confederate army, Samuel Langhorne Clemens had arrived in Washoe with his brother Orion and other territorial officers in 1861. For a year Sam tried mining at Unionville and Aurora. But when Dan De Quille went East on a year's leave, Sam replaced him on the *Enterprise*. To substitute for such an established writer as Dan De Quille was no easy assignment. Though Sam's writings were rough, he was energetic and imaginative. When news was scarce he filled his column with such pieces as "The Petrified Man" [1] and a "Bloody Massacre," relating that an insane man slit the throats of his wife and nine children in an old log house at the edge of the great pine forest between Empire and Dutch Nick's. As usual, California editors copied the piece, but Comstock writers yelled: "The *Enter-*

---

[1] *San Francisco Weekly Bulletin,* October 14, 1862.

prise story is a sensation item, false, a never-to-be-forgotten hoax. Empire City and Dutch Nick's are the same place. No family of the name of Hopkins lives there. No great pine forest, and no murder!"

Like De Quille's article on Nevada's walking stones, some of "mad wag" Sam's accounts were probably true. For example, Clemens insisted that he once rescued himself from an island by pushing a large flat rock into the water and paddling it to the mainland.[2] But to prevaricate was more natural, and soon another paper shouted:

> That mad wag, Clemens, who localizes for the Virginia Enterprise, put a comical speech into the mouth of our representative, Mr. Winters, purporting to have been delivered in Washoe City. . . Clemens yesterday . . . exonerates Mr. Winter from the accusation of having admitted himself guilty of bribery and corruption.

The next Washoe venture of the former river boat pilot was reporting the legislative proceedings. Social life in Carson City during the session was zealously plied. And Sam in starched shirt, broadcloth coat and polished shoes — quite in contrast to his ill-kept appearance as a miner — was lionized by official wives, including his sister-in-law Mrs. Orion Clemens.

On February 2, 1863, Sam wrote his report as usual, but instead of "Josh," signed the piece with the new "Mark Twain," a pseudonym that was quickly accepted. Needless to say, Twain's reports were lively and readable until the *Union* reporter, whose pieces were dully detailed and exact, ridiculed the *Enterprise* accounts. Mark immediately declared Clement Rice's reports untruthful, and dubbed him "The Unreliable," a name that stuck. Though rivals, the writers were really friends, even rooming at the same place,

---

[2] (Reno) *Nevada State Journal*, January 5, 1954, as copied from *Pen*, December, 1953. The light, porous pumice rocks on Paoha Island in Mono Lake really float and Mark Twain actually could have done "just what he said he did."

the White House, until late July when that "recently built and elegantly furnished" hotel went up in a $30,000 fire, which attracted viewers, including Maguire's Opera House audience, who left in the middle of a tense act, necessitating a repeat performance the following night.

2

Of Mark Twain and other Washoe newspaper personnel it could hardly be said that "men for the sake of getting a living forget to live." When Colonel John A. Collins threw open the doors of his three-storied hotel (with its Brussels carpets, spring mattresses, and hot and cold water) and gave a special dinner, the press and other prominent Washoites "sped to the rendezvous" and tossed off the "opening soup with the celerity of lightning, and when the covers were removed — well, did you ever see a hen hawk light on a junebug?"

There yet would have been time to walk the two blocks down to the Opera House, where Mrs. Hayne, Frank Mayo, and O'Neil were appearing in *Retribution* and later in *The Limerick Boy,* but that would have meant missing "the champagne, the wisdom, and the wit." Besides "dashing off" such a stanza as:

> Some breasts may only feel a thrill
> At thoughts for which another bleeds;
> Some souls may only nurse the will
> Which in another grows to deeds;
> By chance, they dare instead of us —
> By chance, we scatter praise and flowers
> On others' graves; Fate rules it thus
> Or they might scatter them on ours.[3]

---

[3] When the editor of the *Reese River Reveille* complained that he was being flooded with "poetic effusions" — not from Joe Goodman's pen! — the *Bulletin* sought to placate the Austin editor by asking proudly, "Who would have expected to find poetry flourishing among alkali, sand, and sagebrush in a region hundreds of miles from everywhere?"

Goodman answered the toast honoring the newspapers by giving an "interesting history" of the press in Nevada, not forgetting to mention that the *Enterprise* was erecting two "magnificent three-story, fire-proof buildings" between Union and Taylor on C, and that mammoth presses from San Francisco were even then on the lot, waiting to be installed.

"But perhaps *the* speech of the evening," wrote a captivated *Bulletin* local, "was made by Sam Clemens. Those not familiar with this young man, do not know the depths of grave tenderness in his nature. He almost brought the house to tears by his touching simple pathos."

3

Sam Clemens was fast becoming a national character and local writers did not neglect him even in such flamboyant writings as:

VIRGINIA AT MIDNIGHT. — Up we went by moonlight, past the Gould and Curry, past the last fence staked out by someone who fervently believes that lots on the summit of Mount Davidson will some day be valuable; up, while the rugged face of the old mountain — wrinkled with the cares of eighty centuries — fairly wreathed itself into smiles of starlight, and moonbeam chuckles. At last we reached the summit, and pulling out the comforter which Mark Twain had pressed upon us at parting, we addressed ourselves to our devotions for a few minutes, while a faint gurgling sound was borne by the midnight breeze far out upon the empyreumatical (see Webster). Then we turned — gods! what a sight. A wreath of silvery smoke lay between us and the sleeping city, like the lace which swells over a woman's neck covering but not concealing its beauties, Virginia lay sleeping in the arms of her rugged bridegroom. The lights of Cedar Hill formed a glittering coronal for her brow, while her anklets of gold burned dimly in the dwindling torches of that sober burg, Gold Hill. The oaths and shouts, and cries, which form the nightly breathing of this sleeping giantess, were filtered by the distances, until they came to us on Washington Peak like the soft sighs of a sleeping babe. And then — Mark Twain's bottle, never full, being empty — we slowly descended into this scene of seeming peace and devotion.

"Here we are on B Street at midnight. A burst of muscle is flashing out through yonder opened door, and with it comes the clink of silver and the trampling of many feet. We enter:"

"Make your game," "all set," "all down," "red wins and black loses." The more you put down the less you take up, with the odds strongly in favor of the men who don't bet. Too hot here! Come out! There is a dozen of these innocent places of amusement all along this street. The transition from them to the station house was not unnatural, and there we found Jack Perry's Deputy, Mark Twain, expostulating with a newly arrested subject, who insisted that Mark had stolen his gin bottle and boots. We don't believe the latter accusation, but for the former — there was a bottle in Mark's pocket in lieu of the one he gave us, and he told us significantly when making the gift, that he was going "prospecting" for another. Then — we went to bed, as you will want to do after reading this.[4]

Scarcely a week passed that Mark Twain did not reach print:

Items. — We have no objections to that young man Wilson, or that sorrow-stricken heart, Sam Clemens, stealing our items from the morning papers; in fact we rather like it. But we do insist that they shall get some new locals from which we in turn can steal.

Another warm day . . . and Mark Twain growled like a bear with a sore head because he had to go down to the Gould & Curry mill and measure that big chimney over again

to settle a local bet. Reporters also resorted to Twain's own verbal barrage to describe "that beef-eating, blear-eyed, hollow-headed, slab-sided ignoramus — that pilfering reporter, Mark Twain."

A theatrical slip on Clemens' part was immediately pounced upon:

A "bill of unusual excellence" might have been offered, Mark, but we didn't see it. The company played in Carson last night, you ignoramus. How these reporters are given to lying!

---

[4] *Virginia Evening Bulletin*, July 11, 1863.

One of "the company" mentioned was Charles Pope, considered "one of the boys" even before he left the stage for mining at Reese. When the *Enterprise* staff (Joe Goodman, Dan De Quille, Steve Gillis, Wilson, and others) planned a joke on one of their members by giving him an imitation Meerschaum, it was Charley Pope they chose to present the gift. Pope did so most effectively. Mark Twain responded with emotion and "treated all around." Later when Twain learned that the pipe-and-party was a prank, he was so hurt that Dan bought him a genuine Meerschaum, declaring that the boys had intended it that way all the time.

4

With Dan De Quille's return to the staff of the *Enterprise* after his extended vacation, a Virginia paper informed Washoe readers:

> MARK TWAIN leaves for San Francisco to-day, and we are sorry to say on account of ill health. Mark has made his mark in a remarkable manner upon the good will of the people of Virginia, among whom he has a host of warm friends. It is said that Mark contemplates making the fearful leap from bachelorhood . . . but true or not, he has our best wishes for his welfare, whether running single or in twain.

In San Francisco the ladies giving a grand ball for benevolent purposes trusted that Washoe's "friend and pitcher Mark Twain" would "not only rival the 'Obese,' but . . . be able to give a good account of the whole affair." Mark did. But before long the Washoites were guessing: "Is he back again? No one could 'lie' under such a load of obligations . . . Scissors!" They were, no doubt, referring to Mark's lengthy article, "Frightful Accident to Dan De Quille." [5] The journalistic bombardment was on again.

When two of the sagebrush editors decided only a duel could give "satisfaction," between acts of *The Three Guards-*

---

[5] Unionville *Humboldt Register*, May 14, 1864.

men at the Opera House, Comstockers passed the dramatic words along: "Navy revolvers, 15 paces, daybreak!" Long before dawn of August 1 all the vehicles of Comstock livery stables had been hired and were "heading for Six-Mile Cañon." But Marshal Perry went too, arriving in time to stop the show. That night the disappointed miners and the unsatisfied editors might have sought diversion with *A Glance at New York* at Maguire's, or at the Melodeon.

Six weeks later, accompanied by seconds, surgeons, and a crowd of spectators, the Comstock editors proceeded to another encounter, which promised to be even more exciting than the fencing match at Maguire's. The duel was "conducted strictly in accordance with the code." The seconds handed five-shooters to the principals and repeated the instructions: ten paces, turn on signal, fire, advance toward each other, and fire at will. Tom Fitch and Mark Twain's editor began pacing. On signal, both whirled and fired — Goodman, low; Fitch, high. With a ball in his leg, Fitch declared himself "fully satisfied." [6]

Less than a year after the Fitch-Goodman "satisfaction," Washoe was agog over another duel. Again the same papers were involved. Laird was now the *Union* editor and Twain, the acting editor for the *Enterprise*. Mark had charged the *Union* with failing to contribute to the "Sanitary Sack of Flour Fund"; then he chided a ladies' group in Carson for diverting some of their "benefit" money to other purposes. Verbal battling reached such intensity that a day in May was set; dueling pistols were chosen.

Suddenly Mark remembered his poor shooting ability, which his second Steve Gillis tried to improve. Then both remembered the territorial legislature had made not only

---

[6] George W. Derickson, who started the *Washoe Times* in the fall of 1862, was murdered four short months afterwards. A few months later (October 31, 1863) General James Allen, proprietor and editor of the paper, fell dead in his office. J. K. Lovejoy then took over.

dueling but sending or accepting a challenge, a penitentiary offense for both principals and seconds. Mark and Steve, deciding they would rather not be guinea pigs for testing the new law, climbed aboard a westbound stage. And "Old Pi" volunteered his benison thus:

> Left yesterday, for bluer skies and more verdant hills, S. L. Clemens, Esq., alias "Mark Twain." Yes, Mark has gone, and amid our fragrant sagebrush, quartz-crowned hills, and alkali hydrants we repose solitary and almost alone. . . We shall miss Mark; his bosom friend De Quille will miss him; Marshal will do ditto; every lunch house in the city, every brewery, and every woman who knew him — and to know him was to love him — will miss him.

"Washoe certainly has some good points," agreed a coast paper. "It sends us bullion and bricks — mark that, and then Mark Twain."

The Little Devil's Share

1

With the departure of theatrical stars Julia Hayne and Frank Mayo, programs of comedy and farce predominated at Maguire's playhouse. No wonder, the new leading lady — brought over from the Temple of Comedy — was the "Queen of Comedy" Mrs. W. H. Leighton, who chose for her opening vehicle at the Opera House *Asmodeus; or, The Little Devil's Share*,[1] and through which — according to Washoe's theatrical critics — she "reaped the little devil's share" of amusement attention that Saturday evening, August 8. As for the afterpieces, *Wife for a Day* and *Sketches in India,* the press insisted that Mrs. Leighton's "exhibition of feet and plumpness" was not without charm, that Mrs. Perry was "enchanting," and that Messrs. Booth and Leman both "played their parts creditably."

With Mrs. Leighton as star, the Opera House troupe brought out on following nights *Captain Charlotte, The Windmill, Podijah B. Peasley,* the two-act musical burletta of *The Barrack Room, The Maid with the Milking Pail,* and *The Yankee Pedlar.*

Looking out over the audience the following Tuesday, Johnny Burns was pleased to note most seats filled, and many by neighbors from "that sober burg of Gold Hill." The reason? At ten o'clock that morning the Gold Hill Theatre had slid into the dump of the Yolo Mining Company and was

---

[1] Early in 1865 Mrs. Leighton and Yankee Locke would begin an engagement at New York's Old Bowery with *Asmodeus.*

now but a mass of bricks and boards. The theatre had hesitated long enough, however, for the hurdy-gurdy girls, sleeping in the back room, to save themselves from a "premature burial." Minus the theatre and the nightly dancing of the girls and seeking anything but "sober" entertainment, the Gold Hill people came up to enjoy Lotta at the Virginia Melodeon and "the side-splitting Yankee Locke, decidedly the feature," at the Opera House.

When next night for the first time in Washoe the Opera House players gave the domestic drama of *Willow Copse*, the critics reported that "Mrs. Perry's rendition of Rose Fielding displayed a fine conception and a finished study of the character. . . Leman was more than ordinarily excellent in representing the loving and heartbroken father . . . occasionally moving some of his hearers to tears. O'Neil made a good obese." But as Meg, Mrs. Leighton showed "a lack of talent with the Yorkshire dialect." Her dancing with Billy O'Neil was applauded in *An Object of Interest*, but there was no encore performance as the "musicianers had fled," no doubt to get an iced julep though the price of ice had tripled.

Succeeding nights left little doubt but that the Opera House was not doing well. Maybe Mrs. Leighton had difficulty; maybe the old troupe, schooled to heavier drama, had trouble. Maybe the *Bulletin* critic had a solution: "Mr. O'Neil is an excellent Irish comedian, but will not do for a low comedian. The gentleman did not act the character of Sampson Low to our satisfaction after having seen Joe Jefferson perform the same part. A good low comedian is wanted at the Opera House. Couldn't Mr. Burns be persuaded to make overtures to Billy Barry? He would afford Mrs. Leighton excellent support."

London Assurance held the Opera House boards on August 13, but "deserved a better audience." The next night Shakespeare's *The Comedy of Errors* with the *Swiss Swains* as the

afterpieces played "to a crowded house," the principal characters receiving the *Bulletin's* praise of "almost faultless," but
other parts were "not ably sustained."

In blackface next night Mrs. Leighton's Topsy "just growed"
in *Uncle Tom's Cabin.* The Washoe production opened with
the Shelbys in Kentucky; took old Tom to St. Clair's plantation; had him die under the whip of Simon Legree; had little
Eva die and angels transport her bodily to heaven. Melodramatic in the extreme, the play was — as President Lincoln
averred — a great weapon against slavery. *Uncle Tom's Cabin*
easily became one of the most popular of plays.[2]

2

Even so, that Saturday evening of August 15 not *Uncle
Tom's Cabin* but another blackface performance "reaped the
little Devil's share" of the amusement business. The Virginia
Melodeon had been newly refitted so that Maguire's minstrels
— just returned from a swing through Silverland — could
render "an agreeable entertainment," which included "the
comicalities of Wallace and Bray, the unsurpassed dancing of
Misses Lotta and Sager, the exquisite singing of Miss Della
Sager . . . and the unrivalled performance of the company generally."

Though next evening offered a real-life by-play when a
duelist was arrested at the theatre,[3] and Yankee Locke, "that
decidedly valuable acquisition" from the Temple of Comedy,
was "in the drunken scene as natural as he was laughable,"

---

[2] Though not a great book, *Uncle Tom's Cabin* was a landmark in our national
history. Since the dramatic rights were unprotected, playwrights brought out many
versions. George L. Aiken did one that played the East for 200 consecutive performances, the actors eating their meals in costume between scenes.

[3] The *Virginia Evening Bulletin* of August 17 reported the arrest: "Captain
Pitcher, who shot Hunter in a duel on Saturday morning, was arrested last night at
the theatre, and held in the sum of $500. The following gentlemen severally held
themselves responsible for the sum: Hon. Henry Edgerton, J. T. Goodman, and
James H. Hardy. The wounded man early this morning was improving."

Ireland as It Was and *Ten Nights in a Barroom* played to a
slim house. Perhaps Comstockers were a "sabbath-observing
people"; yet that did not explain the crowds at the Virginia
Melodeon that night or the next or the next.

To compete with the Melodeon's burlesque of the recently-
departed Julia Hayne, which Comstockers loyal to the actress
thought "abominable," the Opera House condensed *The
Comedy of Errors* into three acts and presented it and *The
Colleen Bawn* "to large and fashionable audiences." *The
Colleen Bawn; or, The Brides of Garryowen,*[4] an Irish, four-
act domestic drama, containing a melodramatic plot with
some stock situations (such as a mistaken identity), interspersed with sentimental Irish songs, good humor, and some
choice lines, was served the next night along with *The Yankee
Duelist* to gain the little demon's portion of patronage. All
the actors were declared "commendable," Mrs. Perry receiving a bouquet of Washoe flowers presented by "a gentleman
who walked six miles to pluck it. Quite a compliment to the
lady." [5]

3

A new comedian, in whom Comstockers took "remarkable
interest," now appeared with the Opera House troupe. What
vehicle would provide sufficient range for testing James
Murray's lingual ability to "call out of the dust of the stage
the works of true Scotch genius"? Sir Walter Scott's "capital
play" of *Rob Roy; or, Auld Lang Syne,* the "grand spectacular

---

[4] While Dion Boucicault was in the midst of a London bankruptcy over earnings
from *The Colleen Bawn,* the actor Charles Wheatleigh, maintaining that he had
the "sole right" to play the piece, had commenced a suit in the U.S. Circuit Court
against Tom Maguire, Mrs. H. A. Perry, Wm. O'Neil, J. B. Booth, and F. B. White
to restrain them from performing the play in California. Maguire lost the suit, but
that did not prevent his presenting *The Colleen Bawn* in Silverland.

[5] As a "substitute for the bouquet" an admirer suggested a custom from Spain:
cigars could have been tossed on the stage for such male favorites as Leman and
O'Neil.

operatic drama of Caledonia," had the Scotch character of
Bailie Nicol Jarvie. Devotees of the Opera House thought this
play would answer for the test. So on August 20 they packed
the theatre to determine whether the former Folsom merchant could "move them to admiration" as he had the "stolid
inhabitants" of Sacramento, where he had played with
McKean Buchanan, whose Rob Roy now was again anything
but disappointing. As for Abilie Nicol Jarvie, Murray played
him "in a masterly manner to the entire satisfaction" of the
large audience. For a few weeks Silverland's legitimate
theatre seemed safe.

Noting the success of Maguire's minstrels in their swing
through Washoe, Henry Sutliff signed a contract on August
18 for the construction of a new melodeon at 68 North C
Street nearly across from Topliffe's (now the Virginia Melodeon). Then Mr. French, the "well-known architect of the
old Metropolitan Theatre of San Francisco," announced plans
to build Washoe a "splendid new theatre," which Charles
Pope would lease. Could Virginia support another theatre or
even another melodeon? Perhaps Henry Sutliff noted that
such legitimate productions as *The Colleen Bawn, The Yankee
Duelist,* and *Guy Mannering,* ("a great play," with Mr. Murray in the role of Dominie Sampson) played to "tolerably
good audiences" while the Virginia Minstrels served "burlesque, farces, comicalities, etc., to crowded houses."

The Opera House fared better with *Richard III* when
McKean Buchanan as the crookbacked tyrant won "considerable applause." Later that night a thief broke into the theatre
and stole a gold chain from a person sleeping there. Robberies
were on the increase, including the stealing of cats, though
dogs overran the towns. "Look to your locks!" warned the
Bulletin and lamented the need of 15 men on the police
force.

4

The Octoroon held the Opera House boards on August 24 and 25. That Boucicault borrowed the story for this play from *The Quadroon* is likely, but he created in Salem Scudder a character seldom attempted by playwrights, that of a stage Yankee with gentlemanly qualities plus the "craft, ingenuity, self-reliance, clear intellect, quick wit, and hard philosophy" of the Yankee himself. "It is hard that a true Yankee of the American drama to be faithfully dealt with, should have to sit for his portrait to an Englishman," lamented *The Californian,* forgetting that Dion Boucicault was a Dublin-born Irishman, who had even persuaded the Congress to pass our first dramatic copyright laws (1856).

In *The Octoroon* Mrs. Perry "never appeared to better advantage" as Zoe, Mrs. Leighton's Dora Sunnyside was "nicely enacted," and Mr. O'Neil's Pete was "highly creditable," but the Salem Scudder of Fred Franks was "tame." However, the *Enterprise* critic called Franks his "favorite" and "one of the best comedians" because he did "humorous things with grave decorum and without seeming to know that they are funny." Nevertheless, the play that "made women weep and strong men grit their teeth in rage" at the horrors of slavery and injustice "against the sable African, the Mulatto, or the almost white Octoroon" attracted only a "fair" house. No wonder! The Melodeon presented "the whole company" in a rapid-paced variety show — "never a dull moment" — and plenty of tuneful music, including the "quite popular duets" of Misses Lotta and Sager.

Though fully aware that minstrelsy was more popular with the average Washoite than the legitimate drama, Maguire hired more actors even if he was busily engaged in defending himself in a legal fight instituted by Edward J. Cook to secure half the lot on which the Opera House stood. Maguire won the case as well as more attendance at his theatre.

Stepping from the incoming stagecoach the following Sat-

urday were Mrs. E. F. Stewart and handsome Charles R.
Thorne, Jr.[6] (later to become leading man at New York's
Madison Square Theatre). Both accomplished actors were
immediately placed on the bills as Lady Macbeth and Mac-
duff in *Macbeth* with all the original music. McKean Buchanan was cast as Macbeth and Mrs. Leighton as the
Singing Witch. But the promised Mrs. Stewart did not appear
that Monday evening or in *Othello* on the next because in a
coach upset or mix-up her wardrobe was being detained in
the Sierras, a not unusual occurrence. *Macbeth,* therefore,
the critic thought, was "only tolerably well performed."

While the Opera House cast prepared *The Duke's Motto*
for J. H. Allen's coming, the troupe gave standard plays, including *The Irish Cousin*[7] for Billy O'Neil's benefit. But on
the day set, August 28, the Catholics gave a fair; the ladies
of Dayton a festival at Doyle's Hall; and a carelessly thrown
match at Pat Lynch's Billiard Saloon started a fire that sped
down A Street to B, on to Taylor, Summit, Union, and on
back, making a square of burning buildings. When the fire
was finally extinguished, the *Bulletin* was without a home; so
were two thousand people — and a small dog, Lazarus the
Second.[8] Nevertheless, Billy's benefit was a "bumper, the

---

[6] Tall, manly, and well built, Charles R. Thorne, Jr., was an exceptional actor,
"who moved easily on stage, and possessed an unusual voice, indeed almost phe-
nomenal," thought the critic Charles Phillips, who insisted Thorne could express in
"subdued tones more than the majority of his contemporaries could obtain through
explosive force or ear-splitting rant." Thorne was so idolized in New York, he did
not need the "star-line so precious to many actors. He was a star without being
starred."

[7] Appearing 70 consecutive nights in his favorite play of *The Irish Cousin* was
a record O'Neil had chalked up to his credit.

[8] Wrote the *Virginia Evening Bulletin* of September 7, 1863: "BUMMER AND
LAZARUS THE SECOND. — Thousands have heard of the celebrated dogs Bummer and
Lazarus of San Francisco, of the circumstances which brought them together, of
their indissoluble friendship, and of their care for each other. But few know that
we have duplicates of these dogs here in Virginia, but such we have. They may be
seen any day at the Court House Exchange on B Street. . ." Less than a month
later the San Francisco Lazarus was dead, and newspapers headed "lengthy obit-
uary notices of the defunct" with "Notable Death."

performance was first-rate, and everybody was satisfied" in spite of the Melodeon attractions and a riot between rival fire companies, in which one man was killed.[9]

The night following the fire the minstrels did a "rushing business"; but so did the Opera House, this being the final night of Mrs. Leighton's season as star of the troupe. *Guy Mannering* and *Retribution; or, A Husband's Vengeance* made up the bill. In *Retribution* Harry Brown appeared as Count Priuli. This was the same Harry Brown who had tried to "do himself brown" when Stark's troupe had disbanded the year before. Comstock critics, however, being kind, called Brown "an excellent actor" and "an invaluable accessory to the company," which now proudly proclaimed J. H. Allen as a new member, who — everyone predicted — would now reap "the little devil's share" of Washoe's entertainment business.

---

[9] More homicides were committed in Virginia City (13 of them) during the reckless, bonanza year of 1863, than all the four years from the discovery of silver (the yield from Washoe mines increased in a year from six to over 12 million dollars in 1863).

I Am Here

1

Evidencing "the most intense interest" in the New York celebrity J. H. Allen, who had by-passed San Francisco to make his western debut in Virginia, the Washoites indicated they would "turn out *en masse* to give him a proper reception" and listen to his salute, "I am here!" The local newspapers exclaimed, "So perchance will one's ears ere long be saluted hourly, 'I am here!' It is *The Duke's Motto,* the last sensation of Paris, London, and New York." [1]

It was Paul Feval's version of *The Duke's Motto; or, The Little Parisian,* ultra-romantic and paying "no respect to probability," that the *Golden Era* ran as a serial and Maguire and Burns served in the Opera House, now fitted with new and elaborate scenery. As expected on opening night, not a seat was vacant. The Comstockers (who had suggested that "actors be clean shaven as during the time of the Regency") were intent to "dive deep into the terrifics and sup their fill of horrors" through the abduction of a little girl, the murder of her father, the hero's vow of vengeance, and his restoration of "the highborn girl to her proper rank after a succession of striking situations and interesting incidents."

Then with complete abandon the Washoites praised the drama, the scenery, and the excellence of the personators of the leading characters: C. R. Thorne, Jr., Buchanan, Mrs. Stewart, Mrs. Leighton, and especially and emphatically J. H. Allen (as Henri de Langardere), who "succeeded to a charm,"

---

[1] *Virginia Evening Bulletin,* August 24, 1863, copied from the Boston *Saturday Evening Gazette.*

possessing an "energy and fire," which not only carried the piece through with success but served "to infuse new vigor into the members of the company, who had, from their too constant and arduous labors, become listless and wearied." The critic concluded his appraisal with the generous compliment, "In Mr. Allen's hands no part will suffer injustice." Then he facetiously injected a local thrust, "The Duke is a sort of ubiquitous animal, and like our city marshal, always around somewhere in the neighborhood."

On the second night of *The Duke's Motto* seats were available since many Comstockers were crowding about the bunting-draped stand before the Collins House to hear the Honorable William M. Stewart. After the pre-primary Union rally and the last "I am here!" at the Opera House, the people joined in a lengthy torchlight procession, dancing with colored lanterns and transparencies that gave off a weird lighting effect as the serpentine parade wound through the Comstock towns while a "pale silver moon bathed the hills around." "A handsome young Pi-Ute" swung one of the lanterns exclaiming, "I, American. I, for Union." To this the reporters chorused, "What a rebuke to the Copperheads, the poor untutored savage more civilized than they." Then Fremont's cannon roared, pistols cracked, the crowds cheered, and dispersed to meet next day at the ballot boxes.

Next night during a tense scene of the second act of *The Duke's Motto* a cry of "Fire" started a rush toward the doors, and soon the actors found themselves playing to empty seats, but the crowd returned next night and saw the play in its entirety. When the "lovers of fun" who generally attended the Virginia Melodeon were "deprived of the talents of Miss Lotta," who was unwell for two nights, they too went to the Opera House to "sup their fill of horrors" (and to enjoy the petite comedy of *My Aunt; or, Love and Champagne*), thus concluding a six-night run of "I am here!"

Acceding to popular demand Maguire and Burns again

brought the Maguire's Minstrels over to Maguire's Opera
House for "fashionable and pleasing matinees for the accom-
modation of ladies and children." For one more night the
minstrels enticed patrons into the Virginia Melodeon, then
set off to please the citizens of Silver City, Dayton, Carson
City, and Washoe City.

2

By September 7 the Virginia Melodeon had been "put in
perfect order" and returned to its original status of Topliffe's
Theatre for J. W. Wilder and Company's "Gigantic Panorama
of the Present War, acknowledged perfectly correct by members of Congress and the War and Navy Departments, profuse with startling scenic and dramatic effects with over 1000
views of the gigantic rebellion, together with a grand moving
diorama of the great naval combat between the iron-clad
monitors." Many Washoites agreed that "the vast and com-
prehensive view of the terrible rebellion brought West from
Niblo's Garden in New York City, was decidedly the very
best artistical work of the kind ever seen on the coast."

Since there was "nothing to offend even the most fastid-
ious," women came and brought their children; paid the
dollar or fifty cents admission; and waited for "8¼ o'clock,"
when Miss Viola, the "highly celebrated patriotic ballad
singer," and Miss Hattie Pomeroy, "the popular songstress,"
opened the program by singing patriotic ballads. John Davies
concluded each show with an educational lecture. For a week
and an afternoon Topliffe's continued "to draw crowded
houses," critics insisting they "heard but one general feeling
of satisfaction" from all who thus had seen "the Civil War
from the dread signal at Sumter to the success at Vicksburg."

3

A glance at the plays given on Maguire's Opera House
stage in Virginia gives some idea of the rigid requirements
troupers were forced to meet a hundred years ago: perform-

ing in one play tonight, another the next, at the same time rehearsing still another. Sunday brought out Kotzebue's domestic play, *The Stranger; or, Misanthropy and Repentance,* for a "tolerably good audience." Leman, Franks, and Mrs. Leighton sought to liven the performance, but the critic felt their "excruciating gags were entirely out of place."

Next night Allen appeared as the brave blacksmith in the Virginia première of *The Blacksmith of Antwerp.* Sparing "nothing to please," Maguire and Burns provided new scenery and effects for this "new sensation drama," which gave such "unqualified satisfaction," it played three nights; and the audiences, including Dan De Quille, who had just returned from the East, expressed their approbation of Allen's "masterly piece of acting" by repeated applause and by calling him nightly before the curtain.

Responding to repeated demand, Allen gave a Thursday night performance of *The Duke's Motto* — "for positively the last time" — but Friday night, assisted by the strength of the entire company, repeated it and also gave the "intensely exciting drama" of *The Orange Girl of Venice,* in which Mr. Allen and Mrs. Perry played "their parts admirably." Pretty Mrs. Perry was further lauded as "a great favorite" with Washoe theatre-goers and extolled "for the correct manner" in which she sustained her various roles.

The "unwarrantable gags perpetrated" by Mrs. Leighton and Mr. Franks, the reviewer found unpalatable, but conceded that "Vive Gallianner" was excellently well rendered by Mr. Westwood. (Could this possibly be Philip Westwood, builder of Washoe's first theatre? If so, it helps explain the critic's slip in calling the Opera House, "the Howard" in one of his reviews). Highlighting the program and "greeted with shouts of applause" was the spectacular sword combat between Allen and Yankee Locke. Mrs. Leighton then came on in *Fool of the Family.* And next night the whole "splendid programme" was repeated.

4

The Opera House season was drawing to a close. It was time Comstock theatre-lovers and the management show their appreciation of J. H. Allen, who had sojourned long enough in Washoe to establish his reputation as an actor "above mediocrity." His admirers selected the play in which Allen had made "a great reputation," the drama from which the Popes had chosen selections for their benefit, the five-act drama translated from the German and adapted to the English stage by Marie Lovell: *Ingomar, or, The Greek Maiden*, the play that had been a hit in Washoe since Stark's Company had presented it in all of Washoe's seven scattered theatres, including the Howard of Virginia City.

Ingomar now became the impetus for one of Mark Twain's pungent critiques, which readers enjoyed in the *Territorial Enterprise*:

"INGOMAR" OVER THE MOUNTAINS. THE "ARGUMENT."

ACT I. — Mrs. Claughley appears in the costume of a healthy Greek matron (from Limerick). She urges Parthenia, her daughter, to marry Polydor, and save her father from being sold out by the sheriff — the old man being in debt for assessments.

Scene 2. — Polydor — who is a wealthy, spindle-shanked, stingy old stock-broker — prefers his suit and is refused by the Greek maiden — by the accomplished Greek maiden, we may say, since she speaks English without any perceptible foreign accent.

Scene 3. — The Comanches capture Parthenia's father, old Myron (who is the chief and only blacksmith in his native village). They tear him from his humble cot, and carry him away to Reese River. They hold him as a slave. It will cost thirty ounces of silver to get him out of sock.

Scene 4. — Dusty times in the Myron family. Their house is mortgaged — they are without dividends — they cannot "stand the raise." Parthenia, in this extremity, applies to Polydor. He sneeringly advises her to shove out after her exiled parent herself.

She shoves!

ACT II. — Camp of the Comanches. In the foreground, several of the tribe throwing dice for tickets in Wright's Gift Entertain-

ment. In the background, old Myron packing faggots on a jack.
The weary slave weeps — he sighs — he slobbers. Grief lays her
heavy hand upon him.

Scene 2. — Comanches on the war-path, headed by the chief,
Ingomar. Parthenia arrives and offers to remain as a hostage while
old Myron returns home and borrows thirty dollars to pay his
ransom with. It was pleasant to note the varieties of dress displayed in the costumes of Ingomar and his comrades. It was also
pleasant to observe that in those ancient times the better class of
citizens were able to dress in ornamental carriage robes, and even
the rank and file indulged in Benkert boots, albeit some of the
latter appeared not to have been blacked for several days.

Scene 3. — Parthenia and Ingomar alone in the woods. "Two
souls with but a single thought, etc." She tells him that is love.
He "can't see it."

Scene 4. — The thing works around about as we expected it
would in the first place. Ingomar gets stuck after Parthenia.

Scene 5. — Ingomar declares his love — he attempts to embrace
her — she waves him off, gently, but firmly — she remarks, "Not
too brash, Ing., not too brash, now!" Ingomar subsides. They
finally flee away, and hie them to Parthenia's home.

Acts III and IV. — Joy! Joy! From the summit of a hill, Parthenia beholds once more the spires and domes of Silver City.

Scene 2. — Silver City. Enter Myron. Tableau! Myron begs for
an extension on his note — he has not yet raised the whole ransom,
but he is ready to pay two dollars and a half on account.

Scene 3. — Myron tells Ingomar he must shuck himself, and
dress like a Christian; he must shave; he must work; he must give
up his sword! His rebellious spirit rises. Behold Parthenia tames it
with the mighty spirit of Love. Ingomar weakens — he lets down —
he is utterly demoralized.

Scene 4. — Enter old Timarch, Chief of Police. He offers Ingomar — but this scene is too noble to be trifled with in burlesque.

Scene 5. — Polydor presents his bill — 23 drachmas. Busted
again — the old man cannot pay. Ingomar compromises by becoming the slave of Polydor.

Scene 6. — The Comanches again, with Thorne at their head! He
asks who enslaved the Chief? Ingomar points to Polydor. Lo!
Thorne seizes the trembling broker, and snatches him bald-
headed!

Scene 7. — Enter the Chief of Police again. He makes a treaty with the Comanches. He gives them a ranch apiece. He declares they shall build a town on the American Flat, and appoints great Ingomar to be its Mayor! [Applause by the supes.]

Scene 8. — Grand tableau — Comanches, police, Pi-Utes, and citizens generally — Ingomar and Parthenia hanging together in the centre. The old thing. The old poetical quotation, we mean. They double on it — Ingomar observing "Two souls with but a single Thought," and she slinging in the other line, "Two Hearts that Beat as one." Thus united at last in a fond embrace, they sweetly smiled upon the orchestra and the curtain fell.[2]

As predicted, Maguire's "every seat, in fact, every spot where a form could possibly squeeze itself, was filled that September night" (September 15) in a flattering ovation to the beneficiary, J. H. Allen, who acted Ingomar "in an admirable manner while the Parthenia of Mrs. Perry was none the less creditable." It was a leviathan bill. Dan Morgan sang a song and Billy O'Neil appeared in his laughable character of "Barney the Baron."

After five acts of *Ingomar* Mr. Allen should have been done. Instead, he came on stage with Mons. Chauvel (proprietor of a local hostelry) in an exciting fencing match that elicited "plenty of applause from the lovers of this art." But the program was not yet over. The curtain rose again. *The Dumb Girl of Genoa*, featuring Allen as the drunken corporal, formed the comic conclusion to Allen's highly successful evening. Completely satiated, the audience left the theatre, but upon emerging were shocked to see flames against the night sky. The Gold Hill Mill was ablaze — and it burned, a $25,000 loss.

5

A "singular freak of nature," on the Placerville road near Lake Tahoe, "a knot in the crotch of a cedar tree" that resembled the head of an old Indian, had been named by the

---

[2] San Francisco *Golden Era,* November 29, 1863, copied from the Virginia *Territorial Enterprise.*

Washoites "Nick of the Woods" from the Indian drama. At
last the play was to be given in Washoe. With Allen as the
Jibbenainosay in *Nick of the Woods; or, The Jibbenainosay*
and as the drunken corporal in the comic drama of *The Dumb
Girl of Genoa* the performance of September 16 was interesting and "tolerably well represented," but did not attract so
large an audience as had *Ingomar*. Some Washoites, starting
for the theatre, got detained on South B Street by "some
Pi-Utes" playing a "singular game of monte," as yet unknown
to civilized gamesters.

Thursday brought out the popular, old comedy of *The
Serious Family; or, Cant and Hyprocrisy* ("acted with immense success 1000 nights in New York" with Allen as Captain Murphy Maguire), and *Andy Blake; or, The Irish Diamond* with Billy O'Neil.

The lovers of legitimate drama pushed past the dangerous
section of the sidewalk on D Street between the Opera House
and Taylor, aware that two accidents had occurred there, and
crowded the theatre Friday night to honor the actress who
"for so long a time" had amused all Silverland with her "inimitable performances." Planché's three-act comedy-drama,
The Pride of the Market, was the opening piece on Mrs.
Leighton's benefit, followed by another three-act piece, *The
Maniac Lovers,* with Allen playing the leads. The evening
concluded with the farce of *The Swiss Swains* as O'Neil had
played in it at the Bowery Theatre under Allen's management
four years before. The laughing lady had a "crowded house
.   .   .   and performed with her usual spirit."

Saturday Mr. Allen and Mrs. Perry, "the lady who was
becoming more and more a favorite," carried the leading roles
in the nautical drama of *Black-Eyed Susan*. O'Neil appeared
in *The Irish Emigrant*.

The Opera House troupe closed their season on September
21, when Thespians of both Maguire's Opera House and

Maguire's Virginia Melodeon — the minstrels had returned
from their Washoe jaunt — and citizens tendered J. H. Burns,
"one of the most deservedly popular managers," with a
"Grand Complimentary benefit." More talent volunteered
than could be used on the stage, manifesting the esteem and
popularity of the manager, who had friends before as well as
behind the footlights.

All that Glitters is not Gold, More Blunders than One, and
Tom and Jerry satisfied the lovers of legitimate offerings.
Lotta Crabtree, Walter Bray, and others of the minstrel
troupe kept things lively and amusing between acts; and the
Lazarus brothers concluded the evening with an exhibition of
the "manly art." [3] It is redundant to state that the manager's
benefit was a "bumper."

Next morning the Opera House troupers boarded stages
for Sacramento to play during the California State Fair. But
Johnny Burns promised Comstockers that the troupe would
return and would bring back with them not only Annette
Ince, but the glamorous, world-celebrated and "greatly talented" Adah Isaacs Menken. Virginia theatrically was becoming world known, second only to San Francisco "on the
western slope," and now boasted four daily newspapers, "most
striking evidence of the prosperity of the place" that had
grown faster than any other "city on the continent."

[3] No unhappy incident marred Johnny Burns' benefit. But several weeks later at
the close of their prize fight in Washoe City, a "row" developed between Harry
Lazarus and a man named Muchach. Unfortunately the audience joined in the
fight, jerked out guns, fired "30 rounds," killed Muchach, and wounded several
others.

Lotta Crabtree

1

Would the Opera House remain dark now with the first day of fall and the departure of the legitimate actors? Quite the reverse, said the manager Johnny Burns, still glowing from the compliment of his "bumper benefit." And having planned ahead so as not to lose a night, he told his patrons they could "expect a chaste and elegant performance on the style of Bryant's in New York and the Eureka in San Francisco, featuring Miss Lotta, the universal favorite, and Walter Bray, the comic son of Momus, plus a whole talented minstrel troupe." [1] Doors would open at seven; the performance would begin at eight. And though he had arranged new staging effects, Burns lowered prices to only a dollar or fifty cents.

More than a flash in the pan, minstrelsy for many months — already four by September — remained a Washoe attraction. Now ensconced in an atmosphere of elegance on the Opera House stage, the troupe — inspired by little Lotta Crabtree — played with more zest and talent than at the Virginia Melodeon. Not more than sixteen, but looking younger in a simple, round-necked, full-skirted dress, but often in costume or blackface, Lotta could sing, dance, and gag through an entire evening with joyous abandon. Her charm, sweetness, and changing moods — pathetic, rollicking, or teasing — endeared her to Washoe audiences.

When Lotta was five, her father, handsome John Crabtree, arrived in California and wandered among the mines while

---

[1] *Virginia Evening Bulletin*, September 22, 1863.

his wife kept the family by taking in boarders in Grass Valley. Here, Lotta came to the attention of the dazzling, but naughty, king's mistress Lola Montez, who taught Lotta to sing, ride horseback, and dance. Soon Lotta was doing intricate steps with such talent, her tiny red head bobbing, that the miners insisted she dance on every occasion.

On the Crabtrees' first barnstorming tour under the management of none other than Mart Taylor, Lotta added to her repertoire. She mimicked the father of the Washoe theatre; she improvised. From Jake Wallace she learned to strum the banjo and sing:

> I can play the banjo, yes, indeed, I can,
> I can play a tune upon the frying pan.
> I hollo like a steamboat 'fore she's gwine to stop;
> I can sweep a chimney and sing out at the top —
> Strike de toe and heel, cut de pigeon wing,
> Scratch gravel, slap de foot, dat's jus' de ting.

Featured with Lotta now were Walter Bray who had left the legitimate stage to become a minstrel, Della Sager — one of the "sweetest songstresses," and others. "So go," urged the *Bulletin*, though no urging was needed, "and see the entire company in all their glory." Washoe minstrel programs, ephemeral bills distributed along the Lode, are unfortunately lost, but a ludicrous angle of a Washoe incident or a bit of gossip about a political aspirant was never overlooked to give local color and interest. Variety was the theme and the Opera House was filled to enjoy it.

Reviewers agreed that "the duets of Misses Sager and Lotta" in "When This Cruel War is Over" and "Bound for the Land of Washoe" were "really charms"; Barnwell had a good voice, but it was "too low to be heard"; Pete Sterling was "unquestionably the quickest-footed individual in the world"; M'lle. Minne was pleasing as a songstress and had "acting talent"; and Schreiner, the violinist, was "one of the best musical leaders ever attached to a theatre." Jake Wallace "provoked considerable mirth in his different acts" and, when urged to do so, accompanied himself on the banjo and called out the "Encore":

> This morning I arose
> From sweet repose
> Put on my clothes
> And out I goes
> In the street, you knows,
> Meets one of my foes,
> His name is Mose,
> He runs wid the hose,
> A quarrel arose
> We comes to blows
> He hits me in de nose
> And down I goes
> In the gutter you knows,
> And the water flows,
> And up I goes
> To my home, you knows,
> To dream of my woes.
> That's all I knows,
> And what I knows
> I know I knows.

2

Since little but good could be said of the minstrels playing at the Opera House, ladies came too, and as nothing offended, enjoyed following programs as well as those of Saturday afternoons. Certainly Washoites were habitués of such minstrelsy as dispensed by the troupe and Lotta, the "talented young lady, the very embodiment of fun and frolic, always whimsical but never vulgar," who on October 2 took a benefit. The theatre was "literally crammed and a great many could not obtain standing room." The ladies turned out in unusual numbers, testifying to the feminine esteem of little Lotta — though the reporters could not understand the tyrannical old jade, Dame Fashion, that would require ladies to walk such narrow sidewalks and "drag their dear dresses along such filthy places" as Virginia streets. "A great army of talent" assisted Lotta in her benefit program, so filled with "hits, drolleries, and smartness, the audience of such a liberal fun-loving community" tossed to Lotta's feet "frequent showers of silver approbation in the shape of four-bit pieces, more than a hundred dollars worth."

No wonder the comedienne eventually amassed four million dollars, which, upon her death in 1924, she left to worthy organizations, including the veterans of the first World War. Lotta, always generous, probably contributed to the fund Washoites raised at this time for the sick and destitute Miss Sterling, the "tall woman or American Giantess," who had been exhibited in Aurora, Virginia, and elsewhere in Washoe — as also in California. But it was Washoe generosity that paid for the medical aid of the theatrical skeleton.

When Lotta was ill several days, the Comstockers expressed concern as they also did over the loss of her valuable breast pin. An army captain "during his perambulations" to amusement spots of Virginia located the missing jewelry "adorning a danseuse of a very much lower grade in a hurdy-gurdy establishment on C Street" and through the police had Miss Lotta's property returned to her.

Next evening while doing her inimitable grotesque pas in the "walk around," Lotta, like Julia Hayne, received a "substitute bouquet" (Mark Twain seems to have kept the secret this time), a "silver bar of considerable weight if judged by the kir-flump with which it fell on stage," causing the *Bulletin* reporter to fear that "had the bar fell on Miss Lotta's toes it would have knocked all the nimbleness out of them. This custom — for which it has become here — of throwing silver coin or bars on the stage, must be very 'pleasong,' as the Frenchman would call it, to the recipient." In this instance, the esteem and generosity and "the novelty of the 'token' so overcame her phelinks" that the little redhead could not complete her number.

3

In the audience on her benefit night, Lotta may have noted the drivers of the camel train in from the Humboldt salt mines and the author-lecturer J. Ross Browne, who would "by request" next night entertain at Topliffe's Theatre with his lecture on Iceland. Having written "Sketches of Life in Washoe," Browne was back now to gather additional material for *Harper's Magazine.* "Scarcely had I descended from the stage," related Mr. Browne, "when I was greeted by several old friends. . . 'Your sketch of Washoe,' said they, 'was a capital burlesque. It was worthy of Phoenix or Artemus Ward! A great many people thought it was true.'" [2]

To advertise his lecture, Browne had secured a bill-sticker, who "agreed for the sum of six dollars to make me notorious, but," moaned Browne, "a lady popularly known as 'The Menken' . . . was about to favor . . . Virginia with a classical equestrian exhibition entitled 'Mazeppa.' She was represented as tied in an almost nude state to the back of a white horse, which was running away with her at a fearful rate." The bill-sticker evidently enjoyed Mazeppa "a flaming and gorgeous bill" in colors of "the most florid character, and he posted it accordingly. First came Mazeppa on the mustang horse; then came the Trip to Iceland and myself!"

But the posters paid off. Unlike the sparsely filled house for the billiard match, Topliffe's was packed. Comstockers, paying $2.50 for lady and gentleman or $1.50 for a single admission, viewed the "panoramic shots of life, character, and scenery in that wonderful region" of Iceland and greeted Browne's experiences and dry humor with bursts of laughter and applause. "But never again . . . will I undertake to run 'Iceland' in the vicinity of a beautiful woman tied to the back of a white horse," declared Browne [3] as he climbed

---

[2] "Washoe Revisited," *Harper's New Monthly Magazine,* June, 1865.

[3] Each entertainer saw the Comstock, of course, through different eyes, but no one went away unimpressed, least of all J. Ross Browne. To him Virginia was a

beside the driver on an outbound stage only to be plagued by the one line of a song: "When this cruel war is over."

Determining to enjoy the "amenities of social life in Aurora," Browne viewed a "badger fight" and, along with "a large number of people," a shotgun duel between Dr. Eichelroth and B. E. Draper, editor of the *Aurora Times*. But when a man throwing brickbats at a house came near getting "shot dead" in front of the Sazarac Saloon,[4] Browne hurried on to Bodie and so out of the territory.

4

Back in Virginia the minstrels continued doing a rushing business. "So they ought," insisted a local critic, "such talent, such a variety of performances, and such a comfortable house, 'twould draw a crowd anywhere. Remember . . . an unusually good bill for to-night." On October 8 the great Momus representative Walter Bray would take a benefit. To promote

conglomeration of tunnels, dumps, and puffing steam-engines with belching smoke-stacks; subterranean blasts and crushing rock; sawing, ripping, and nailing; fruit peddlers and freight wagons; ubiquitous saloons with men "swilling poison"; auctioneers, speculators, and men shouting off the stocks of delinquent stockholders; minstrels, organ-grinders, and hurdy-gurdy girls, especially those in Bell's Opera, opposite the Opera House, where the "orgies keep up till nearly daylight disturbing the whole neighborhood"; newsboys crying, "Papers!"; stages dashing off for "Reese" or in from "Frisco"; Wells Fargo distributing letters, packages, and papers amid tempting piles of silver bricks and $20 pieces. Virginia presented confusion; this was 1863.

Yet a visitor's ears could hear meaningful music, not the "Sardinian Polka" nor the "Maggie Mitchell Waltz" — new sheet music sent up from the Bay — but the music of steam whistles that "fill the air with harmony, forming a sort of calliope" that well could vie with the Mormons' new organ at Salt Lake City. ("The community of saints," so the *Bulletin* told readers, was "having the largest organ ever built in the United States made for their new tabernacle by a celebrated builder in Boston.")

4 The good claims Aurora had to its being the site for the capital of Washoe were "submerged," the *Aurora Times* had to admit, "under the reign of terror set up by barbarian sway." To which the *Bulletin* sympathized, "Aurora is certainly a beautiful town, and the surrounding country exceedingly romantic as well as rich in mineral and agricultural resources. What a great pity that such a country should be thus 'submerged.' Are there any ladies in Aurora? We presume not — a few importations of this kind might tend to dissipate the darkness of the barbarism. . ."

interest Bray promised to give "a really splendid gift, a silver trumpet," to the fire company selling the most tickets. On display in a C Street jewelry store window, the trumpet, "its design exquisitely chased" and surrounded by a gold scroll, was such an attraction that days before Bray's "gala night," the fire boys had sold more than a thousand tickets at a dollar each. "Remember," admonished the *Bulletin,* "new songs and dances will be introduced and Bray himself will make a speech, preach, and perform some tall braying to please the public, all of whom are expected to be there."

Hardly "all" were there, yet every part of the Opera House was "rammed, crammed, and jammed full." What an ovation to a comedian late from the Shakespeare stage! The performance drew ringing applause, Walter this night exceeding all former efforts. "A sweet-toned Bray," little Flora, the comedian's petite step-daughter, also did "very well indeed for a first appearance on any stage," singing and dancing several numbers.

Another diminutive piece of femininity, "about twice as high as 50 dollars worth of four-bit pieces," sang the "Flag of Our Union," and had such a shower of Uncle Sam's currency flung at her that she was compelled to take off her tiny shoe in which to collect it, "much to the amusement of everybody." Possibly the brightest point of the evening was the beneficiary's presentation of the silver trumpet to Eagle Engine Company, No. 3, accepted "to wild applause" [5] by their foreman Tom Peasley.

Though Johnny discontinued the "fashionable and pleasing matinees . . . for the innocent amusement of ladies and children, who could not be 'out o' nights,' " the evening fun went on, especially that of October 10, when "three cele-

---

[5] Not to be outdone, the staff at the *Enterprise* office presented their editor-boss with a belated birthday gift: a cane "of fine gold," the head of which was set with choice California quartz and carried the inscription, "The Printers to J. T. Goodman, September 18, 1863."

brated Terpsichoreans" — Lotta, Johnny Mason, and Tim Darling — engaged in dancing matches, the prizes being silver cups. Comstockers generally backed Lotta for no reason except that "when a woman's toes or tongue are well trained, those of no mortal man can keep pace." October 14 was Lotta's last night in the territory and it was a big one for the soubrette, the troupe, the audience, and Johnny Burns.[6]

5

With Lotta gone, Maguire and Burns gave the Opera House over to "Divine services" on Sunday mornings (the first speaker being a former chaplain in General Grant's army, the Reverend O. W. Briggs of the Baptists) and for evening programs made changes. Charley Rhodes, the famous banjoist, and Miss Fillmore were brought up from San Francisco; Jake Wallace was substituted for Darling "on the end," which proved a "judicious move"; and L. Loud, veteran of the Battle of Bull Run, was featured on the tenor drum with the Opera House Brass Band, where patrons had noted his "rattling expertness."

Burlesque, unceremonious take-offs of regular plays, which now took over the Opera House, employed exaggeration, humor, puns, and gags. The operatic burlesque of *Bone Squash Diablo* was served Comstockers on the benefit night of W. D. Corrister. The evening was such a success, Washoites demanded more, especially "the great burlesque of The Ghost," which had so invaded theatres that everything else "had to give way." And Burns "spared neither pains nor expense" in putting on the weird fascination in "unsurpassed style," including the unique Washoe touch of "a ghost under ground" in a benefit for the Washoe Guards.

Aping Walter Bray's device for creating interest, Burns also

---

[6] The prize conundrum from Gilbert's New Idea (where Lotta would keep her San Francisco engagement), "Why is Lotta superior to the Planet Venus?" was answered: "Because Venus is the Evening Star but three months out of six, while Lotta is always the Star of the Evening."

offered a prize for the most tickets sold: a silver brick, which
was won by a handsome young lieutenant of the Guards,
much to the "special delight of the ladies." And those ladies
"loving to be squeezed" must have been pleased, observed a
local reviewer, who was "unable to get nearer than six feet of
the door." "We have never seen such a 'scrowdging' in our
life, but judging from the terrific yells and shouts of applause
it is reasonable to suppose that it was satisfactory. We con-
gratulate the Guards."

It was a climactic close to a long and successful season of
minstrelsy in Nevada Territory. And the "capital" troupers,
welcoming rest, were disbanded. Walter Bray, Pete Sterling,
and Barnwell left for the Bay, but the "balance of the troupe
remained in Virginia" perhaps "to enjoy their otium cum
dignitate," unhurried by the pressure of meeting an entertainment schedule.[7]

6

Flaming handbills now announced the First Annual Fair
of the Washoe Agricultural, Mining, and Mechanical Society,
which the *Sacramento Bee* praised as "highly creditable to
the intelligence and correct view of the people of the territory." Though the *Bulletin* assured its readers, "our reports
may be implicitly relied upon for accuracy,"[8] one wonders at

[7] Since the minstrels were gone, musicians Evans and Shultz planned a grand
ball at their hurdy-gurdy hall adjoining Topliffe's Theatre, but Marshal Perry
arrested the barkeeper, the musicians, and three of the girls for failing to pay the
city license. As a test, the case went to the Supreme Court of the territory. The
musicians lost; the girls went "back to jail."

[8] When the *Virginia Union* puffed that it gave "a fuller report of the Fair
. . . and contributed as much or more than any other paper," the *Bulletin*
retorted that "in a multitude of words there is not wisdom." Cause of the journalistic "tremulous nervous excitement" was the premium to be awarded for the best
reporting of the fair. Under an item entitled, "The Generous Few" the *Bulletin*
also noted that "less than 50 public spirited citizens" gave funds and made the
arrangements for the fair, including the printing, the prizes, construction of the
pavilion, etc.

A happier note was contained in another news item: "All gentlemen whose stock
gained premiums at the Fair generously donated the said premiums to the fund
for the prizes at the next Fair."

cabbage that would "gladden the heart of a Dutchman in Faderland"; beets that absolutely "can't be beat"; carrots, "reaching over the head of a tall man"; pumpkins weighing nearly a hundred pounds each; and potatoes that "surprised, astonished, dumfounded but highly delighted" visitors from September 12-16 during the "great event in the onward and upward progres of Washoe."

Of course the horses ran; and a scrub race with horses of doubtful prospects (as irregular an affair as Siena's Palio from thirteenth century Italy) outshone all others. The final day of the fair opened with a grand parade of the prize livestock, preceded by a "splendid brass band, whose dulcet sounds gave so much satisfaction all during the fair." Then, the exhibits removed from the huge pavilion, Schreiner and Millington and their dance bands arrived as did gentlemen with their more than two hundred ladies "in every style of beauty, form, and adornment," the very sight of whom struck one youthful reporter with the shock of a "galvanic battery." [9]

---

[9] Remembering Minerva Morris's criticism (in a letter to the *Gold Hill News* of October 13) that newspapers carried gallantry too far in not mentioning the ladies and giving them credit for their refining influence in Silverland, column on column the reporters described those ladies — their beautiful faces, their coiffure, height, feet, dress, hoops, and their "polkaing and waltzing, oh!"

Thalia

1

When *The Ghost* had completed its run, Maguire, who had been standing by with a new troupe, now took over the job of proprietor of the Opera House. He selected C. L. Graves as stage manager, and presented Miss Fanny Morgan in the starring roles along with the prima donna, Madame Biscaccianti, the already popular Mrs. H. A. Perry, J. B. Booth, C. R. Thorne, Jr., W. Stephenson, and others,[1] including "a first class musician and composer of the celebrated 'Fireman's March,'" Charley Shultz, now leader of the orchestra. "The advent of the newcomers is anxiously looked for by our citizens," greeted the *Virginia Evening Bulletin*.

On October 20 the Muse of comedy and joy opened the Opera House with *As You Like It*. "I didn't like it," wrote a hypercritical reviewer of Miss Morgan's San Francisco debut. "Delicate sentiment, exquisite diction, and the utmost attainable perfection . . . are demanded for the *role* of Rosalind." But how would the Washoites receive "the dashing and beautiful songstress and actress" as Rosalind?

Australian-born, Fanny Morgan, "tall and comely in figure and superabundantly joyous in look and manner," had arrived in the bay city the middle of August. Nine years before she had appeared in New York with Edwin Booth and Laura Keene; and by 1872 she would star at the Denver Theatre

---

[1] Others of the troupe included Miss Lulu Sweet, Mrs. Claughley, Miss Fanny Howard, L. F. Beatty, D. R. Anderson, J. W. Thoman, F. Woodhull, C. L. Graves, F. Alexander, C. S. Runnells, and H. Macklin.

along with the Civil War actress-spy, Major Pauline Cushman, who also would visit Nevada.[2]

Although Comstockers admitted the comedy queen sometimes attempted roles beyond her ability, "unequivocally
favorable" they now said of her initial Silverland personation
of Rosalind — Comstockers did like it. They also liked her
celebrated "Cuckoo Song" and her interpretations of Miss
Thistledown and Maggie McFarland in the afterpiece of *The
Bonnie Fish Wife*. In fact, all actors were "up in their parts,"
said the reporter. "Maguire certainly is making a hit by engaging so talented a company." Next night Comstockers
enjoyed the comedy of *Masks and Faces* with Miss Morgan
as Peg Woffington to J. B. Booth's Triplet, and a repetition of
The Bonnie Fish Wife. But the promised Madame Biscaccianti did not appear.[3]

2

Though Maguire had "new scenes painted for each of the
sterling comedies . . . and added several first-rate musicians to the orchestra," he provided no heat in "his beautiful
little theatre," for at ten cents a stick for firewood, he would
(as the *Bulletin* pointed out) have to own two feet in the
Gould and Curry to break even. However, next night when
Miss Morgan appeared as Nell Gwynne in "a splendid speci-

---

[2] Scout and spy with the Army of the Cumberland, Pauline Cushman — because
of her daring exploits during the War — was allowed to wear a Northern uniform
and use the complimentary title of "Major." When the actress-spy died in San
Francisco in 1893, the Grand Army of the Republic honored her with a military
funeral and burial in their plot in the presidio. (See the *Territorial Enterprise* of
November 17, 1872, and an account by Margaret Watson in *The Nevada Magazine*
of June, 1948.)

[3] While the audience awaited Madame Biscaccianti, a Teuton and a Celt began
a conversation. "Shure, an ave yees heard as how we'v shtruck it in der Get-up-
and-Git?" asked the Hibernian. "Och! by der powers, but we'v shtruck it ov der
biggest kind, an so we ave."

"Mine Gott!" said the Teuton. "I'sh ave two feets in dat glaim, bud von tam
proker he sheets me out of dem." Even when told to "dry up" by those sitting
near, the dialogue continued.

LOTTA CRABTREE

The child wonder, whose flying toes, gags,
jokes, and rollicking songs — including
"Bound for the Land of Washoe" — made her
"the universal favorite" in early Nevada.

The rare Topliffe Theatre Playbill. From the collection of William Miller, and reproduced with his permission.

TOPLIFFE'S THEATRE!

Under the Management of.. W. H. LEIGHTON
A. R. PHELPS.. Stage Manager
A. FISCHER,... Leader of Orchestra
C. L. GRAVES,... Prompter

Grand Complimentary Benefit

Tendered by the Citizens of Virginia City to

MRS. W. H.

LEIGHTON

MONDAY EVENING, - - - - - SEPT. 22, 1862,

The performance will commence with the Fine Comedy, in Two Acts, entitled

ALL THAT GLITTERS
IS NOT GOLD.

Stephen Plum .... A. R. PHELPS
Jasper Plum .... D. C. ANDERSON
Frederick Plum .... C. L. GRAVES
Sir Arthur Lascelle .... W. STEPHENSON
Toby Twinkle .... YANKEE LOCKE
Harris .... Mr. WOODHULL
Martha Gibbs .... Mrs. W. H. LEIGHTON
Lady Leatherbridge .... Mrs. H. A. PERRY
Lady Valeria .... Mrs. G. E. LOCKE

COMIC SONG, : : : : : : : MR. WOODHULL.

To be followed by the One-Act Comedy of

THE WINDMILL !

Sampson Low .... Mr. WOODHULL
Marquis De Boueville .... D. C. ANDERSON
Peter .... C. L. GRAVES
Marian (with Songs) .... Mrs. W. H. LEIGHTON
Marchioness .... Mrs. G. E. LOCKE

FANCY DANCE, - - - MRS. H. A. PERRY

To conclude with the Laughable Farce of

THE FOOL OF THE FAMILY !

Bell .... (with Songs) .... Mrs. W. H. LEIGHTON
Tom Jackson .... YANKEE LOCKE
Augustus Gumption .... W. STEPHENSON
Mr. Saunders .... C. L. GRAVES
Lucretia .... Mrs. G. E. LOCKE

TO-MORROW, BENEFIT OF "VIRGINIA CITY GUARDS!"

On which occasion a Magnificent Bill will be presented, and Positively the Last Appearance of the Company in this city.

DOORS OPEN AT HALF-PAST SEVEN.—CURTAIN RISES AT EIGHT.

ADMISSION, : : : : : $1 00.

TERRITORIAL ENTERPRISE JOB PRINT, C STREET, VIRGINIA CITY.

men of acting" in *Court and Stage*, "the unusually large number of ladies" present found a stove in the parquette.

So from October until December the Washoites filled the Opera House to enjoy such legitimate productions as *Masks and Faces, She Stoops to Conquer, Court and Stage, A Duchess for an Hour, A Roland for an Oliver,* Shakespeare's *The Merchant of Venice* and *The Taming of the Shrew,* Tobin's *The Honeymoon,* Cherry's *The Soldier's Daughter,* the serio-comic drama *Sharp Practice, Evadne,* and *The Stranger.* But it was the "side-splitting" afterpieces that wrought the greatest merriment.

On Saturday the "renowned prima donna" Madame Biscaccianti made her first Washoe appearance with the "great star company." *A Duchess for an Hour* and the musical farce, *The Loan of a Lover,* were presented, between which Mrs. Perry danced, affording no "slight amount of merriment by a step not usually given in an Irish or any other kind of lilt." But the cantatrice was the feature. For days she had been billed and expected. There was reason why Biscaccianti, once the toast of operatic circles, "didn't come to time."

Elisa Biscaccianti had been pictured ten years before by a California critic as an attractive Italian lady, petite with large lustrous eyes and a "luxuriant flow of jetty ringlets falling over her delicately moulded shoulders." From stage distance she was still lovely to the Washoites though they were not unaware of her alcoholic weakness and of her performances in one of the lowest melodeons of San Francisco. "It is a pity to condemn such a voice to the purgatory of melodeon cigar smoke and the dissonant cry of 'More lager this way,'" the *Call* had lamented.

But under Maguire's direction and Washoe's sympathy, Biscaccianti now "created an enthusiasm among the lovers of song in the Silver Land over the Sierras" (though again in San Francisco she would drop back to her old indisposition). "It is a long time," observed a reviewer, who had heard "The

Thrush" in *Lucia*, "since we heard Madame Biscaccianti sing as well as she did last night." Three times encored, she sang a different song each time.[4]

One evening at Maguire's before Biscaccianti gave her lilting "Cavatina," J. A. Wright presented a thousand-dollar bar of pure Comstock silver to the winner of the first prize in a daring gift entertainment.[5] "A crowded and fashionable audience" enjoyed Sunday evening's comedies and farces, as they also did *The Merchant of Venice* on October 26 and on Tuesday, when actor-turned-miner Charles Pope — in Virginia briefly from Reese, "where he has been engaged in the 'feet' business for some time past" — may have been seen in the audience.

On Wednesday the troupe served the "beautiful drama" of *The Soldier's Daughter*; "Cavatina," twice by Madame Biscaccianti; "Par Espagnol" by Miss Fanny Howard; and the farce of *My Neighbor's Wife*. "If all this is not sufficient to please," the *Bulletin's* theatrical critic insisted, "then there is no use in trying." Nevertheless, "the irrepressible" Maguire continued improving productions, "determined to merit the very liberal patronage his establishment is receiving at the hands of the public," continued the reviewer. "And he is playing a game that will be sure to win." But not without difficulties.

---

[4] A year later during a season in South America, the Peruvians, "not satisfied with the most lavish patronage of the singer, went to the length in their enthusiasm of taking the horses from the carriage and conveying her in triumph to her hotel." Peru and Washoe were evidently better places for Biscaccianti than San Francisco.

[5] Both women and men enjoyed the Gift Enterprise that offered chances or prizes so daring and varied that the schemes were long popular in Washoe. J. A. Wright led the field with his $10,000-enterprise that included "410 magnificent gifts." Tickets were "only a dollar" and they sold so fast Wright was forced to hold the fall "drawing" earlier than planned. Finally on October 24, a Saturday afternoon, with the Opera House packed, the selection of lucky ticket holders took place, but the first prize was saved — as noted — for the more auspicious presentation from the stage of the Opera House.

3

A rival troupe was now ensconced in Topliffe's Theatre and the weather also brought troubles. Halloween stirred up a wind so stiff that the news of any "shooting scrape in the territory" failed to reach print and brought down the "lofty flag pole on Union Street." By night the Washoe Zephyrs had subsided into an earnest snowstorm. Comstockers next morning looked out on unfamiliar scenes. But snow meant sleighs "darting about at a 2:40 rate" and youngsters snowballing all whom they dared, mainly the poor Chinese. The talk turned again to stoves, more stoves.

Pat Holland upon re-opening Topliffe's as a melodeon brought in "plenty of stoves to keep the room completely warm . . . and good liquors and cigars for those who desire them" and fast-paced variety entertainment served up by a good minstrel troupe. But to properly burlesque *Mazeppa* — a sensation piece Adah Menken was giving on the coast — Pat borrowed "the famous ass belonging to one of the Celestials" so that November 2 "for the first time" at Topliffe's Mazeppa rode through the evening "with extraordinary eclat and numerous additional incidents" to enthusiastic cheers.

But by morning Mazeppa's mount had produced a new commotion. Chinatown inhabitants, pigtails bobbing in anger, sought Officer Downey, who with little difficulty "tracked the missing quadruped" to the melodeon on C Street. But Holland was not inclined to part with the "borrowed" creature of such "gifted sag-ass-ity" until *Mazeppa* should be "played out." The Chinamen vowed they would take their donkey off the stage. The "likelihood of a very pretty muss among the Mongolians, Mongrels and all kinds of mortality" brought out greater crowds to Topliffe's on following nights.[6]

The snow seems to have silenced the *Bulletin's* theatrical

---

[6] *Virginia Evening Bulletin,* November 3, 1863.

notes except when local people were involved. Could it be
that this paper was too engrossed in the affairs of the Constitutional Convention to include the theatre? The convention
took the front-page space. Or had some misunderstanding
developed? The only extant Comstock paper came from press
day after day without mentioning the large, fine company
dispensing legitimate dramas and merry comedies at Maguire's. However, this paper noted that "A CARGO OF CATS"
arrived "safe except one which had the misfortune to lose an
eye"; and during a fight at the Opera House Officer Perry
arrested a man, who "will have to pay a good deal more to
get out of the lock-up than he paid to get into the theatre."
Again, ignoring the arrival of "the talented" Miss Annette
Ince, the *Bulletin* gave complete details of "another row in
the theatre" when a "gentleman in the dress circle" slapped
the face of another and found himself being taken "off to the
calaboose."

4

Nevertheless, on November 6 Miss Ince, taking the part of
the Countess in Knowles' play of *Love,* made her initial Virginia appearance, replacing Miss Fanny Morgan as star of
the Opera House troupe. Considered "a bright young star"
and recognized by some critics as even a rival of Julia Dean
Hayne, Annette Ince as early as 1857 had drawn praise from
Stockton theatre-goers for her "sincere endeavors to raise the
moral purity of the drama." On her repertoire now un-
doubtly was *East Lynne,* in which she had recently appeared
in San Francisco. (One wonders if the actress again demanded Maguire get her a "real bed" for her dying scene in
the lachrymose drama.)

Though concerts and balls received more *Bulletin* attention
than the theatre during November, this does not mean that
Maguire's was any less important in the amusement lives of
the Washoites. Colonel Rogers included an Ince-and-troupe

performance in "one of the most social parties that ever took place" in Virginia. And an omnibus, charging a fare of 50 cents, made numerous trips each evening between Gold Hill and the Opera House.

One night the carriage got stuck at the corner of D and Taylor Streets, causing a local observer to rhyme:

Tell me, ye winged winds that round my pathway sweep,
Is there any spot on this wide earth where the mud
becomes so deep?

No mention was made as to what performance the mud-entrapped ladies had enjoyed. However, some simple prank at the theatre brought out details.

When a joker having made something resembling a pair of lorgnettes from soda-water bottles amused the audience by imitating certain other theatre-goers, another man, "ambitious to imitate his neighbor," took the instrument, "but was hustled off to the calaboose and fined $22 for disturbing the performance." A fortnight later lorgnettes were scarcely needed; Maguire's theatre glowed with gas lights; the gas manufactured in Virginia.[7]

Though still using oil, S. J. Millington opened his large ballroom on November 13 with "a grand social hop." Here the Germania Glee Club held soirées, the "pleasure of which lasted long after midnight." "To favor the dancing portion of our community," Charles Cardinell established "new dancing schools" in Virginia; Professor Sweet did likewise for Carson, Dayton, Como, and Galena.

---

[7] From near and far the Washoites came night after night to view the "brilliantly illuminated" Opera House; Wells Fargo; and Gillig, Mott, and Company. And studying their parts, actors too, re-echoed the rhymer's

Brillyant Flame!
The nites was next to darkness when you came.
But candles has vanisht before you,
And lard oil gone to grass;
Every greasy nuisance has been banisht
Hurraw for Gass!

For the "November 23d benefit of the Masonic Charity Fund," the *Bulletin* turned a spotlight briefly on the Opera House with the following: "Miss Annette Ince and the Star Company will appear together with the Virginia Glee Club and the Germania Glee Club! For particulars, see bills of the day." Charles W. Cooke had charge and "from the manner in which he conducted the heavy business of the Old Howard Theatre, we may confidently expect the benefit to be a complete success." It was, the theatre crowded to its "utmost capacity." *Evadne* with Miss Ince as the heroine was the Opera House contribution, as well as a fencing match between Booth and Mons. Chauvel.

The following night one of the "grandest affairs ever gotten up" in Silverland was given at Millington's Hall for the benefit of Washoe Engine Company No. 4. Next night too, overflowed with entertainment, music lovers enjoyed a "rich feast" when Hubert Schreiner took a benefit, for which every good musician in the territory volunteered. A brass band of thirty instruments, "the most effective and complete ever heard in the territory, discoursed sweet sounds" outside the Opera House before the performance began. During the evening an orchestra "upward of 20 pieces" played the popular quickstep "When This Cruel War is Over" and the new overture "The Groves of Blarney," which were "most deservedly encored by the large and appreciative audience."

Interlarded between the Opera House contribution of *The Stranger* with Miss Ince and J. B. Booth in the lead characters was a fast and humorous "Grand Musical Olio." The Star Company concluded the evening with the musical farce of *The Swiss Cottage*. The box office receipts revealed the orchestra leader's decided popularity.

Thanksgiving, designated by Lincoln and Nye for November 26, was filled to overflowing with events, all the more enjoyed because of the "gladsome news flashing over the wires" that Hooker had taken Lookout Mountain. "To keep up kindly feelings among the citizens of neighboring towns," a Thanksgiving Party for the Sanitary Fund was enjoyed in Doyle's new "largest hall in Dayton," intended for meetings and "theatrical performances, . . . a fine lot of new scenery having been painted for just such use." In Virginia Pat O'Conner opened his new Oriental Hotel with "a most agreeable" grand ball. "No pains were spared" either to make the Cotillion Party opening Gold Hill's Vesey House a "decided success."

At Galena a "jolly set of mortals" enjoyed a wedding, but "there came pretty near being a grievous mar to the hilarity when an old cannon . . . flew all to smithereens. By a miracle nobody was hurt." [8] Then Evans and Schultz (previously arrested for failing to pay the city license) gave the "Hurdies of Virginia . . . a high old ball."

After almost five months of full-time activity that "was successful beyond parallel," Maguire's Opera House closed on November 30 with a benefit for Miss Ince. A Virginia paper of December 1 listed the principal actors' names among the passengers departing the Comstock "via Pioneer Stage" for Maguire's Metropolitan Theatre in Sacramento to support Miss Menken, whom the Washoites avidly awaited. [9]

[8] Shortly after the Proctor marriage, "the first suit for breach of promise in the Territory" was instituted by Gertrude Syckoff demanding $10,000 of Alexander Paul, both "respectable citizens."

[9] With the Thespians departure, local newspapers told readers that Sandy Bowers was building a mile of iron fence around his "magnificent residence on the shores of Washoe Lake," where a beautiful white swan glided by for the enjoyment of passers-by; Grafton T. Brown, a Negro artist, was canvassing subscriptions of his contemplated lithograph of Virginia; a telescope was set up on C Street; Virginia's 80-acre cemetery needed fencing to prevent "cattle and hogs from rambling over and disturbing the graves of the dead"; and Storey County's hospital under Drs. Pinkerton and Tucker had treated "upwards of 400 patients" since opening in 1862 and was now "fitted up with every convenience."

5

A new establishment, the Niagara Concert Hall above Lynch and Hardy's Saloon on B Street, now moved into the amusement picture. The opening long and carefully planned by Lynch, Hardy, and Connor did not take Comstockers by surprise. For weeks Washoe papers had reported the progress of construction; then told readers that "artists from San Francisco" were "decorating the walls and ceiling and adorning them with paintings"; that chairs, "a great improvement upon the uncomfortable narrow benches that one is compelled to sit on in the other places of amusement in the city," and other conveniences, such as six or more "waiter-girls to furnish the thirsty with good liquor," would be added.

Of the entertainment at Niagara Concert Hall, Washoites learned they "must look out for fun" as manager Pat Holland — he had returned the Chinamen's ass for burlesquing *Mazeppa* — was in San Francisco engaging "13 efficient artistes," including Señorita Maria, the thirteen-year-old "celebrated Spanish (born of Americans in Sacramento) danseuse," who had "appeared in all the principal theatres" of Europe, the United States, and South America. An immense favorite in San Francisco, she was "pronounced the most correct and graceful danseuse living."

The Gallotti operatic singers would appear also on the Niagara Concert stage, Sig. Gallotti having the reputation of being the "best harpist in the state." Otto Burbank, the celebrated Ethiopian delineator and jig dancer" was sure to be a hit. Sam Knowles was a "good end man." Miss Isabella was a pleasing balladist. Others of the "first class artists" included Miss Clarissa, Madame Larue, M'lle Celeste, M'lle Arabella, Tommy Peel, and Ned Ward. Mr. Oldfield was an able pianist; Henry Pugh, a good cornet player; and Mr. Strakosch, a fine violinist. John M. Davies (father of Señorita Maria) would act as stage manager; and the price of admission would be "50 cents and one dollar."

In spite of the next-to-the-last-night-but-two at the Opera House, Niagara Concert Hall was packed so full that many could not get inside to enjoy the "immense attractions":

Songs

Dances

Pantomime

Burlesque

Farces

Ethiopian Extravaganzas, etc., etc.[10]

Noting this success the Virginia City Council passed an ordinance fixing the license of melodeons at $250 per month.[11] Pat Holland paid the tax, and as the only amusement house — other than hurdy-gurdy — the Niagara played to such large audiences that Washoites on many evenings could not "obtain even standing room." Perhaps another hall was needed.

And as if foreseeing such business possibilities, Henry Sutliff was readying at 68 North C Street "a fine building, lofty and wide" to serve the Comstock's constant passion for social gatherings. Designated by various enthusiasts as "a melodeon," "music hall," "dance hall," or "theatre," Sutliff's had a 75-foot front on C and ran 104 feet back to D. Built thus down the slope, the C Street end was one story high; two on the D Street end, thus giving sufficient room for stores and a large saloon. Interior dimensions of the main hall were a nice size, 50 by 80 by 20 feet, with a "fine floor," which Eagle Engine Company No. 3 enjoyed in a concert and grand ball when they dedicated the building the last of November.

Committees of arrangements included Governor Nye and Secretary Orion Clemens. Nearly five hundred people paid ten dollars each for tickets, which, however, included the

---

[10] *Virginia Evening Bulletin,* November 30, 1863.

[11] The penalty for giving "exhibitions without said license" was a fine not to exceed $500 or imprisonment in the county jail for 250 days at the "discretion of the police magistrate."

concert, dancing, supper, and transportation. Sutliff's new
Music Hall was "almost too full," according to "those who
went to enjoy the pleasures of the mazy dance." But what a
sight greeted them that evening! As a ballroom, Sutliff's
glittered with lights, mirrors, pictures, banners, and garlands,
guests pointing out those presented by Mrs. H. A. Perry, Mrs.
T. J. Taylor, and others, as well as the silver trumpet from
Walter Bray. Not only was the dancing enjoyed but "every
delicacy provided in profuse abundance" for the midnight
supper.

Virginia and Dayton were not alone in boasting new entertainment houses. A new theatre in Gold Hill — to replace the
one that slid into the glory hole of the Yolo Mine — was so
well along in construction of "building, scenery, and upholstery" that the Gold Hill *News* felt safe in saying the
theatre would be ready by Christmas. But until Sutliff secured
a troupe for Music Hall and Artemus Ward briefly reopened
Maguire's Opera House, the main Comstock amusement
house continued to be Pat Holland's Niagara Melodeon.

20

Wax Figgers and Snaix

1

Temporarily forgetting the coming of humor-man Artemus Ward with his "wax figgers and snaix," the Washoites watched the "political cauldron of their embryo state seethe and bubble." Actor James Stark, "not the least conspicuous member of Nevada's first Constitutional Convention, did more than any other delegate to shape the political course of Silverland," insisted Washoe's correspondent to the *Golden Era.* "In the discussion of suffrage . . . Mr. Stark made a speech, which commanded profound attention by its oratorical power and beauty, and great ability. The *Territorial Enterprise* pronounces it one of the best specimens of eloquence ever delivered." [1]

Those favoring ratification of the Constitution [2] crowded

---

[1] Among the delegates to the Constitutional Convention were lawyers, merchants, farmers, newspapermen, miners, mill owners, a sign maker, a coach maker, and the actor James Stark. Henry G. Worthington, who won the Congressional seat from Stark, was one of the active pallbearers at Lincoln's funeral.

[2] When the *Washoe Times* died with its editor, a "venerable gammon named Lovejoy" brought it to life "under the outrageous name of *Old Pah-Ute.*" A "telegram," flavoring the usual Washoe joke, was directed to this paper, but the *Bulletin,* which had confidently stated earlier, "Let no one doubt for a moment but that the Constitution will be carried by an overwhelming majority," now flared in all seriousness, "Read this wretched roorback, and ask yourselves whether President Lincoln would condescend to send a dispatch to the drunken editor of a scurrilous newspaper?"

TELEGRAPHIC! Editor of Old Piute —

My Dear Sir: — I understand that bogus dispatches are in your Territory, purporting to come from Chase, Conners, and Higby. Permit me to say there is nothing to it. We don't care a damn about it, whether you become a State or not.   Yours truly, A. LINCOLN

N.B.   Bill Seward is with us.   A.L.

the Opera House to its "utmost capacity" — but not quite as full as it soon would be for Artemus Ward — "to hear Judge North and Bill Stewart blacken the characters of each other." Next night the Comstockers surged into Sutliff's Music Hall for more emotional politics. At last, the excitement and the elections over, the people learned they had "decided by their votes" to remain a territory (Ruby Valley was the only precinct favoring the constitution at this time).[3]

To recuperate from their "herculean labors," many delegates and reporters (including Mark Twain) drove to a "veritable habitation of the gods" — Lake Tahoe, which, Twain jested, was a Paiute word meaning "grasshopper soup." J. Ross Browne insisted Tahoe meant "whiskey"; if Artemus Ward had a definition, it is not recorded.

Already through the *Territorial Enterprise* Mark Twain had sent

GREETINGS TO ARTEMUS WARD

We understand that Artemus Ward contemplates visiting this region to deliver his lectures, and perhaps make some additions to his big "sho." In his last letter to us he appeared particularly anxious to "sekure" a kupple ov horned todes; alsowe, a lizard which it may be persessed of 2 tales, or any komical snaix. . . I would like a opportunity for to maik a moddel in wax. . . Could you alsowe manage to gobbel up the skulp of the layte Missus Hopkins? I adore sich footprints of atrocity as it were, muchly. I was roominatin on gettin a bust of mark Twain, but

---

[3] Though many Washoites took their politics too seriously, the constitution delegates themselves did not neglect devilry and fun. After suspending the rules and omitting the prayer since it was "never listened to by members of the First House anyway," the delegates elected Mark Twain president of the funny Third House. Mark "arose, and without previous preparation, burst forth in a tide of eloquence so grand, so luminous, so beautiful, and so resplendent with the gorgeous fires of genius, that the audience were spellbound by the magic of his words."

A group in the Humboldt Mining District did a funny version of the Constitution of the State of Buena Vista, "proclaiming the right of Kangaroo Court to remain undecided forever" and their motto be *Buena Vista go Unum, E Pluribus Braugh, you bet.* Then copying the Carson delegates, they presented their speaker a mountain mahogany cane with a tin foil head and adjourned *sine die.*

. . . they tell me down heer too the Ba that the busts air so kommon it wood ony bee an waist of wax too git un kounterfit presentiment.

We shall assist Mr. Ward in every possible way about making his Washoe collection and have no doubt but he will pick up many curious things during his sojourn.[4]

2

Everything conspired to make Ward's entry and stay in Silverland spectacular. Fairly drooling, the Washoites recalled that the author, newspaperman, and lecturer Charles F. Browne (Artemus Ward) while in the East had received a telegram from theatrical magnate Tom Maguire, shrewdly asking what Ward "would take for 40 nights." Maguire expected some monetary statement. Instead, the reply telegram simply said: "Brandy and water," a joke that appealed to the Washoites, and was the best and cheapest advertising Maguire ever got.

Immediately Comstock papers began shadowing "the great, the incorrigible Artemus" with such items as:

A. Ward . . . delivering a lecture in Boston did not reach his subject. . . He said he should continue it in California, and all who were present in Boston should have free tickets. . .

and reprinted such of Ward's lectures as "The Ghost," "Artemus Ward on the Negro," and "The Babes," with which Walter Bray was then making a hit through burlesque in San Francisco.

Early in November the press announced that "the world-renowned, wax figger showman" had arrived in San Francisco and would come to Virginia to "speak a piece, probably a good many of 'em." Arriving first was Ward's "agent and avant-coureur," a man of "much cleverness and scholarly attainment," who made arrangements with various Washoe

---

[4] This seems to be the only time, fortunately, that Mark Twain used Ward's misspelled form of writing. (The funny piece was copied by the *Golden Era* and thus saved for Nevada's amusement history.)

theatre managers and left a "goodly number of tickets" with newspapermen, one of whom wrote that he understood Artemus had "secured the services of Mark Twain and Dan De Quille to personate the babes, and would have a painting of the 'great pine forest at Dutch Nick's' to represent the woods."

Artemus Ward arrived in Washoe via the "classic Horace Greeley-Hank Monk route" the middle of December intending to stay three days. He stayed as many weeks. Yet his first Silverland appearance, at Carson, was far from a happy one. The only interesting thing Ward saw about Johnny Moore and Charley Parker's Saloon Theatre was a sign near the main entrance to the theatre part, which read: "No Washybums admitted here" — meaning that additional money was needed to go from the saloon on into the playhouse part, which Ward found dirty and too poorly ventilated for the mass of people packed into it to hear his "Babes."

Of the lecture the Carson *Daily Independent,* thinking no doubt to ape Mark and Artemus, ran a vacuous rambling review that dealt with crime in Nevada, a flea-ridden dog named Jack that insisted on occupying the stage with Ward, "the Menken," Charley Parker's suspenders, the usher's confusion in not knowing where to seat the audience, and winning back the dollar admission by playing the gambling tables at the entrance to the Saloon Theatre.

3

Disappointed with his Carson reception, "the great Artemus" boarded the stage and — his "wax figgers unblemished and his 'babes in the wood' looking as pleasant as ever" — arrived "all safe" in Virginia, where "expectation was on tiptoe," to be greeted as an old acquaintance by Mark Twain, Dan De Quille, Joe Goodman, Steve Gillis, and the Comstockers generally. Fun-loving Governor Nye, "reposing special trust and confidence in the ability of Artemus Ward," appointed him "for the term of natural life Speaker of Pieces" to the Washoites.

Everything Ward now saw "called forth a joke or a quaint saying." He spent much of his leisure in the editorial rooms of the *Enterprise,* in saloons, and with the miners, who "received as large a share of his attention as did the millionaire owners." No wonder the miners gave Ward a gold chain, but one so heavy he could not wear it with comfort. A man would gaze at Ward "for a moment in blank amazement," explained De Quille. "Then the oddity of the thing would prove too much and he would be obliged to 'let go all holds' and indulge in a regular explosion of laughter — Artemus the while more solemn than ever gazing from face to face as though astonished and somewhat hurt at being interrupted by the sudden outburst."

Of Ward's humor Bret Harte wrote in the *Era,* "It is the humor of audacious exaggeration, of perfect lawlessness, a humor that belongs to the country,   .   .   .   which is met in the stage-coach, rail-car, canal- and flat-boat, which bursts out over camp-fires and around barroom stoves — a humor that has more or less local coloring, that takes kindly to and half elevates slang that is of to-day and full of present application."

4

Two days before Christmas Maguire's Opera House — dark during December except for political gatherings — twinkled with lights when "about 1000 individuals, a goodly number of whom were ladies — good-looking, well-dressed ladies" — crowded into the playhouse, but hundreds of other Washoites could not gain admission to hear "the Babes" that Artemus "trotted out" for the occasion. Though Ward made no reference to the "poor innocents" who wandered in the woods "till death did end their grief," he did talk around and about fifty other things. "Death is like sleep, and so are stones like rocks, but I prefer being rocked to sleep to being stoned to death," said Ward. "I have the gift of eloquence. I have not got it bad, but I have got it some. I have a great love for novelties, and like everything new, except neuralgia. . ."

The *Bulletin* found the lecture "indescribable," but thought
Artemus "young, rather good-looking and unmarried." Ward's
hair at this time was yellow and straight. Not until after his
Washoe visit did he curl it. An illness of mountain fever in
Salt Lake left his face so thin that ever after he wore curls
to soften his features.

"Ward is as great a follower of Barnum, the Prince of Humbugs, as Brigham Young is of Joe Smith," deduced the *Bulletin*. "Ward made everyone laugh because everybody went
to the theatre for the purpose of laughing. They laughed
when he spoke, and when he didn't. One enthusiastic individual went so far as to propose three cheers for Artemus
when he first appeared on stage, and the audience laughed
when he said, 'Oh, don't 't.' Artemus probably made a
thousand dollars by his lecture last night and he deserved it,
for he really did amuse." Yet the reviewer could not resist a
veiled dig: "His lecture is like medicoelectricity or laughing
gas, one dose of which is enough for a lifetime."

Answering "insistent demand, the illustrious son of Momus"
repeated his lecture at Maguire's, but he gave it on Christmas
night, thereby having to compete with the Masons' Prom-
enade Ball at Sutliffe's New Hall, a dance at Topliffe's Theatre, the minstrels at Niagara Concert Hall, and smaller
Christmas parties, dinners, and dances along the Lode. He
also had to compete with so cold a theatre one patron remarked, "The parquette reminded us of Steamboat Springs
at a distance. Every joke got off by the lecturer was not only
heard but seen in a jet of vapor."

Though shivering, the audience enjoyed the lecture along
with Mark Twain, who later wrote, "The man who is capable
of listening to the Babes in the Wood from beginning to end
without laughing either inwardly or outwardly must have
done murder, or at least meditated it." To which the *Bulletin*
retorted, "That accounts for . . .   Mark's solemnity. The

Yourn till Deth,

Artemus Ward

CHARLES F. BROWN — ARTEMUS WARD
From a photograph, about 1857; the great American humorist as he
appeared to the Comstockers during the Civil War. The Austinites
— especially those of the mock Indian scalping party — were the last
to see the "wax figger showman" with straight hair. An illness in
Salt Lake City left him so thin he curled his hair to soften his
features — and ever after wore curls.
Courtesy, the Bancroft Library.

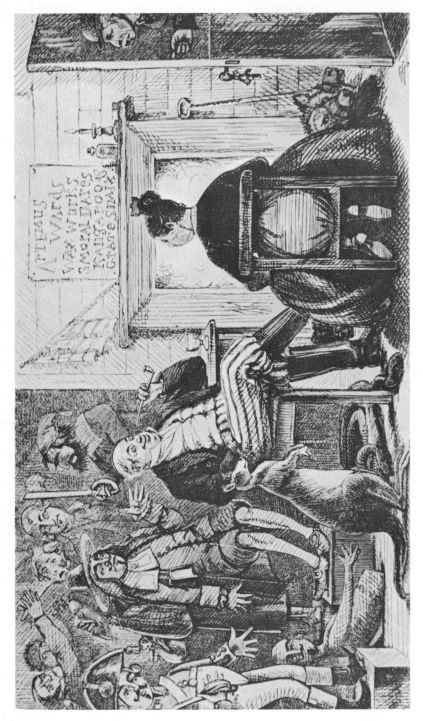

"Wax Figgers and Snaix" — an Artemus Ward advertisement

Courtesy, the Bancroft Library.

remembrance of his murder of the Hopkins family must have been preying on his mind."

Slighting none of the Lode towns, Ward delivered his comic oration to a large Silver City audience; to an equally packed Vesey's Hall in Gold Hill; then back to Virginia to deliver "The Babes" again, to dine with the newspaper boys, and to fight the tiger with them at the local saloons.

5

One night Ward did an unusual thing. Always fond of actors and theatrics (Artemus had even started writing a play in which he hoped to appear), he gave way to a long-suppressed urge to try his talent with the minstrels then playing at Niagara Hall, many of whom he knew. Maybe it was on a dare or a wager, as he later said.

Anyway, the humorist blacked his face and came on stage as end man in the "Three Black Crows," making much fun "of a kind that was fresh and droll," and leaving much that could be detected as Ward's in later melodeon programs. As soon as the audience recognized Ward, they demanded the "Babes." He responded with a short, funny lecture; and said he "would have the pleasure of seeing them in New York City," adding that he "hoped they would all be sober," implying that he was not — or so the *Call* reporter interpreted it. Later the paper retracted, feeling that it had "unwittingly injured the gentleman."

But the *Call* was right; for Artemus writing to Mark Twain "from Austin, N.T." lamented that after dinner in Virginia with the *Enterprise* boys he got drunker than Alexander the Great, blackened his face, and at the Niagara Melodeon made "a gibbering, idiotic speech," which he feared the *Union* would pounce upon. Ward probably had reason for concern. He had "neglected to read a 'satirical pome,'" one the *Union* had "wished him to peruse." But "the reading of the first six lines had such an effect on his nervous system," Ward had confided to the *Bulletin*, "that it required 14 cocktails, six gin-slings, and about a score of brandies straight to set him right again."

Because Ward was indiscreet, Comstockers not only saw and heard him as a lecturer, but in blackface, a treat not accorded any other audience. And the comedian need not have felt remorse for his act. Other theatrical people — before him and after — fell in with the easy comradeship of Virginia.

6

With the departure of Artemus Ward, Maguire's Opera House remained dark; Topliffe's opened only on occasion. And regarding the immediate future of Sutliff's newly completed hall, the *Call* could not resist a pessimistic forecast, "I don't think it will pay. The chances are strong against professional success in this city this winter." Hundreds of men were returning to their old haunts in San Francisco "quite down in the mouth!" Instead of talking "feet, dips, spurs, and veins" with the importance of millionaires, they again "became pensioners upon the free lunches of generous saloon-keepers."

"Unquestionably many disillusioned miners returned to California," conceded the *Bulletin;* "however, we know a few who would not leave till their locks are silvered o'er (ore)." And the *New York World* extravagantly wrote, "the mine wealth of Nevada Territory will be sufficient to pay a national debt of $20,000,000,000 and to give every returning soldier a musket of silver." C Street was still congested, drivers blaming this on those "stock-brokers and feet dealers" who insisted on holding office in the middle of the street in front of the International Hotel.[5]

Argentoro conceded, however, that Concert Hall was "get-

[5] The International now boasted a "double front," that on B Street, the principal entrance, "being four stories high and 40 feet wide." Ornamented with cornice and heavy moulding, giving it an "elegant appearance," the International boasted "one hundred rooms, furnished with the most approved style of furniture," 30 persons to attend upon patrons, cooking facilities to serve 100 people, and gas lights.

ting along well." Comstockers, therefore, were not without diversion of an imported variety. Imported too, were the turkeys, nearly two hundred of them — who made "such a gobbling coming over Cedar Hill they were their own advertisement" for Washoe holiday dinners.

Besides the "phunny phellow who spoke inimitable pieces" twice at Maguire's, the Comstockers had numerous attractions, including A. Budd Smith's lecture on the "Civil War" requested by those who desired coming into Virginia to hear it Christmas night at Sutliff's; and the Masonic Ball, which was "crowded with the beauty, wealth, intelligence, and elite of the territory."

"The American citizens of African descent" gave a "grand celebration ball" at Selfridge's Hall on B Street. Most of the gentlemen wore "white kids and patent leather boots, and several had long tail blues with gorgeous buttons." The ladies all wore colored gowns, but which did "not expose their charms quite so freely as the white folks are in the habit of doing." Though the dance began pleasantly, when enough of the "adulterated article" had been taken, a general row started, involving the "shattering of crockery at a fearful rate" and one dancer yelling that some "yeller fellow put on airs with him and he'd make him apologize or give him the satisfaction that one gemman has a right to demand from another."

The aftermath of Washoe celebrating was often unpleasant. The twenty or more "unfortunates" arrested for "taking too much Christmas" marched forlornly next day to the police court. Many, however, who got "well squeezed between whiskey and Christmas" reached only the streets, where "one would imagine at least 2000 men must have done what the whale did to Jonah after that privileged individual had remained in his intestines for three days."

Dayton's festivities included a gigantic outdoor Christmas tree loaded with gifts and treats for all, which "took the shine out of anything of the kind ever got up in the Territory."

Churches held pageants, carolings, and special services. Como in the Palmyra District celebrated its year-old anniversary with a ball at the National Hotel, which left "nothing to be desired." After parade and drill, the "happiest-, healthiest-looking lot of men" at Fort Churchill also celebrated in holiday fashion.

7

The great American humorist now paid his "devours to the good people" of Dayton, Reese River, and "from thence to Salt Lake City, dropping fun and humor," wrote one critic, "as a poodle-dog drops sweetness after emerging from a dirty puddle." [6] But the Austinites greeted Artemus nearly as heartily as the Comstockers had.[7] Clifton too, with its eight saloons and a billiard table would also hear the humorist. Why not? Austin's sister town claimed to having had "the first sermon ever preached in the Reese River mines."

A white curtain thrown over the bar fixtures in Johnson's Saloon shut out "terrestrial spirits." His Reverence chose "none of these things move me" as his text and delivered "a very pleasing and instructive discourse," to which the audience gave "marked attention." [8]

Since there were "about 1000 men to one woman," the "gay young bachelors of Austin," considering it a "luxury to dance with a female," welcomed the "four fat, good-natured hurdy-gurdy girls," who arrived from Virginia to "carry on

---

[6] The English paper *The Spectator* praised Ward before and after the lecturer's premature death in Southampton, March 8, 1867.

[7] The first mine of Reese had been discovered early in May of 1862 by a former Pony Express rider, William M. Talcott. Even before Ward's arrival, the six-month-old *Reese River Reveille* had been informing Silverland that Austin boasted several stories, laundries, blacksmith shops, two express companies, a livery stable, shoe shop, dairy, and an assortment of other businesses, some still with canvas roofs, though the newspaper would soon move into "a stone house of its own." The *Reveille* claimed 450 citizens for Austin as well as 20 dogs for each man, five saloons, and one billiard table.

[8] Though no church, the town had a Sunday School with R. C. Gridley, its superintendent.

their Terpsichorean vocations without paying a heavy tax."
Sponsored by the Austin Brass Band, a Thanksgiving Ball —
held a month prior to Ward's arrival — was an event to embrace though it followed two murders, one fatal stabbing, the
running down of Indians suspected of stealing horses, and
general baths that consisted of "two inches of cold water, a
piece of brown soap, a towel about half the size of the
Reveille, and — a dollar and a half." "The youth and beauty
of Austin" that now included "some 25 or 30 ladies greased
their boots, donned store clothes and biled shirts," filled the
new building on Main Street opposite the Austin Restaurant,
and "tripped the light fantastic . . . till broad daylight." [9]

One recorded 1863 Christmas event never occurred. This
was a purported Indian uprising that involved the "ordering
out of one hundred thousand men" to make a "harrowing
march" and fight the New Pass Indian War. The fake fight
was recorded in the *Reveille* by Austin's first, and perhaps
only, war correspondent.

Recalling, perhaps for the humorist's benefit, that Reese
also experienced the "big rush of 1863" with 75 to 100 people
"arriving per day in wagons, stages, buggies, horseback and
afoot" (some walking all the way from Virginia City), the
Reveille editor worried about the "chances of starving this
winter." No wonder the Austinites longed "for a 180-mile
railroad into the Comstock" and welcomed the "merry jingling of 'Mountain Schooners' " and the crunch of heavy freight
wagons drawn by 40-ox teams "strung the length of Main
Street" loaded with provisions, lumber, and liquor. The people would eat, and enjoy entertainment, including that dispensed by A. Ward.

[9] One account of a Reese River dance Artemus Ward probably enjoyed. Four
ladies were present, "three and a half of whom were of the Pi-Ute persuasion."
Music "was tortured from a cracked fiddle and an Indian drum. Supper consisted
of tule roots, pine nuts, and roasted mountain rats. For dessert all hands chewed
pine gum!"

8

Then came a piece of intelligence that conjured up amusement possibilities for the humorist as well as for Austin, "the hub of the universe." Announced the *Bulletin:* "We are informed that certain parties well-known in the theatrical profession intend to erect a theatre at Austin immediately." Before Ward should arrive, C. B. Lovell also planned completing a theatre, one that George Chapman would manage. In fact, the *Reveille* insisted, Mr. Chapman was already "getting up a troupe of performers to take out to the Reese River country." Virginia might be "more than well supplied with places of amusement for the coming winter," but Austin too would have resorts "higher than lager beer saloons."

Yet when Ward arrived the last of December there was no theatre, no hall suitable. Where could the humorist speak his piece? Sheriff Tabor had begun a new hotel back of his office, but it was not finished. The courthouse, though available, was too small. Then someone suggested a building nearly completed. Although the plastered walls were still wet, Ward and Hingston finally chose Holbrook's new granite store. And that New Year's night, Artemus, followed by his audience, many with chairs, carried a lighted lamp from Austin's International Hotel over to the new store and delivered his "Pioneer Lecture in the Shoshone Nation." So pleased were the Austinites in, at last, having received theatrical recognition, they started a dance and kept it going until nearly dawn.

Monday night (January 4) the proprietor of "Wax Figgers and Snaix" gave his piece again so that those who could not get into Holbrook's store on the former occasion might also hear the "Pioneer Lecture." Even this was not enough. More and more Reese River people demanded to hear the incorrigible Artemus.

With some hesitancy Ward finally complied with another request. He drove deeper into Shoshone country; at the bottom of his poster added the words, "Admission, One Scalp;

Front Seats, Two Scalps"; and delivered the "Pioneer Lecture in the Shoshone Nation" to the miners of Big Creek, a mining camp 12 miles from Austin. The saloon where Ward spoke was packed. The barkeeper went on serving drinks, but interrupted this service at propitious points to yell, "Bully for Artemus Ward. Ain't he sweet! Ain't he hell!"

The way back to Austin after the Big Creek lecture was far from uneventful. Made up like Indians, some Austin men stopped Ward's carriage on the lonely road, forced him to get out, and, on threat of scalping, ordered the talkee man to "Talkee, now talkee!" Ward, his voice quivering, complied, but got little appreciation, the Indians maintaining a stony silence at the humorous passages, but howling with glee at chance points, finally making so much noise Ward was forced to talk louder and louder until he was almost shouting when an Indian cried "Bosh" in a white man's voice that gave away the joke.

To compensate, the pranksters supplied hot toddies and escorted the lecturer back to the International Hotel, where next day the humorist learned through the *Reveille* that Canyon City people considered him "as sensible as the rest of human kind," and although "not a very good judge of water," his opinion of Big Creek as "a very nice stream" accurate enough. After five hilarious days in Reese, Ward and Hingston boarded Ben Holladay's stage and left the territory.

But so intrigued were the Washoites in the florid adventures of the proprietor of wax figgers and snaix that through letters and newspaper accounts they followed him to Salt Lake City, across the continent, and thence to Europe. Ward's letters to Mark Twain reached print in the *Enterprise* and those to theatre-man Pat Holland were read from the Niagara Hall stage.[10]

---

[10] Artemus Ward's Washoe lectures netted him a good return: around $1060 in box office receipts at Virginia, $400 at Carson, $300 at Silver City, $200 at Gold Hill, an unstated amount at Dayton, and $275 at Reese River.

21

The Marsh Juveniles

1

The year Nevada attained statehood dawned with all towns greeting the new 1864 with "a devil of a noise" that included steam whistles, brass bands, and pistol shots — the "balls making the dust fly as they glanced off the brick walls and struck the streets."

Two performances before those of New Year's Eve, R. W. Marsh, the founder and "well known director of the juvenile comedians," opened Maguire's Opera House with legitimate drama. Although certain dramatic critics labeled the presentations of the Marsh juveniles — ages seven to seventeen — "saccharine" and parrot-like, reminding one of "dancing dogs, learned pigs, or performing monkeys," many competent reviewers rated young George and Mary Marsh (born Guerineau) as "stars," George, a comedian of "more than juvenile ability," and Mary, "an uncommonly attractive child, bright eyed, graceful, fresh, and fair," a light and graceful dancer.

A large Comstock audience — an "appreciative" one, too, the *Virginia Union* happily reported, "judging by the enthusiastic applause that welcomed each scene of the entertainment — enjoyed the rich Irish brogue of Billy O'Neil; the grotesque actions and quaint sayings of Master George W. Marsh, who "convulsed the audience with laughter"; the peerless acting of "that saucily beautiful little fairy Jennie Arnot"; and the general competence of Mr. Marsh, Mr. and Mrs. Beatty, and others. In short, the Marsh Troupe could be relied upon for a "brilliant engagement"; and further inducement was Maguire's comfortably warm theatre, which during Ward's lectures there had been "as cold as Greenland."

On January 4 the Marsh players served another "superb bill" of three pieces, including the laughable farce of *Poor Pillicoddy*. After the last act many Comstockers went over to Millington's Soiree, some still chuckling and aping Master George's "great impersonation of Captain O'Scuttle in *The Toodles*, O'Neil's Pat Rooney, or commenting upon the huge Virginia-built wagon used in hauling ore.

Next evening the farce *To Paris and Back* "called forth frequent applause" at the Opera House, but from a small audience. The reason? It was snowing and the streets were bad — not bad enough to prevent an "immense crowd" from enjoying a street fight between well-trained bull terriers and a "grand fist fight," the usual Washoe aftermath of such sports. Niagara Hall also attracted its quota of patrons desiring to see their favorites before they departed for San Francisco. Besides, Mrs. Cutler's concert at the courthouse was "well patronized" at a dollar a seat for Carson education.[1]

"The Battle of Waterloo," the *Union* insisted, "was the *chef d'oeuvre* of the evening and seldom better rendered," Mrs. Cutler's "powerfully rich and finely cultivated voice thrilling every member of the audience," as it also did with her cavatine from *Tancredi*. The Germania Glee Club afforded amusement by singing with their mouths shut. Mrs. Chappell "did exceedingly well" as did Professor Grambbs, Mr. Maguire, and Mr. Studeman. By special request — "from the ladies, we presume," teased the critic — some amateur gentlemen sang the delightful ditty, "Kissing on the Sly," to end the evening.

---

[1] Not until the papers were signed on the successful bid for constructing a fence around Nevada's capitol, did the legislators learn that H. K. Clapp was a *woman*, Hannah Kezia Clapp, who put men to work on the job and inspected the work between classes while principal of Sierra Seminary. An advocate of women's rights, some years later this pioneer educator became a member of the faculty of the University of Nevada when it was moved from Elko to Reno.

While some seven hundred Anti-constitutionists and their opponents fought political battles at Sutliff's, the Marsh troupe presented a first-rate performance, which the lovers of fun patronized very well since the Niagara Melodeon was closed for remodeling and the construction of five additional private boxes. *Ireland As It Is* with Billy O'Neil as Ragged Pat and little Jenny Arnot as Judy O'Trot, and the comedy of *Slasher and Crasher,* young Marsh playing Slasher and old Marsh, Crasher, made up the program.[2]

2

For Billy O'Neil's benefit Signora and Signor Gillardi, Señorita Maria, Rhodes, Knowles, and Durand came over from Niagara Hall to do the interlude. In *Andy Blake* O'Neil, of course, played Andy, Jenny that of Mary. The evening concluded with *The Wandering Minstrel* in which Master George impersonated "Jem Baggs with song of Villikens." Surely the January 8 benefit for the "delineator of Irish character not surpassed by any actor on the Pacific coast" was a success.[3] Next day the Marsh Troupe, plus the Beattys and Billy O'Neil, left to serve Silver City, Dayton, and Carson City short seasons of the legitimate theatre.

Even with the Marsh company elsewhere, the Opera House did not close. Instead, Tom Maguire presented the magician, "the Man with a Great Name — Professor Simmons, the Basiliconthaumaturgist." And the Washoites paid five and 10 dollars for private boxes, one dollar for orchestra seats, or 50 cents to sit in the parquet, and watched "Professor what's-

---

[2] Next day the Utah Mine north of Virginia on the Geiger Grade celebrated a grand opening that included roast duck, boiled ham, egg-nog, and champagne before the engineers started the huge mine machinery so guests could hear the "beautiful manner" in which it performed.

[3] Comstockers were generous. The employees of the Sandy Bowers Company gave their superintendent a watch and chain valued at $225; those at Central Mill presented their chief a massive gold seal and buckle. The Chinese gave Officer Downey a diamond ring, perhaps because of his efforts regarding the Mazeppa jackass.

his-name knock the spots out of spiritualism and all other humbugs by showing how their tricks are performed."

With such advance press notices as the *Call's* "Other like entertainers are mere apprentices to an art of which this man is master," the King of Conjurers from January 9 to 13, in spite of a "rather unhappy style of address," dumfounded the natives and astonished some "stolid old Pi-Utes and shrewd stockbrokers," even allowing himself one evening to be securely tied, then freeing himself before the audience. As a grand finale Simmons promised he would "cut off his own head, put it in his pocket, catch himself by the stump of the neck and throw himself away. . . But as we perhaps made a slight mistake in this matter," conceded the *Bulletin,* "everyone had better go and see for himself."

3

At the remodelled Niagara Concert Hall on January 11 Pat Holland introduced a new troupe, not the least of whom were Johnny Tuers, the popular variety player; Tommy Peel, the celebrated clog and jig dancer; Lew Rattler; Miss Emma Paster; and Miss Emma Norton — all old hands in California, but new to Washoe audiences. Between the rounds of applause that night Pat came on stage with a letter from the former one-night, blackface end man, Artemus Ward, writing from Austin about Reese and "Tebits Hanah," his lecture there.

By the middle of January, Niagara Hall performances were becoming a habit with certain Virginians; Sutliff (renting his new hall for balls, concerts, political meetings, and lectures) promised, however, that Music Hall would be "ready soon" for theatrical performances; J. Wells Kelly numbered the houses in Virginia; Professor Simmons and Johnny Burns followed Artemus Ward into Austin, Simmons to treat the Reese Riverites to his exhibitions before presenting them to

the "harem of B. Young," Burns to see about building a
theatre in Austin; and the Marsh Troupe returned to Virginia from a professional swing through Silverland to help
the "deserving" Young American Engine No. 2 pay off the
indebtedness on their engine.

Players from Pat Holland's troupe also volunteered. In
response to requests for O'Neil's Irish comicalities as Ragged
Pat, *Ireland As It Is* was substituted for *The Serious Family*
and played to a "full house and immense applause" in spite
of the muddy streets. Charley Rhodes' banjo solo, George
Marsh's comic song, and *The Two Bonnycastles* were also
declared "first-rate." The engine was paid in full.

4

Since October the Washoites had been waiting to draw
their prizes in "Wright's Mammoth Gift Enterprise." By New
Year's, ticket holders were so insistent that Wright set the
drawing "positively and precisely" for January 15, when
Maguire's was jammed full within five minutes of opening.
Mr. Marsh informed the crowd he held the only ticket not
sold. A lady in one of the private boxes outbid all others.
While she counted out the 12 silver dollars, Master Marsh
and Miss Arnot entertained with songs and sketches "for
which the crowd paid them liberally by a shower of Uncle
Sam's silver currency." Then from a huge turning wheel little
girls drew the winning tickets, redeemable at 11 North C
Street.[4]

---

[4] Besides the *Bulletin* reporter Charles A. Parker, George Marsh chose George
Eells, George Lyman, Mr. Selfridge, and Mr. Adams to superintend the drawing
of the prizes. Ticket no. 6277 won the $1000 cash award; a $30 prize went to a
poor man with six children.

Noting the zeal evidenced for Wright's lottery, other opportunists launched
bona fide gift entertainments: I. Frederick and another jeweler on North C Street
sold their entire stock of goods through lottery; Winn and Center raffled off oil
paintings done by a Washoe artist; and Battersby and Elmer also held gift enterprises.

5

The Phantom opened the week of January 17 at the Opera House, and the next evening Billy O'Neil played Larry Hoolegan with the Marshes in *More Blunders Than One.* Thursday was the benefit day of the National Guards, a Washoe organization scarcely two months old. Expecting the "miserable parade generally made by volunteer companies," the Comstockers stared in appreciative astonishment as the fifty-four "brightly dressed" men executed "one of the finest pieces of military parading and precision marching ever witnessed in Virginia." Down to Gold Hill and back marched the Guards preceded by McClusky's 10-piece brass band, headed by their drum major Smith Schneider. And though "somewhat jaded, they went through the manual of arms again with fine exactness," disbanded for dinner, and met at the Opera House for their benefit. What a workout! But it brought results.

Comstockers crowded Maguire's both upstairs and down; cheered L. F. Beatty as Sergeant Austerlitz and others of the Marsh troupe in the advertised play of *Old Soldier* (or was it *The Cross of Croissy* instead, as the *Union* reported?); applauded the Guards as they *again* went through the manual exercise; joined in the singing; listened to Governor Nye; applauded Mrs. Cutler's "Address to the American Flag," and the performance of *Andy Blake,* featuring O'Neil with the Opera House troupe. Assured that the Guards' treasury was now replenished, the audience and those Guards with enough remaining energy finished off the night's fun at the Fancy Dress Ball in progress at Topliffe's Theatre.[5]

Having given, at least, two civic benefits, Mr. Marsh decided to take a benefit himself on the closing night of the

---

[5] Next night at Carson the first ball of the legislative session brought out "much of the youth and beauty of Carson." Also attending were Governor Nye, the venerable A. Curry, and Frank Perkins, J. J. Musser, F. M. Pixley, H. F. Rice, J. H. Kinhead, W. W. Rose, Mr. Retiker, and "their ladies."

company's engagement. But a "splendid new theatre," Sutliff's Music Hall, was opened that same January 23 and against such attractions even the famous Marsh family could not compete. Though they performed an "excellent program," the *Union* reported only "a fair audience" to enjoy it while the *Call* insisted Mr. Marsh dismissed the audience "because there were so few present," but the company had been "liberally patronized" previously throughout Silverland. Next day the Marsh Juveniles climbed aboard California-bound stages, leaving the Opera House dark. The two melodeons, Niagara Concert Hall and Sutliff's Music Hall, now took over the principal theatrical business of the Comstock.

22

Washoe's New Theatre: Music Hall

1

On the east side of C Street not far above Topliffe's Theatre, an uptown location the *Union* thought unfortunate, but which made for accessibility, was Washoe's new theatre. Of oriental style surmounted by a striking cornice, unlike any building near it, Sutliff's Music Hall was "one of the strongest frame buildings in the city." And Comstockers, remembering the Washoe Zephyrs' attack upon Maguire's Opera House, were relieved to learn that the new theatre was constructed of large timbers secured by iron bolts with a self-supporting roof.

Suspended from the ceiling twenty feet over the heads of the audience on each side of the 29-by-50-foot stage, five large boxes were so placed that the occupants could view the stage without being seen from the floor (maybe Sutliff was considering Julia Bulette and other such females). There were lower boxes too, fourteen in all. Painted by an Eastern artist, the scenery — considered the "best in the territory" — included mountains, Alpine glaciers, lakes, tropical gardens, fountains, statues, streets, interiors of castles, kitchens, apartments, rooms, and parlors.

Lamps could be withdrawn and covered to produce almost total stage darkness. Everything, in fact, was "finished off in fine style with white paint and gilt moulding." To secure warmth in winter, Sutliff had the back of the stage battened

with flannel, all "apertures closed in with the blanket stuff,"
had put down a double floor, and installed large heating
stoves.

Although Washoites, attending political meetings and
dances there, had admired the new hall, it was not until
January 23 that Sutliff and his musical director H. Oldfield
announced the "Grand Opening Night!" And those Comstockers who managed to squeeze in, after paying the same
prices as at Maguire's, saw and heard the celebrated Irish-,
Dutch- comic-singer J. C. Williams; the comedienne Miss
Emma Williams; the already popular danseuse Señorita Maria
from Niagara Concert Hall; the Irish nightingale Miss Joey
de Vere; Tom Greely in one of his champion jig dances; John
Collins the celebrated Brother Bones; tambourinist John
Howards; the "people's favorite" John H. O'Neil; Johnny
Edwards; "and other popular favorites."

Entertainment "of a higher grade than usual (free from
that vulgar lewdness usual to melodeons)" kept the huge
audience appreciative and happy. To the *Union* critic's ears
the dancing of Señorita Maria and the singing of Joey de
Vere received the loudest applause. Certainly for such an
array of talent in such a fast-moving, varied program no
claque was necessary. Disregarding the fact that Virginia
schools, overcrowded with 118 pupils to a room, needed
financial help; seemingly oblivious to the miserably muddy
streets; but excited that Mike Bradley had challenged prize-
fighter Dwyer of San Francisco; and that the Savage Mine
had declared a $50-dividend — the Comstockers packed
Music Hall night after night, eager and insatiate for the
"mirth, fun, and laughter" dispensed there, encoring the
farces, dances, interludes, and songs "as many as four times." [1]

---

[1] *Virginia Evening Bulletin*, January 25, 1864.

2

On the 27th Billy O'Neil was featured along with the equally famous banjoist Charley Rhodes who, however, got into a quarrel with his former boss of Niagara Hall. Rhodes pulled a pistol on Lynch, but did not shoot. So, no corpse! Nevertheless, Rhodes was disturbed that newspaper accounts of the affair used only the word "pistol." "It was a Derringer pistol!" the musician insisted.[2]

Vying with Niagara Hall, Sutliff kept Charley Rhodes in the news; piled more $20-cordwood into his stoves; lowered the price of drinks to the smallest coin used in Washoe; secured O'Neil to do his Irish characters and to introduce his "Darlin' Biddy step" into Gowan's Reel; and gave such attractive programs that Comstockers could not resist this amusement house, now featuring not only O'Neil but Señorita Maria, whose talents, a Washoe critic insisted, "should give her a higher position than before the footlights of a melodeon." Several nights later the danseuse returned to Niagara Hall. A promotion? Anyway, Lynch enlarged the stage and made several other improvements to fill seats in his melodeon.

Sutliff also made changes. G. W. Boulten became business manager; J. H. O'Neil, stage manager. Mr. and Mrs. Beatty and others were engaged "to appear in a new class of entertainment" — or so Sutliff announced, possibly to offset the coming Opera House attraction of Adah Menken, already advertised to "perform the *Ursa Major* feat" for the Washoites.

---

[2] The reporter should have known his gun-conscious public even then were enjoying a gunsmith's window display of "one of the most beautiful pistols . . . ever seen in this territory," a Smith and Wesson, over which Comstock men argued the new patent's improvement on the original Colt and admired the electro-plating of silver.

3

Having on the first Sunday in February dedicated the new Methodist Episcopal Church, "the finest in the territory, built of brick and stone" at the corner of Taylor and E Streets in Virginia, the Reverend M. G. Briggs, asking a dollar admission to help furnish the church, lectured on "Human Nature Read Backwards," which "afforded considerable amusement and instruction." But others wanted to help with the money-raising. Under the direction of "that sweet songstress and accomplished musician" Mrs. E. H. Wiley, some forty amateur musicians brought "the embodiment of Old New England into the sagebrush" in an Old Folks Concert.

When the entertainment moved over to the Opera House under the experienced management of N. A. H. Ball, the concert changed somewhat. Whereas the church party had exhibited piety, costumes, and cookery, the concert at Maguire's that February 13 portrayed manners, courting, curiosities, and eccentricities "of the good folks who did so much toward making us a nation." Professor Grambbs furnished appropriate music on a Steinway (the grand piano that was to be given away during Wright's next gift entertainment).

The Opera House was crowded, reviewers agreeing that of home-talent productions the Old Folks Concert was decidedly the best of the season. That Governor Nye in the audience enjoyed the concert is doubtful. His thoughts were occupied with reports of murder and lynching in the Esmeralda District.[3]

---

[3] Angry Aurora citizens erected a scaffold in front of Armory Hall and forcibly took four prisoners from the jail. (One wonders: was the former actor James Stark in that vigilante audience? No, if reports are correct, he was playing a limited engagement at the Metropolitan Theatre in San Francisco, and would, according to rumor, leave for the East by March 2.)

The governor arrived too late. Only the scaffold with its empty swaying ropes greeted him. But Nye had "the devilish machine removed"; ordered all saloons and public places closed at nine each evening; declared gambling prohibited; "enjoined both the officers and the populace" to maintain order; threatened martial law; and as a further precaution gathered up some "150 muskets, 50 sabres, and

4

Mazeppa was still "attracting a great deal of attention" at
Niagara Hall — not on the Chinaman's donkey, but on a
"wild horse in the shape of a jackass, not much larger than a
sagebrush rabbit." *Mazeppa* should have been finished; for
Pat Holland had had it on and off the Niagara boards since
early November. Perhaps, as at the Bella Union in San Francisco, he used a different actress in each scene to entice male
patronage.

The performances at Sutliff's were not to be ignored either.
Boasting an array of "actors of merit," including Kimble and
Peck on the double trapeze, Music Hall patrons found the
atmosphere such as to amuse. The singing, dancing, jigs,
jokes, comicalities, conundrums, songs, and sayings kept the
audience laughing through the evening and chuckling on the
way home.

Ever "on the alert for novelties" and not to be outdone by
Pat Holland, Sutliff also entered into a season of burlesque
that culminated on February 17 with a ludicrous take-off on
Mazeppa planned to run until the Menken herself should
appear *in propria persona* at Maguire's Opera House and
give "as large an exhibition of female loveliness as the law
allows." As done now at Sutliff's, *Mazeppa* was a "serio-
comical, equestrian, ass-anine, canine, melodramatic," fun
piece with the obese J. H. O'Neil performing a double part,
in some scenes playing a thieving Paiute, in others a long-
tailed Chinaman, while Charley Rhodes personated a "lovely
female." Lashed to the back of a fiery untamed steed, "which

----

a like number of pistols, all United States property, but before in the hands of the
people," and drove through the night with them to the capital.

Nor was all peace in other sections of Silverland. The ranchers of Truckee and
Washoe valleys had banded together, shot one man, wounded others, and let outsiders definitely know that jumping ranches in Washoe was unhealthy. Over in
Humboldt County the people of Dun Glen also found it necessary to adopt rules
that drove town lot jumpers out of the area in a hurry.

turned out to be the quietest of well-behaved mustangs,"
Mrs. Beatty and Miss Sally Henry, dressed in "less than two
yards of calico," both played the part of Mazeppa, riding
backwards and forwards *a la cavalier,* as some Washoe "politicians rode the political fence, astraddle."

"Mazeppa, as played at Sutliff's must be seen," cried
Charley Parker. "It cannot be described." Certainly there was
weird variety. Through the last scene stalked "Chinamen,
Pi-Utes, Niggers, Mazeppa, Phelim McTwain, Winnemucca,
Count Cast Iron, Buffalo Jim, Skerilous Zemelia, Sentinel
Gould & Curry, a milk-white steed, two Chinese jackasses,
and the bow-legged dog Bummer, all brilliantly illuminated
with red fire."

Considered "indescribable" and "the grandest theatrical
success ever witnessed in this city, "Mazeppa, attired mighty
scantily," was next proclaimed sole monarch of Empire City.
The burlesque was a must to all Washoe males, especially
since the Menken herself would "positively arrive" by the
third week of February. Dame rumor even reported rooms
reserved for her at the International Hotel. And she certainly
would appear at the Firemen's Washington Day Ball.

<h2 style="text-align:center">5</h2>

Thus with eager anticipation, Young American Engine
Company No. 1 saluted February 22 using Fremont's old
cannon; then staged a parade and a dinner at which Governor
Nye was presented with a "magnificent wine pitcher and six
goblets made of Washoe silver," a gift so pleasing His Excel-
lency responded "in his happiest manner."

Regarding the theatrical part of the festivities, Charley
Parker remembered "the tremendous crowd at Sutliff's and
that the Governor and his staff were there too"

to view the points of the female form divine — so many and so
much of which are nightly to be seen. Mrs. Beatty and Miss Henry
have both got good legs and feet, busts and — all the rest — and
men as well as boys love to gaze on them and ruminate.

But *Mazeppa* did not end the fun. A formal ball at Maguire's Opera House, "fitted up with great taste and elegance," beckoned the "elite of Washoe's stalwart men and lovely women." Miss Menken did not appear, but No. 1's ball was a success as was the one benefiting the First Infantry Regiment of Nevada Territorial Volunteers.

Mazeppa at Music Hall continued to be the major attraction. O'Neil as middle man varied his act with songs, jigs, dances, and ended in a grand walk-around. "The Washoe canaries and the bowlegged wolf" plus "the creditable manner in which each character was dressed" — though for some of the ladies "mighty scantily" — made the "really capital burlesque pass off as slick as grease."

Finding competition with Music Hall too keen, Lynch & Hardy's troupe gave other Washoe towns a treat of their *Mazeppa* burlesque. So crowded was Doyle's Hall many could not get inside to see the Mazeppas ride the wild horse up the dizzy crags, so had to be content with horse-racing, cock-fights, prize-fighting, and the saloons.

A Niagara Hall troupe performance of *Mazeppa* on Friday evening, February 27, in Carson City nearly ended in tragedy when Carrie Chapman, evidently playing the part of Mazeppa, was accidentally struck across the temple during a sword encounter. The other actors carried her limp body to the greenroom and sent for a physician while the manager quieted the audience. Fortunately Miss Chapman was soon able again to delight Carson melodeon-addicts.

In Virginia on the same night as Carrie Chapman's accident, Mrs. W. K. Cutler was giving competition to Miss Sallie Henry's scantily-clad Mazeppa. In the first series of "Three Literary and Musical Entertainments," Mrs. Cutler assisted by Mrs. Wiley, Mr. Studeman, Mr. Sturm, Professor Grambbs, Mr. Franz, and Mr. Rudolph entertained those who paid "five dollars for the course, admitting two persons" into the new Methodist Church.[4] The programs received good reviews, good crowds, and such good box office receipts at Virginia, Dayton, and Carson that the home talent entertainments were declared a definite benefit for education. A short time later the ladies of Jackson, likewise inspired, gave "a calico party" to help their schools — but, needless to say, more than "two yards of calico" were required to make the dancing frocks of these ladies.

[4] The complete program was published in the *Virginia Evening Bulletin* of February 27, 1864.

Menken and Mazeppa

1

The report that Adah Isaacs Menken and suite had reached Lake Tahoe and soon would arrive in Silverland kept the burlesque of *Mazeppa* on its "wonderful run" at Sutliff's Music Hall, thereby whetting appetites all the more for the real *Mazeppa*. But the "shape artist" could not open her sensation-season at Maguire's Opera House with that vehicle, reporters told a Washoe public "on tiptoe" to see her, because her horse had not arrived and new scenery was not yet "prepared equal to any in San Francisco." There the Menken had assumed so many parts in *Three Fast Women* she confused her audience on the sex of her characters.

"Prudery is obsolete now," observed a theatrical critic, "the Shakespearian 'modesty of nature' has a new interpretation." To this another wrote, "Adah's abundant charms and wealth of muscle need no encomiums from my pen. As she takes no pains to conceal them, they speak for themselves." No wonder the Washoites followed the checkered career of Adah Isaacs Menken Heenan Newell even before she steamed in through the Golden Gate on August 7, 1863.

Born Rachel Adah Isaacs about 1839 in New Orleans, she had made her debut there as a danseuse at fourteen. By 1852 she was traveling with a hippodrome and becoming an expert equestrienne. Legend said she was captured by Texas Indians and upon her escape wrote poetry;[1] then married a southern Jew. Becoming bored she returned to the stage to assume male characters. And now the "more undressed actress than any other tolerated on the American stage" had "with two immense cigar boxes full of clothing" really arrived in Washoe as the following advertisement indicated:

MAGUIRE'S OPERA HOUSE

| Thomas Maguire | . | . | . | . | . | . | Proprietor |
| L. F. Beatty | . | . | . | . | . | . | Stage Manager |

THE MANAGER TAKES PLEASURE IN ANNOUNCING to the citizens of Virginia that he has effected an engagement with the celebrated and popular artist

MISS ADAH ISAACS MENKEN!

Who will make her first appearance on Wednesday Evening, March 2d, 1864,

IN HER WORLD-RENOWNED CHARACTERS

in the Thrilling, Musical, and Spectacular Drama in Three Acts of
THE FRENCH SPY!

Supported by the following array of talent:

Mr. Charles Pope,	Mr. L. F. Beatty,
Mr. Walter Leman,	Mr. L. Brown,
Mr. J. N. Griffith,	Mr. W. Morrill,
Mr. H. Rivers,	Mr. J. V. Bowes,
Mr. H. English,	Mr. H. Mackin,
Mrs. H. A. Perry,	Mrs. Geo. Chapman,
Mrs. L. F. Rand,	Miss Hattie Johnson.

A splendid Orchestra, under the leadership of HUBERT SCHREINER, with numerous auxiliaries.

---

[1] While in New York, Adah often met with a literary group that included Walt Whitman. In the West, Bret Harte, Joaquin Miller, and Mark Twain encouraged the poetess, so while awaiting the arrival of her "fiery steed" for *Mazeppa*, the Menken ensconced in the International penned

CORALGIA

O long not, worn feet, for the days that are squandered,
  Or the flowery paths that in childhood we trod;
The years have been many through which we have wandered
  From pleasure, from happiness, virtue, and God.

The breast that is buoyant may court nature's gladness,
  But stricken, it turns from such mockery apart;
Here, where nature lifts her pale features in sadness;
  Is the home for the world-weary, desolate heart.

In consequence of the great expense attending the engagement
of Miss Menken, the following Rates of Admission will be observed:

Dress Circle and Orchestra . .	$1.50
Pit	1.00
Private Boxes . . .	$5 and $10 each [2]

Even with the advance in prices, Maguire felt compelled
to cancel the free list — with the one exception, of course, of
the press. For those who wished reserved seats — though they
cost no more than when bought at the door — Maguire opened
the box office at the theatre on Monday, February 29, from
ten to four. Twenty supernumeraries were needed for the
Corps de Ballet and young ladies and gentlemen of the Lode
towns who wanted a taste of stage life could "inquire of Mr.
Beatty at the theatre."

The Washoites had been "warned they should prepare to
be astonished at a rare exhibition of mental and physical
development, an intellectual muscularity when this petted
child of genius drops down among you"; for "compared with
them limbs and *that bust,* all the 'feet' in your Territory are
as nothing." Hence, every seat in the theatre was sold the day
before the lady, who "fenced with a strong wrist and Bowery
dexterity," made her Virginia debut. The house was sold out
the next night, and the next too, ladies seeming "to take as
much interest" as the men in the actress who believed that
"beauty unadorned is adorned the most." For five consecutive nights Comstockers saw the Menken as Henry St. Alme,
Hemet Carmauly, and Mathilde De Merio in the "Thrilling,
Musical, and Spectacular Drama" of *The French Spy,* a risque
leg-show.

2

Although Music Hall noted a marked difference in patronage the first nights of the reopening of the Opera House,
Sutliff's was doing well again by the benefit night of Mrs.

[2] *Virginia Evening Bulletin,* February 29, 1864.

Beatty, when the troupe burlesqued *The French Spy*. With Mrs. Beatty as the spy, George Chapman as Mahonmed the wild Arab from Desert District, O'Neil as Achmet Dey, Miss Henry as Murad, Miss Paster as Marie Duborg, "and soldiers, vivandieres, Arabs, etc.," the performance at Sutliff's was "received with repeated bursts of laughter and applause."

On March 5 *The Spy* burlesque was repeated. Even after *Mazeppa* opened at the Opera House, *The Spy* continued at Music Hall and was, according to the *Union* "in some of its parts superior to that" presented at Maguire's. Though the plot of the Sutliff production was as naughty, the drill of the soldiers at Music Hall was "a masterpiece" and the varied details of the play were "carried out in an almost perfect manner, which excited no little astonishment" from those aware that many of the Sutliff troupers were novices.

The Niagara Minstrel Troupe, returning from good houses in Carson, Washoe City, Dayton, and Silver City, were — unlike Sutliff's — unable to stand the *Mazeppa* competition and so closed the melodeon on C Street "for improvements."

Monday night, March 7, the shape artist appeared in the long awaited racy drama of *Mazeppa,* a rather poor play, the work of a mediocre dramatist, who had been inspired momentarily by Byron's poem of the Tartar prince Ivan Mazeppa. Because he dared to love the daughter of a Polish nobleman, Mazeppa was "condemned to be bound by hempen lashings to a fiery, untamed steed" which, upon release dashed for the distant hills. Finally horse and rider reached Tartary and the King recognized in Mazeppa his long-lost son. Together they led an expedition on Poland — Mazeppa still with nothing to wear, "not even a shirt collar or a pair of spurs" — defeated their enemies, and Mazeppa carried off the heroine. But the climax of the play was the scene of the helpless rider, bound to the back of the "wild, untamed horse of Tartary" plunging at breakneck speed up the steep, almost "convincing rocks." Dummies were usually used; the Menken was the first performer bold enough to allow herself to be tied to the horse.

Though the Washoites longed for a sprinkling cart to "down the dust," they packed the Opera House on *Mazeppa's* opening night and hundreds more had to be turned away. Mark Twain and Dan De Quille wrote such lavish praises of the performance, the *Humboldt Register* protested:

> MENKENIZED — The local of the Enterprise is awfully spooney in his comments on Menken's performance. He had better take some of Mrs. Wilson's soothing syrup and get to bed earlier of nights.

The *Union* reviewer also thought the Menken disappointing, but that the characters of the Khan of Tartary, Haman, and Castellan were "well taken and aided materially in carrying the plot of the play to perfection." The scenery was good, but in some scenes did present a rather "poverty-stricken appearance." Schreiner and his orchestra, however, were highly praised for the new "Mazeppa Medley Overture"; in fact, the critic went so far as to say, "The music at this theatre is worth all the balance of the performance."

The *Union*, becoming more critical with each presentation, finally called Maguire's "a Hippotheatron" and the Menken's performance "a scandalous, obscene exhibition, a defamation of a historical character whose ghost might well exclaim: 'To what base uses may our name be turned?' " But for Music Hall he had praise, especially for O'Neil's handling of *The Spy* and another new burlesque, *Alta Skeesicks Blenken*, in which Mrs. Beatty, O'Neil, Rhodes, and Miss Marietta appeared for the benefit of Miss Sallie Henry.

By the second week of the Menken's run even the *Enterprise* did not "pile it up quite so steep. Guess Dan has discovered that she wears drawers," observed the Unionville editor. And Bay city papers stated that a most remarkable exhibition on the Opera House stage one evening necessitated "the dropping of the curtain before the act was concluded."

3

On St. Patrick's Day, Adah Menken "managed to offend the people" of Carson. Her peevishness stemmed from having to dress by candlelight or because of a small audience due to a severe storm that was raging, bringing "the moisture Washoites had long awaited." But snow "to come down softly as a mother's kisses was not Washoe." Instead, "the impalpable powder" hurled through the streets struck the cheek like splintered ice,[3] but the Menken felt this to be no excuse for Carsonites to stay away.

After playing the first act, she refused to go on with the performance and the curtain was kept down nearly an hour while manager Johnny Burns coaxed her to go on with the second act. Of course Adah was unaware of Washoe patronage of home talent and local benefits so could not comprehend the success of Mrs. Wiley's concert-and-dance that same blusterous night.

Adah's benefit next night at Maguire's Opera House was also "poorly attended" — because of the big dance of the night before, one correspondent explained. But this seems a lame excuse for fun-loving Washoites. Either the storm was responsible or the Menken was failing to attract.[4]

---

[3] Some camels, many with sore backs and bleeding feet, and loaded with desert salt intended for the mills on the Comstock, encountering snow in Six Mile Canyon, stopped in confusion, cried, and shivered with the cold, but were forced to go on into Virginia.

[4] Of legendary interest is the frictional byplay of the Menken's Silverland season. Writing from memory rather than factual notes, Sam Davis unintentionally in his *The History of Nevada* gave a story that would be copied far too many times by later writers. Before Adah arrived the newspapermen of the *Enterprise* had agreed to deride her, but when they actually saw her on the stage, they all wrote accounts so glowing as to excite the jealousy of the rest of the company, some Maguire players even putting gags in their lines about Goodman and his paper. This so angered Adah, she stopped the play and insisted the Opera House manager make a public apology to the *Enterprise*. When Burns refused, she would not go on with her part and the audience had to be dismissed. At the next performance she relented and was rewarded by Mark Twain in a special notice, which, Davis said, was widely copied.

However, no such Twain account has to date been located. Stars always re-

Had the Menken been on the Lode for St. Patrick's night, she might have fared as unhappily as she had in Carson. Since the first week of February local papers reported the extensive plans for the occasion, which turned out to be "one of the finest" in spite of trouble brewing between Comstock military and fire companies.[5] The day passed off quietly for all except theatreman Henry Sutliff, who left Virginia in a hurry with Officer Green on the chase of one of his former employees, who, it seems, had mounted the "noble steed"

---

ceived the acclaim; lesser players expected this. Nevertheless, even after the Menken had left Silverland, Davis had friction continuing. If players came to Virginia, he said, they received no notices in the *Enterprise*. Poor players were so abused, many actors hesitated coming to Washoe.

Playing the feud to a dramatic close, Davis had the *Enterprise* stubbornly remain loyal to the Menken until the Opera House manager was dismissed and the free list and the advertising again resumed. Walter Leman, a member of the cast, mentioned no such phases of the Menken's Washoe season in his biography. The *Virginia Union*, Carson *Independent*, *Gold Hill News*, *Old Pah-Utah*, *Humboldt Register*, *Reese River Reveille*, and California papers wrote of the Menken's Washoe season, but all fail to put the Davis account into fact.

[5] In keeping the St. Patrick's Day celebrators under control, perhaps no little credit is due a rugged, 250-pound, big-hearted giant, Father Patrick Monague, who opened the festivities with a solemn prayer. Towering six feet, three inches in height, the leader of Virginia's Catholic Church had been a California placer miner before studying in Paris and entering the priesthood. The Reverends Franklin Rising and Ozi Whitaker of the Episcopal Church, like Father Monague and other Washoe pastors, straightforward, energetic, and tolerant, exercised strong influence on the side of peace, law, and order in Washoe.

After the prayer and a colorful parade led by the Metropolitan Brass Band with Smith Schneider as drum major, the "immense assemblage" pushed into the Opera House, up the stairs, and into seats on a temporary floor below. Judge Tilford had scarcely begun speaking when some of the latter gave way with a tremendous crash and, "what with the alarm of the persons thus rudely precipitated from their seats" and the shrieks of the ladies, "panic well nigh ensued." Finally quieted, the audience listened to more oratory until another part of the floor went down, this time bruising several people. Lecturer and audience then adjourned to the Catholic Church.

The Grand Military Ball took place however as planned at Maguire's; for the military organizations hurriedly repaired the shattered floor, decorated the theatre, brought in musicians, and held their dance, which "passed off in a happy manner" with no further accidents. Also that night Young American Engine Company No. 2 held its Second Annual Ball at Sutliff's, where the 69 committeemen removed the seats, decorated the theatre, engaged Schreiner and the Metropolitan musicians, and prepared "tempting viands" expertly decorated with the St. Patrick motif.

with which the burlesque of *Mazeppa* had been performed at Music Hall and ridden eastward toward Fort Churchill and Reese carrying theatrical props and theatre funds along.

4

Sutliff recovered Mazeppa's mount and continued the burlesque of *Alta Skeesicks Blenken* to its "usual run," which explains in part, at least, the reason for Adah's occasionally slim audiences at the Opera House. Although Lynch and Holland had closed Niagara Hall because of the "powerful attractions elsewhere," Johnny Tuers, "champion flat-foot dancer of the Pacific coast," [6] believing otherwise, reopened the Niagara; gave it the name of the New Idea; lowered the admission price to "two bits" — although to sit in orchestra chairs cost 50 cents; and engaged "La Petite Soledad, Ned Buckley and lady, and Carrie Chapman" among others to entertain nightly.

Virginia rejoiced in three theatres now: one presenting the legitimate, Maguire's Opera House; one high-grade variety, Sutliff's Music Hall; and the third, low-grade variety, Johnny Tuers' New Idea, which with the passing weeks degenerated into a place "about as beastly as can be imagined." Nevertheless, of March 19 — the last night of the Menken's *Mazeppa* on the Comstock — the *Union* wrote: "The New Idea is attracting unusual attention and larger houses than for some time. Ida May and Ned Buckley are among the performers."

John Dougherty's 180-hour walking performance (without sleep or rest) opposite Maguire's could scarcely have detracted from the Menken's audiences. But Sutliff's did when *Black-Eyed Susan; or, All in the Downs* (a safe, old, stand-by nautical drama containing empty puns) was put on the boards at Music Hall. But the troupe made charming changes in the drama, inserting new and popular songs and dances,

---

[6] This was the same Johnny Tuers who later accidentally shot a San Francisco theatre manager.

Shape artist Adah Isaacs Menken, the Marilyn Monroe of Civil
War times, intrigued Nevadans with her confusing male interpretations, and a daring horse act that set off *Mazeppa* burlesques,
which kept Washoites titillating for months.

Courtesy, the Henry E. Huntington Library.

$40,000 ! $40,000 !

—:o:—

Attention, Everyone!

J. A. WRIGHT'S
THIRD
MAMMOTH GIFT ENTERPRISE!

Of $40,000,
TO BE GIVEN AT

Maguire's Opera House, Virginia, N. T.

2,058 Rich and Elegant Gifts!

TO BE DISTRIBUTED TO THE AUDIENCE, COM-prising the largest collection of rich and superb California Jewelry, with an endless variety of the finest Works of Art. And, altogether, comprising the largest assortment ever distributed on the Pacific coast, or any other coast, gratuitously, among ticket holders.

The FIRST GIFT will be

A WASHOE SILVER BAR !

[Weighing 1,738 40-100th ozs.]

Theall & Co.'s assay—Gold, .928 fine ; Silver, .965 fine. Value—Gold, $1,006 ; Silver, $2,169. Total, $3,176 18.

Second Gift—$1,000 in Gold Coin!

One of STEINWAY & SON'S celebrated

PIANO FORTES,

Purchased for the occasion from Messrs. Dale & Co. of this city.

Jewelry,
Diamonds,
Pearls,
Onyx,
Stone,
Cameo,
Etc., etc.,

Ranging in price from Twenty-five to Six Hundred Dollars.

Diamond Crosses,
Rings, Pins,
Diamond-backed
Watches, with
Chatelains to match.

A large amount of fine GOLD and SILVER

PATENT LEVER WATCHES,

Massive California Gold Chains,

Washoe Quartz Jewelry.

An endless variety of SOLID SILVER WARE, consisting in part of Goblets, Cups, Fish Knives, Forks, Dessert, Butter and Pie Knives, Ice Cream Sets, Salts and Spoons, Ladles, etc., etc.

A Free Gift to the Virginia Fire Department of two Solid Silver Fire Trumpets—magnificent articles—purchased of Tucker, of San Francisco, for the occasion. Also, One Hundred Dollars to the Storey County Sanitary Fund.

These goods were purchased and manufactured expressly for this Gift Entertainment, by the well known firms of Messrs. Lovison Bros., R. B. Gray & Co., and A. Kohler, and are in every particular of the latest and most approved patterns, and just as represented on the list of gifts. The proprietor defies any similar enterprise to show a superior quality of goods, or any that can begin to compete with them. They need only to be seen to be appreciated ; and I invite any one and every one to call and examine these beautiful goods, which are all to be given away on or before the Fourth day of July next.

The drawing of this Enterprise was set for the 30th of April, but owing to the dull times and the short space of time set for the sale of 40,000 tickets, it will be an impossibility to consummate it by that time.

I will place myself under $80,000 bonds to redeem each and every ticket, at $2 each, if it is not drawn by the 4th of July next, or as much sooner as the tickets can all be sold.

This Enterprise will be drawn by a committee of gentlemen appointed by the ticket holders, and that same fair and square principle will be strictly observed with which my former ones have been.

Tickets, only One Dollar each,
IN COIN ;

7 Tickets for $ in Greenbacks—15 for $20.

All orders promptly attended to by the proprietor,

J. A. WRIGHT,
VIRGINIA, N. T.

April 28, 1864.   ap29-td

"Gift Enterprises," Nevada's earliest lotteries, were exciting entertainment — distributing by chance assorted jewelry, musical instruments, gold, bars of silver, and real estate, totaling tens, then hundreds, of thousands of dollars. From the *Daily Old Piute*, May 17, 1864.

keeping "just enough of the story to flavor the scenes." Señorita Maria did a sailor's hornpipe, which had received "approbation both in this country and in Europe." Miss Marietta sang a favorite ballad that drew "repeated applause." "The Neapolitaine" was Mrs. L. F. Beatty's contribution to the evening. Misses Emma Paster and Nellie Carpenter and a host of others including Johnny O'Neil performed "with rare gusto." *Black-Eyed Susan* convinced the Menken it was time to change her performance at Maguire's.

On March 20 she introduced *Dick Turpin* and played the dashing highwayman with her accustomed spirit, but keeping "the equestrienne business under control." As a result the Opera House was filled. But so were the houses at the New Idea and Sutliff's, which that afternoon had given a "regular performance" as a matinee for those who did not "want to brave the cold tonight." Next evening to offset *Dick Turpin*, Sutliff introduced a "new, splendid, scenic, operatic, and terpsichoric drama" never before played in Virginia, entitled *The Lake of Killarney; or, We May Be Happy Yet.*

5

A week before the close of the Menken's 29-day Washoe season a notice appeared in the *Enterprise* tendering the shape artist a benefit. Under it was the Menken's card accepting the honor. Later it was learned the signatures were not genuine. Someone had perpetrated a theatrical joke, but the men chosen "to stand the punishment" of the expense for such a benefit got "madder and finally became pretty hot." They stalked over to the *Enterprise* office, investigated the original card, and found that the Menken had really accepted the benefit a day before the offer had been made. The actress finally "repudiated the whole affair."

As if to compensate the Menken, the Virginia "Fire Huskies" of Engine No. 2 elected her to honorary membership and gave her a massive silver belt as a token of their esteem. The actress thus became, in the language of the boys, "one of 'Two's fellars.'" On the Monday prior to his and the Menken's departure, J. B. Booth,[7] for whom the public entertained "the highest regard, not only for his social and gentlemanly deportments, but also for his superior qualifications as an actor," took a farewell benefit.

On the last day of March the colorful Adah — who had "taken Washoe by storm," risen to the peak of popularity, declined with temperamental outbursts, then soared again — and her current husband Orpheus C. Kerr stepped up into the Pioneer Company's stage and were carried out of Nevada Territory while the *Enterprise* made its final laudation: "Miss Menken played a variety of characters, and she was better in all of them than in each that preceded it if possible which, hardly seems reasonable to believe it yet nevertheless so." To this the *Humboldt Register* sarcastically remarked, "Is a sentence remarkable for its felicitous wording and corresponding beauty."

But the Menken was gone, bound for Australia "and the continent."[8] Her departure, however, inspired a literary admirer to do the following quatrain:

> Menken, adieu! No more shall lusty "boys"
> Applaud Mazeppa, till hoarse throats grow
>   hoarser;
> No more shall they, mid lights and horrid
>   noise,
> See that *fine* form outspread upon a courser!

---

[7] A few weeks later "June" Booth was in New York associated with his famous brother Edwin at Niblo's Gardens. All three Booth brothers were theatrically engaged in the East now, but before a year passed John Wilkes would have fired the fatal shot into the brain of President Lincoln and thus brought death to himself and disgrace to the Booth family. Edwin and Junius suffered professionally. Depressed and worried for years over his brother's act, J. B. Booth killed his wife and committed suicide in England on December 7, 1912.

[8] While playing Paris four years after her Washoe advent, the Menken failed to report for rehearsals. Her producer, believing her absence of several weeks another temperamental outburst, went to court to compel the actress to return to the cast. When officers forced her apartment door, they found her dead.

Fires, Fights, and
Four Bald Heads

1

With April all forms of activity increased. Even after the Petaluma *Argus* pleaded with California men, "Don't all go to Washoe!" still they came and demanded space for business and living as well as for amusements. Professor Millington gave a farewell soirée and turned over his dancing academy to the Virginia Board of Brokers. Mr. Vesey permitted the Turn-Verein Society to use his ballroom for "a delightful dance"; then "cut it up into bedrooms." Only the Gold Hill Theatre was left for dances, meetings, or troupes in Gold Hill.

Gambling houses, closed all winter, reopened throughout Washoe. Faro and monte tables, pianos, banjos, and bones, and in fact, "every allurement to entice the unwary" was in evidence again. Billiard tables were used for rondo playing with women dealers "still more unpracticed" than the professional gamblers, who now returned to fleece the greenhorns.

The "comical Frenchman" appeared again on the Lode with his "two-wheeled ice cream cart, his tin horn, and the identical donkey, who was so well accustomed to following his master amid the maze of quartz teams, prairie schooners, omnibuses, and vehicles of every kind."

Visitors were "struck with the determined energy" with which Silverland people pursued their pleasures. "The ladies," Pigeon Wing wrote *The Californian*, "think nothing of driving a dozen miles to a picnic over rough roads, narrow and dangerous, in open carriages . . . with the dust flying through the air in fine impalpable alkaline powder that covers everything with a gray ashen hue."

When headed for fun, the Washoites went, regardless of the hardships, stayed all night if need be, and in the cold of early dawn drove back into town, which at that hour "had a dissipated, slovenly look, as if it had sat up too late the night before and had not yet been to the barber's." Like Artemus and Adah, the lady correspondent thought Virginia a "most hospitable place," where the ladies could "stand more fun and the gentlemen more champagne than any other people" she ever saw.

2

The Opera House made its spring opening now. Since March 23 Tom Maguire had been adding to his troupe, which would take over when the Menken departed "for a more salubrious climate." On March 30 the proprietors Maguire and Burns along with Thomas McKeon, the new stage manager, presented such "talented artists" as Virginia Howard, Frank Lawlor, Agnes Perry,[1] and McKeon himself — the latter in a first appearance in Virginia. In fact, Mr. McKeon had been engaged for the express purpose of producing the "celebrated and highly successful sensational drama" of *Aurora Floyd*, which McKeon himself had written.

Nevertheless, the Opera House on opening night was poorly attended in spite of Maguire's advertising and the performance of "a beautiful piece" that held the "mirror up to nature with truthfulness and absence of exaggeration rarely witnessed on the stage." Even the *Union* praised the players, the

---

[1] While Adah Menken was being elected to honorary membership in a Virginia fire company, Agnes Perry was led to the front of the Opera House stage by Charles Pope, who read a note handed up to him from the audience expressing admiration of the lady's talents and wishing her continued "success and good fortune." A fire chief then handed the actress a large, six-inch gold star "encircled by a wreath of roses, attached to which was the badge of each fire company in the city." It was a gracious gesture and Mrs. Perry was greatly pleased.

playwright, and the play. Why then that Wednesday night did the Comstockers stay away?

Weather! "not very great aids to theatres." Though the *Bulletin* thought *Aurora Floyd* "as performed at Maguire's . . . worth going through the mud to witness," audiences became so small by April 1 and 2 that the piece was not given — this according to the *Union.* The *Bulletin,* however retorted, "the nearly 300 ladies and gentlemen who witnessed the admirable performance on that evening can form some idea of the re-lie-ability of that paper. If Maguire were to advertise in the *Union,* we should not be apt to hear so many disparaging remarks about his theatre" — had the *Bulletin* forgotten its own lack of Opera House support? Hoping to induce Comstockers to brave the mud, Burns reduced prices. A seat in the parquette now cost only 50 cents; in the dress circle, a dollar. Thereafter, these were the standard admission charges at the Opera House.

Though the frigid weather drove "nearly all the perambulating population off the streets" and Music Hall's warmth, the "goodness of the liquor, the prettiness of the waiter girls," and the varied stage performances were strong drawing factors, Sutliff too had to reduce prices to "only 25 cents." And the New Idea, presenting a "ludicrous comedy," put prices so low it "generally drew fair houses."

Nevertheless, another amusement-minded individual opened Topliffe's Theatre, renamed it the Old Bowery, and presented a company of minstrels, including four female performers. "With four shows in full blast," observed the *Union,* "we will be well supplied for the summer." Changes would take place, however, before April passed into amusement history. By Sunday the Old Bowery was exhibiting "a demoralizing dog fight." Then one of the partners "sequestered all the receipts." Another proprietor and a performer John Edwards, ended a dispute with a "shooting match."

Noting Washoe's theatrical difficulties as well as his own,

Johnny Tuers closed the New Idea. Sutliff's now as the sole melodeon on the Lode continued to attract, but not to crowded houses. This was something for the Opera House with "new scenery and supernumeraries" and "great legitimate bills" to accomplish.

3

Tom Maguire, again leading the amusement field, served Silverland for the first time, April 4, the five-act sensation drama of *Leah the Forsaken*, which theatre-lovers of New York had been enjoying for weeks. To Comstockers the fact that Dr. H. M. Bien, who was then opening a seminary in Virginia, was author of "the beautiful play" made the production as enacted by Virginia Howard, Frank Lawlor, and Thomas McKeon in the principal roles all the more acceptable.

The *Bulletin* felt compelled to say, however, that "Leah, though a really splendid lady, full of lofty sentiment and exhibiting many beautiful exemplifications of woman's intense, self-sacrificing love, is not of a character to suit the tastes of a Virginia audience." Even so, *Leah* was repeated the next night and yet again on the next, forcing the *Bulletin* critic to state diplomatically, "As all things intrinsically good, though not quite to our taste on first acquaintance, force themselves on our admirations so the beautiful play *Leah* is forcing itself on the good opinion of us Virginians."

Although *Romeo and Juliet* was presented "in a manner never equalled before in this Territory," Frank Lawlor had a "somewhat brawny and huge form for the sighing, sentimental lover," thought the *Bulletin*. Mercutio and the Friar by Leman and Aldrich were "excellently played." For Miss Howard as Juliet the *Bulletin* reserved its highest compliment: "a most natural performance." [2]

While romantic tragedy served the Opera House, Music Hall audiences applauded *Home for a Day; or, A Hero on Furlough* and laughed at the drolleries of the Sutliff troupers.

Next night the "lovers of good dancing" helped Señorita Maria enjoy her benefit.

Sutliff repeated the burlesque of *Mazeppa* to compete with the Reverend Taylor's lecture on "Sinai and the Holy Land" and the Opera House's sensational *Aurora Floyd* for "positively the last time." To round out the week Maguire presented the domestic drama of *The Stranger* and the comedy *All that Glitters is not Gold.*

The week of April 11 opened at the Opera House with Lawlor's benefit and last appearance. The actor played Hamlet to Miss Howard's Ophelia. Regardless of his having been billed on occasion as a "new star" and as an "amateur," a local critic insisted, "What would appear as a puff for others, was but justice for Frank Lawlor." Comstockers felt so too. They "absolutely jammed" the theatre, broke into frequent applause, and called Frank before the curtain again and again until he recited Samuel Lover's "Tale of the Rebellion of '98" in his fine rich voice. Even the *Union* admitted that Lawlor's Hamlet was "without rant . . . or insipidity. . ."

Next night another sensation drama, one which had played a London theatre with "unabated interest for 300 consecutive nights," held the Opera House boards. This was *The Ticket of Leave Man*, "a real novelty, a play true to nature and founded on fact." Promised the reappearance of "the general favorite Mr. Charles Pope," the Comstockers had "certain proof that the play" would be "rendered to perfection." It was. Completely in sympathy with the actors and the play, the audience — a more fashionable one than formerly — wept, laughed, "clapped their hands and stamped their feet." Not

---

2 Apparently nothing extraneous detracted from the regular presentation of Miss Howard and Mr. Lawlor that April 7 at the Opera House; nevertheless, Comstockers were amused at an incident during a "recent performance" of the sentimental lovers in Massachusetts — as related by the *Bulletin*. When the fair Juliet in the soliloquy before taking the sleeping draught asked, "What if this mixture do not work at all?" she was answered by a small urchin in the pit, "Then take a dose of pills." The effect on the audience can be imagined.

a person present but knew of such a kind-hearted, talkative old lady as Mrs. Willoughby and of such a wild, scamp son as Sam to get "inveigled into crime."

Robert Brierly, hero of the piece as done by Charles Pope and May Edwards, the sacrificing wife as played by Virginia Howard [3] were both declared "most perfect." Mr. Leman (the detective) and Aldrich (the thief) were "exceedingly well played," according to the critic, who believed with Shakespeare that players ought to " 'Hold the mirror up to nature' and teach the young the dangers they run by keeping company with the vicious and depraved." Hence, the next night, and again on the next, Virginians filled Maguire's to run the emotional gamut and learn through nature.

4

Sutliff now resorted to a Mazeppa modelled on the character of Julia Robust, kept Tommy Peel and Señorita Maria doing their double jig, and presented the romantic musical drama in two acts and seven tableaux, entitled *The Brigands* — a piece laid in Italy. The characters represented robbers, French students, dancing girls, the governor and the secretary of Rome, and an assortment of travelers.

The benefits of Charley Rhodes and Señorita Maria were "crowded affairs," Maria appearing for the first time in Washoe as Charles II in *Faint Heart*. Next night a new sensation, *The Quaker City*, was the attraction at Sutliff's Music Hall.

"Virginians are not niggard in their patronage of merit such as possessed by Miss Howard," stated the *Bulletin* in announcing her benefit for the middle of April. The choice was *Fanchon the Cricket*, which Charles Pope translated from the French especially for the beneficiary since it gave a "fine opportunity of exhibiting the range of her ability." Cricket as an insolent, rude, ragged girl, wild as an untamed colt, was an

---

[3] The Virginia Probate Court had that day granted the former Mrs. Charles Pope a divorce from Pete Cunningham and the right to resume her maiden name of Virginia Howard.

extreme contrast to the Cricket as a refined, polished, gracious lady. Miss Howard pleased her audience as both, and she fairly "brought down the house in that singular dance with her shadow." Every character was well performed and Schreiner's "Nightingale Overture" was "as usual" encored. The benefit concluded with *The Taming of the Shrew*.

Half the people of the town next night rushed to a fire in the northern part of Virginia while the only fire bell clanged, whistles blew, and "volumes of smoke" belched from Gould's Mill. The fire out — if not the dread of it — theatre-goers hurried back to Maguire's and enjoyed *The Ticket of Leave Man* for the fourth time within the week.[4]

Another regrettable thing happened that night, not another fire, but a fight, and unfortunately it took place on the stage of the Opera House. A "pitched battle between two actors," Louis Aldrich and Jimmy Griffith, stopped the show. Even after the curtain fell and they were being "formally dismissed," the audience could hear the "tumultuous noise" of continued fighting. Aldrich, whom some blamed for the trouble, was "stamped into a condition of insensibility." At the Old Bowery that same evening a shooting occurred between two or three professionals. No wonder actors' nerves were on edge, some had been playing continuously since early March.

Schiller's German tragedy of *The Robbers*, "admirably performed" with Miss Howard as Amelia, Pope as Charles de Moor, and Leman as old de Moor, closed the week at Maguire's. The troupe now took a one-night rest while the Germania Singing Society, the Virginia Glee Club, and local theatrical amateurs bestowed on Comstockers "a musical treat" as well as "heaps of fun" with *The Four Bald Heads*.

---

[4] One evening with the cry of "Fire!" and the accompanying rush of Comstockers into the streets, two men of Eagle Engine Company No. 3, trying to take their machine down Taylor Street, lost control. The heavy engine gained momentum, threshed about, nearly crushing the firemen in charge. Then escaping them, it chased two screaming ladies, gained velocity, rounded the corner into busy C Street, scattered the crowds, sheered off at another corner, and finally landed side up in a cellar excavation.

Performed "for the first time in the Territory," the comic opera of *The Four Bald Heads; or, Misery Loves Company*, composed by Carl Musch and especially arranged by Professor F. Grambbs, was "fully appreciated by the hundreds of ladies and their cavaliers, who paid a boosted price for admission to the Opera House. Done entirely in German, the "comicalities and excellent acting" of the comic opera were, so Virginia newspapers declared, "a great success, the most perfect thing of the kind in dress, acting, and singing ever before seen." San Francisco's *Call*, however, reviewed Virginia's amateur performance of *The Four Bald Heads* as "a ridiculous affair."

By special request the professionals at the Opera House repeated *Fanchon the Cricket* and *The Taming of the Shrew*, patrons afterwards attending a Sanitary Ball at the Gold Hill Theatre and at the What Cheer Saloon. It was three in the morning. The night shift had gone into the mines, but at both dances the floors were filled with revelers. Suddenly a scream of "Fire!" stampeded everyone into the streets. The What Cheer was blazing and the flames were spreading, streaking the sky with a "ruddy glare." Mine whistles wailed. People roused from sleep pushed frantically into the streets. Red-faced and panting local firemen arrived through the mud with their engines. Virginia fire companies came down to help battle the fire with water and axes. Fortunately the *Gold Hill News* building escaped; as did the new theatre, but $25,000 worth of property lay in ashes.[5]

<h2 style="text-align:center">5</h2>

For weeks Comstockers had been anticipating the arrival of Mr. and Mrs. S. M. Irwin, who had just completed "a long

---

[5] One good came from the disaster: the city fathers of that "sober burg" of Gold Hill ordered hydrants and iron pipe for water lines to help battle future fires. Then, in appreciation of the "almost superhuman efforts" of the Virginia fire companies — Eagle Engine No. 1, No. 3, and Hook and Ladder — in fighting the recent fire, Gold Hill sent the Virginia "boys" several baskets of champagne.

engagement at Salt Lake City." Artemus Ward [6] had seen them there, not unaware that the Austinites "hoped" the Irwins would favor them with, at least, one evening of entertainment. Though they had "elicited golden opinions from all sorts of people," the Irwins did not stop to gather them in Reese River, but hurried on to keep an engagement at the Opera House, where they "came fully up to their reputations" in *Evadne* and the comedy of *In and Out of Place*, Mrs. Irwin sustaining six characters — even Menken did no better.

Although the Great Star Company "never acquitted themselves more admirably" and Mrs. Irwin in her six-character burletta "kept the house convulsed with laughter," still the troupe at Maguire's that April 21 "played to a slim house." The Washoites, observing their unwritten rule of local patronage, were attending a benefit for the military at Sutliff's, where Captain Murphy was presented a sword formerly belonging to "one of Guerrilla Morgan's men." While a lively Scottish dance, Ethopian wit, and a laughing burlesque were being applauded at Music Hall, a mine fight was going on underground that night, workmen having broken into the tunnel of a rival company, though the timbers over which the men fought had saved their lives from eighty-four feet of water.

To keep Comstockers laughing rather than fighting, the manager of the Opera House offered an "attractive bill": the petite comedy of *A Day in Paris*, the genteel comedy of *Perfection*, and the comedietta of *The Married Rake*. The audience laughed, and they went home laughing. Comedy was needed to fill seats at the legitimate theatre.

---

[6] A letter arrived from Artemus Ward and E. P. Hingston telling of their "big business" in Salt Lake, Denver, and Central City, and supposing that the story of their capture by the Indians (as related in the *Missouri Democrat*) had reached Virginia.

Winn and Center, taking advantage of continued interest in Ward, advertised now in Comstock papers as though quoting the "great Wax-Figger Showman" as "never better treated nor oftener in his life" and the Babes as "delighted with the attentions shown them," of course, at Winn and Center's Saloon.

Topliffe's Theatre (recently the Old Bowery) reopened now. Renamed the Athenaeum with Pat Holland as manager, a troupe of minstrels — all of them female — presented "variety programmes of choruses, ballads, songs, repartees, jigs, dances, walk-arounds, etc."

6

On the tercentenary of the birth of William Shakespeare, the Opera House presented the five-act tragedy of *Othello*, featuring Pope as Othello, Irwin as Iago, Mrs. Irwin as Desdemona, and Miss Howard as Emilia. Sutliff's offering that April 23 was *The Bard of Avon* as arranged by L. F. Beatty and such specialty acts as a sparring exhibition and the gymnastic stunts of two good French performers. "Appreciative audiences" responded to the efforts at both theatres.

Of the next Maguire offering, *Nick of the Woods,* a Virginia critic labeled it "a miserable burlesque without plot or point or language to recommend it," but he praised the performance of *Pocahontas* and mentioned an accident at Maguire's that morning during the drawing of prizes in Frederick's Gift Enterprise — the wheel broke throwing 20,000 stubs all over the stage. On their way to enjoy the Irwin's sixth night in a laughable three-piece bill, the Washoites noted approvingly that the new city jail and marshal's office were taking shape opposite Maguire's theatre, former site of Benham's foul-smelling livery stable.

After a Grand Celebration of the I.O.O.F. members, including the dedication of the new Dayton Theatre on April 26, the admirers of Mr. and Mrs. Irwin came in "fashionable dress" to honor the Salt Lake Thespians on their benefit and last Virginia appearance. A Washoe première, *The Marble Heart*, a sensation drama, held the Opera House boards and was followed by the humorous operatic extravaganza of *Po-Ca-Hon-Tas,* which reviewers thought was "alone worth the price of admission."

7

With the Irwins gone, Maguire advertised "the unprecedented success of Virginia Howard, Charles Pope, and Walter
Leman and the entire talent of the company" in *Ingomar* and
the laughable comedietta of *Box and Cox,* which had titillated
California audiences since the gold rush.[7] Although devoid
of direct feminine interest, this light farce held Comstock
attention through a series of fast, humorous surprises, involving a quarrel over the room in which Cox, the journeyman
hatter, slept by night and Box, the printer, slept by day. On
April 27 the troupe played to a small audience. The *Bulletin*
reporter did not admire the wild and improbable *Ingomar*
"very enthusiastically," but insisted the company was "really
a very meritorious one" and he was "astonished that they
were not better patronized by the lovers of amusement."

The next two nights the Opera House was filled when *The
Wife's Secret,* considered "one of the most beautiful and soul-
touching plays on the English stage," was performed with
"consummate knowledge of the characters being personated."
And as evidenced by the "roars of laughter, the audience saw
Box and Cox anew in the hands of Jimmy Griffith."

The last day of April was the Nevada première of *The
Mormons; or, Life in Salt Lake City* and the "side-splitting
farce," *A Kiss in the Dark.* But those Comstockers who did
not see *The Mormons* but went to Sutliff's instead (the troupe
had returned that day from a swing through the territory)
laughed at the farce of *Irish Corroberee,* applauded the jig
dance, and gasped at the flying trapeze act of Johnny Tuers
and M. J. Quinn.

To compete with Maguire's and Sutliff's that last day of
April the Athenaeum took from both its competitors, Pat
Holland, having engaged Mr. and Mrs. L. F. Beatty, Ida May,

---

[7] Players often found it next to impossible to secure dramatic scripts, once paying an ounce of gold dust for one copy of *Box and Cox.*

and Joey De Vere,[8] presented an amusing burlesque of *The Mormons*. The evening was going well, "everything lovely and the goose hangs high," when suddenly a man in the audience shouted an insult at an actress on the stage. Another man fought the insulter all the way to the door, where Peter Larkin and his pistol also got involved. No one was killed.[9]

Several wandering Italian minstrels, playing "soft voluptuous music" at Comstock street corners, reminded the *Union* editor of "morning air laden with orange blossoms." To which the *Bulletin* retorted, "and garlic . . . bad macaroni, filthy cheese, old clothes, and time-gone poverty. If these wandering musicians would confine themselves to such airs as 'When this Cruel War is Over,' 'John Brown's Body' . . . or even 'Der Bully Lager Beir,' 'Der Bolat Soulger Boy,' and the like, we could stomach them on most villainous, untamed catgut."

The "wandering minstrels" neglected Genoa, but this slight was hardly noticed so busy were the patriotic people of Nevada's first town raising money, buying a gift with it, and planning a "Grand Presentation Ball, including heavenly dancing and a gorgeous supper." After presenting Captain Wallace and Company G, First Regiment of Nevada Territory Volunteers, a "splendid flag" and a "splendid sword," the citizens and their guests "set the chairs back, tuned up the fiddle, threw care to the dogs," and went in "for a good time," only to be interrupted by two "loud-mouthed traitors," who were arrested at a near-by saloon. The patriotic dancers thereupon collected enough money to send the Copperheads to Fort Churchill, where soon they were "engaged in packing sand" around the quadrangle.[10]

---

[8] In Judge Atwill's chambers a few days later Miss De Vere was "joined in holy bonds of padlock" to a Virginia man, Joseph Elridge.

[9] Another melodeon episode of Virginia to reach print was that of "a much noted ballad singer and admired barelegged danseuse," who " 'left for parts unknown' with divers and sundry small and large bills unpaid in the hands of the poor dupes who were carried away by her sweet alluring smile."

[10] *Gold Hill Daily News*, May 4, 1864.

25

May 1864

Slim Houses and Fat

1

The first nights of May *Charles II, Don Caesar de Bazan,* and *The Honeymoon* played to "slim houses," though that fact probably was not the cause of John Burns' suffering a stroke at the Opera House. However, the reduced box office receipts may have kept Tom Maguire from paying all his bills; for A. & T. Torning had instituted a suit "to recover a balance of $417 . . . for work done and traveling expenses for painting the Opera House sashes, floors, casings, etc., in San Francisco and at Virginia City."

A performance at Maguire's for Hook and Ladder Company received a "goodly attendance." At Charley Pope's grand complimentary benefit too, "every seat was filled," testifying to Washoe's high regard for the actor as "one of the most gentlemanly, talented and deserving" in the profession. Pope, playing his "famous character in *Richard III,*" was frequently applauded. Mr. Beatty, a volunteer from Sutliff's, now came on as did the Germania Singing Society, and Professor Dobbs and lady. A "grand musical melange" and *A Kiss in the Dark* concluded the "most successful" evening, for which the former Washoe miner thanked the audience "in a neat farewell address."

Dion Boucicault's *The Octoroon* played to "very slim houses" both nights of May 4 and 5 in spite of excellent performances. Virginia's streets, dark, muddy, and dangerous, were undoubtedly a deterrent [1] as may have been the dance at Huffaker's.[2] But business was no better for *The Lady of Lyons, Paddy Miles' Boy,* or the Washoe première of another Boucicault drama, *The Poor of New York.*

Attendance picked up sharply at the Opera House on May 9, when "most of the leading men" of Storey County tendered a benefit to Miss Howard [3] for her "uniformly lady-like deportment and her accomplishments in the histrionic art." For her "last appearance but one prior to her departure for the States" Miss Howard chose "the most beautiful and soultouching play" of *The Wife's Secret* and the three-act comedy of *The Serious Family.*

---

[1] Had the contract for 16 lamps (at $15.50 per post, payable in scrip at 10 per cent) been completed, theatre-goers — and the young lady who lost her "nice India-rubber overshoe" in the mud on C Street — would have greatly appreciated the light.

[2] Some Virginia people enroute to the dance at this popular place in Truckee Meadows were injured when their team, frightened by a rabbit, bolted, dragging the buggy down a forty-foot deep canyon.

[3] Since the Opera House was closed one Sunday, Miss Howard, along with Mayor Arick and other "distinguished civil and military" guests, enjoyed a fashionable wedding at Steamboat Springs. On their return to Virginia the whole party — having, like present-day Nevadans, an antipathy for umbrellas — got drenched in a heavy downpour. As a result, the *Bulletin* composed and published a dozen timely verses such as the following:

ALL ABOUT UMBRELLAS
Dear editor, I'd have you know
    I'm a soft hearted "feller";
Abused, because I can't refuse
    To lend my new umbrella!

It rains, and I must stay at home!
    For Jack — confound the "feller" —
Last night, to go to Tom Maguire's
    Must borrow my umbrella.

I had one once, I lent to Miss ———
    Her foolish pride did tell her
'Twas new, and had a genteel look
    That handsome silk umbrella!

She went to some grand country ball;
    An accident befell her,
Some one purloined it; and I lost
    That valued silk umbrella!

WALTER M. LEMAN
This popular character actor wrote
the dedicatory address for the
opening of Maguire's Comstock Opera
House, and played many seasons
along Nevada's early theatrical circuit.

THE COMSTOCK'S GREAT FLOUR SACK PROCESSION
Losing a Reese River election bet, Reuel Gridley triggered a chain
of events that included these processions, a rash of public auctions
and dances, a unique seal for Austin, national recognition of
Silverland, and culminated in raising thousands of dollars for the
"Sanitary Fund" — the Red Cross of Civil War times.
Courtesy, Los Angeles Public Library.

STEPHEN MASSETT
Globe trotter, actor, writer, singer,
lecturer, and mimic, who entertained
"large and fashionable" Washoe
audiences with serio-comic programs.
Courtesy, University of California.

SAM WELLS
The famous basso profundo, versatile
leader of the hilarity-provoking
Minstrels, plunged Nevada into sorrow
by his accidental death while riding
horseback to the theatre the night of
his own Comstock benefit performance.
Courtesy, Harvard College Library

But mud lay a foot thick in the streets again and the papers, aware that ladies could "scarcely be expected to be present," felt that hardy miners, rich merchants, prosperous stock-brokers,[4] and the "masculines generally" would be there. They were. Maguire's "was better filled last night that it has been for a month previous," remembered the *Bulletin* theatrical critic, who was astonished too at seeing "so many ladies as well as Governor Nye in the audience."

When Mr. Leman came on stage with a telegram announcing General Butler's capture of Petersburg, the audience rose, lustily cheering. The orchestra played a special overture, Josie and Mattie Aldrich did a double Irish jig, Professor Dodds and lady performed their intriguing "ethereal suspension act" without wires, and the benefit concluded humorously with *The Serious Family*. "To say that the performance was excellent were superfluous," the reviewer concluded.

Next evening the treasurer, doorkeeper, and other attachés of the Opera House were honored with a benefit; and again Comstockers packed the house to enjoy the last appearance of Pope as Richelieu in the Bulwer play of the same name, Miss Howard as Julia de Mortimer, and Mr. Leman. Many novelties were introduced by volunteers from Sutliff's and the Athenaeum. And Professor Dodds did brass ring tricks.

2

Although Miss Howard, Pope, and Leman had made plans to leave for the East, stopping at "Reese River, Salt Lake City, and Denver for performances," they were prevailed upon to accept a re-engagement for "three nights more" (May 11, 12, and 13). With Mr. Beatty, brought over from Music Hall, the troupe presented *Damon and Pythias*, the comedietta of

---

[4] When cold, wet, and uneasy miners milled in C Street one evening that week, it was Thomas Barclay, president of the Virginia Stock Market, speaking from the balcony of the International, who reassured them with a promise that on Saturday speakers would "discuss the matter of taxing the mines as proposed by Congress."

Sketches in India, and the tragedy of *Macbeth,* for which "the favorite comedian, C. Chapman, volunteered."

Thirty-eight habitués of the Opera House, considering Walter Leman a gentleman and an artist "without a superior anywhere" in social life and "in his line of characters without a peer" and desiring "to manifest in a substantial manner their high appreciation," requested Leman to name a benefit. Deeply touched by the kind words and the offer, the actor chose his favorite character of Sir Peter Teazle in *The School for Scandal.*

No doubt there was truth in a critic's appraisal of this play as the "most delightful comedy" in two hundred years of British playwriting, especially with Mr. Leman as Teazle, Miss Howard as Lady Teazle, and Pope and Beatty in the parts of Charles and Joseph Surface. Professor Dodds again suspended his lady in a reclining position several feet above the floor of the stage — "like a good many fellows who knock around Virginia without any visible means of support." At the close of the program, Leman feelingly addressed his friends, and when he made reference to the "Bright Star of Nevada," the house went into a "perfect furore of applause." "If Walter Leman ever entertained a doubt of his popularity with the mass of theatre-going public of Virginia," observed the *Union,* "he most certainly had that doubt removed from his mind last night."

3

Again the engagements of the three outstanding professionals playing at Maguire's were extended, until June 17 the bills promised. But the star of *Jack Sheppard; or, The House-Breaker of the Last Century,* hailed as "one of the greatest hits of the season," was the "really meritorious actress" Madame Marie Duret who had, however, "a powerful company, in fact one of the most extensive and best that ever appeared in our city" to support her. As Jack Sheppard, a character with a genius for selecting a house worth robbing and for breaking in and out of same, Marie Duret, who never appeared to better advantage on the stage "than when she dons the unmentionables," not only "picked a pocket and a lock with equal dexterity," but "scaled a wall as expeditiously as a fish-wife did a herring."

Having for six years starred in the spectacular piece, dreadful with gallows and death, Duret took special care at the Opera House not to get the rope about her neck too tight as she had once done in California while enacting the hanging scene. Though Mrs. Sheppard (Miss Howard) had her romantic moments, and Winnifred Wood (Mrs. Chapman or Mrs. Beatty) and Mr. Wood (Leman) important roles, the last scene was the thriller. Then Blueskin (Pope) hurled from him the body of Jack Sheppard (Mme. Duret); the soldiers fired into the mob charging with sticks and stones; Blueskin shot and wounded the thief taker (Beatty); an officer killed Blueskin; and the curtain fell on shooting, uproar, and wild confusion.

The Opera House was "crowded" all three nights, and resplendent, too, with uniformed men from Fort Churchill. And Virginia's new paper, *The Daily Old Piute* (the *Bulletin* had just died), gave an earthy review: "Our people are rank, spank, plum deranged in not witnessing the rendering of Mr. J. Sheppard, Esq., the celebrated English robber and his conferees." [5] Even editors Lovejoy and Gillespie admitted, "We have abused Maguire's when we thought their performances bilks, and they got mad about it, and now they have done well we'll say so, and they can get mad and be d--m--d."

For the evening of May 17 the Opera House announced

---

[5] To each actor or his performance the *Old Piute* editor assigned such descriptions as "unequalled" (Madame Duret), "unparalleled" (Mrs. Chapman), "splendidly" (Pope), and for Leman's Mr. Wood, "nine cheers." In fact, the editor felt "disposed to jump . . . onto the stage and hug the women one at a time so as to make the maneuver 'a link of lengthened sweetness, long drawn out' and order cigars and things for the male performers."

"the glorious success of the favorite artiste Marie Duret in her great impersonation of Miami, the Huntress of the Mississippi" in Buckstone's romantic drama of *Green Bushes.* How long Miami held is not known. The troupe had in preparation *The Old House on the Bridge* and the new sensation drama of *Cartouche, the Terror of Paris.* But other than with her initial opening piece of *Jack Sheppard,* Mme. Duret seems to have played to slim and slimmer houses.

4

For more riotous fun the Washoites went over to Sutliff's to enjoy a grand suspension act "a la Dodds" by Tuers and Quinn; the farce of *The Mischievous Nigger,* in which Comstockers were convinced "that Tommy Peel and Señorita Maria can dance better than anyone." Audiences also enjoyed T. F. Barnwell "the well-known tenor singer," who with Kavanagh and Miss Florence never left the stage "without a rousing encore"; the Hanlon Brothers performing feats of daring; the farce of *The Dumb Belle;* and on May 19 *Robert Macaire; or, The Two Murders,* which was "put upon the stage in good shape."

Silver City, Dayton, Fort Churchill, Carson, and Genoa enjoyed melodeon fare when entertainers from Sutliff's and the Athenaeum made brief one-and two-night visits. Back in Virginia the Athenaeum with "a high old" company that catered to lower tastes — at least, Miss Emma Paster left the company suddenly, so rumor said, because "she could not stand the vulgarity of that stage" — played a few nights then closed its doors.

Though Music Hall as the sole melodeon drew the fattest houses, Washoites were not averse to attending the "Listerian Performances" of the sprightly little woman famous as Lisle Lester, "intelligent, a rare genius, and personified brightness" at the courthouse. Here, too, appeared Miss Emma Hardinge, who — "though an English woman," apolo-

gized the *Union* — had become "intimately acquainted with
manners, peculiarities and institutions of many people from
a long experience and travel in many countries," so that once
heard, Washoites "desired to hear her again." And they did
so on ten different occasions, paying for each a dollar admission to enjoy such lectures as "George Washington and
Napoleon," "Life and Times of Satan," and "The Battle of
Waterloo."

Maguire's was in temporary doldrums. Nevertheless, on
May 23 it rated even a *Union* review, but only because it was
the benefit night of the First Regiment of Nevada Territorial
Volunteers. For a time it seemed that two theatres would be
required, Maguire's for the program and the Gold Hill Theatre for the dancing. The latter house was finally deemed
unnecessary, but a Gold Hill merchant advertised a new stock
of clothing with "So dress yourselves gallus, ye gallants all,
and dance the cat-choker at the Volunteer's Ball."

The theatrical part of the evening (*The Morning Call,
Queen of Abruzza,* and *The Serious Family*) was "a complete
success, the theatre filled to overflowing, and the actors, as is
always the case upon such occasions, performed their parts
better than usual." But the program lasted until after one
o'clock, which was rather late, "especially for us 'outside
barbarians,'" grinned the *News* editor, and those who "delighted in the mazes of the dance" wanting "to get down to
the business of the Grand Civic and Military Ball." Certainly
the Nevada Volunteers reaped a good harvest, aided as they
were by some six hundred soldiers with their "brass buttons
and prompt military bearing" on leave from Fort Churchill

---

[6] The question of metallic versus greenback money caused dissension in Washoe.
Gold Hill citizens with torches, anti-greenback transparencies, and mottoes (one
read, "Teamsters: not a team stirs without pay in gold and silver currency")
paraded through the Lode and up to the anti-greenback meeting in Virginia. In
Reese River "rowdy" money meetings, however, did not keep miners from finally
agreeing that with a raise in wages they would accept greenbacks as pay. Business

for "a big time" with nine-months pay — if in greenbacks [6]—
in their pockets.

Next night J. D. McGowan made his reappearance on the
Opera House boards "after an absence of seven years and
was well received." But at Sutliff's the audience, asked to pick
the best hornpipe dancer and the best big shoe dancer from
Peel, Mason, Tuers, O'Neil, and six Cornish miners, became
so excited and noisy that nothing could be decided. The curtain was dropped to end the show.

When next day Major Ball paid off the cavalry, "Virginia,
Dayton, and Carson City vomited forth a flood of sports and
gamblers," who set up business in Fort Churchill, but when
drunk they received the same cure as the soldiers — time in
the guard house. Several well-known minstrels also went over
to the Fort "to give exhibitions," expecting "to reap a golden
harvest as long as the money lasted."

Though the *Golden Era* reported, "Madame Marie Duret
is doing a fine business at Maguire's in Virginia," it would
seem the "fine business" really referred to benefits, especially
the one for the Emmett Guards, which netted them "upwards
of $700" and another for Sutliff's Señorita Maria, which was
a "most gratifying affair," the Opera House "being crowded,
in spite of one of the heaviest rainstorms of the season, and
the mud knee-deep in the streets." Mme. Duret appeared as
King Charles opposite Mr. Beatty's Guy Gomez in the petite
comedy of *Faint Heart Never Won Fair Lady* and introduced
a new piece called *The Creole,* in which she "never appeared

men published cards stating that they did not want a currency change, but, as
Virginia and San Francisco merchants were accepting greenbacks, they felt compelled to do likewise.

A local Shoshone, who owed an Austin merchant two dollars, changed his lone
silver "cart wheel" for two greenbacks and cancelled his debt. This Indian shrewd-
ness amused everyone but the merchant.

Most Washoites favored metal coin and ridiculed anyone paying in paper. However, "to accommodate those who wished to get rid of greenbacks," especially the
soldiers, J. A. Wright offered tickets for his forthcoming gift lottery in both coin
and greenbacks. If bought with metal coin, tickets cost one dollar each; with paper
money, they sold seven for $10 or 15 tickets for $20.

to better advantage." Between the two plays the beneficiary in "La Zingralla" and the Spanish dance of "La Morena" almost "excelled herself and won the applause of every person present."

To compete with Señorita Maria's benefit, Music Hall featured a prize clog dance between Mason and Peel for $100 a side. Interest was at fever heat; for more than $1000 had been placed in bets by members of the audience. Peel probably was the better dancer, but Mason had more friends, "which in this Territory makes a heap of difference," observed a local critic. Later the judges declared the match a draw; and Mason immediately challenged Peel to another clog contest at $150 a side — so more Sutliff excitement appeared in the offing.

5

Exciting too, were the events surrounding a sack of grayish, coarsely ground flour. Even an Austin duel [7] rated neither the newspaper space nor the interest, which ultimately reached national proportions, of a 50-pound bag of ordinary flour that swelled the Sanitary Fund to unprecedented amounts. Reuel Colt Gridley, an Austin merchant, had made a bet regarding the election of the first mayor of Austin (Democrat David E. Buel against Union man Charles Holbrook). The Union man won the election.

Following the conditions of the wager, Gridley shouldered the flag-and-ribbon-bedecked flour sack in its buckskin cover and, preceded by the Austin Brass Band playing "Old John Brown," started his march, but was soon joined by local politicians and cheering crowds while mill whistles screeched approval. What inspired the next event no account makes clear, but Mr. Gridley began an auction by bidding $200 for

---

[7] A four-month-old dispute over an election at Amador (near Austin) grew to dueling intensity. At daybreak 400 Reese Riverites witnessed the exchange of shots. The affair turned out pleasantly; the duelers left the field as friends.

his own sack and turning the money over to the Sanitary Fund.

The sack sold again, and again. "What with money, scrip, stocks, and town lots, it appeared as if the whole town of Austin was about to be swallowed up in the maelstrom of the Sanitary Fund." The grand total from the mining town "yet obscured by sagebrush" is commemorated in the city seal of Austin: a picture of the sack of flour and the figures $5000 encircled by the words, "Sanitary Fund." [8]

Though hardly so spectacularly, other Washoe towns helped the Fund, but the usually generous Virginians were adamant until the chairman A. B. Paul called another mass meeting. Then an "immense concourse of civilians" followed the military companies, a color guard from Fort Churchill, and the Metropolitan Brass Band into the already packed Opera House. By the time the glee clubs sang, Tom Fitch spoke, Miss Hardinge reported first-hand experiences of wounded soldiers, and the many gifts (including a silver brick, jewelry, and mining stock) had been sold and resold, Mr. Gridley, himself, entered the theatre to such long applause the chairman feared "it would shake the building down." Further sales brought the total to $5,262.50.

---

[8] (Austin) *Reese River Reveille,* April 26, 1864; March 18, 25, 1950; March 21, 1953. Although not a man of wealth nor a Northerner by birth, Gridley auctioned his sack in the principal areas of the West and in every important city of the East. His efforts netted the Sanitary Fund over $170,000, no small amount when one considers that daily wages then were nearer two than twenty dollars. President Bellows of the Sanitary Commission wrote the *Reveille* predicting that Gridley's sack of flour would be "more renowned in history than any other sack since the sack of Troy."

Never a robust man, Gridley did not return to Austin; instead, he sought to recuperate in the milder climate of California. A *Reveille* editorial of 1867 inspired veterans of both the North and the South to arrange a benefit for the sick and impoverished man. Held in the Methodist Church, the evening's speaking netted $700. Three years later Gridley was dead. Today in the Nevada Historical Society one may see the famous sack, still decorated exactly as Gridley carried it. The Gridley store in Austin on Highway 50 is a historical landmark.

But at ten the next morning Paul, Gridley, and reporters climbed into carriages and followed the Band and some two hundred men to Gold Hill and Silver City for lively auctions and "the moistenings" of many throats. By four o'clock "the Army of the Lord," as Mark Twain called it, arrived at Dayton "with flags flying and music blasting." [9] Judge Haydon as auctioneer declared the bag was "self-raising flour" that would "raise itself to Richmond."

Upon returning to Virginia, Paul climbed the speaker's platform on C Street and informed some two thousand assembled Comstockers that (in spite of "the amount of lager beer drank by Marshall of the *Union*, Clemens of the *Enterprise*, and Gillespie of the *Old Piute* while on their journey with *that* sack") $10,000 had been subscribed.[10] Then with cheers for "Gridley, Paul, General Grant, Abe Lincoln, and the Austin sack of flour," the Washoites started Gridley on his way to California and national fame, and to Nevada immortality.[11]

---

[9] Mark Twain later did his version of the flour sack in *Roughing It*.

[10] Pickpockets did not fare well that exciting Monday. More of them than usual were caught and "taken to the station-house."

[11] For another of the many accounts of the Sanitary Fund drive, see the *Virginia Evening Bulletin* of May 16, 1864.

Beginning Borrasca Days

1

The three popular professionals, Virginia Howard, Charles Pope, and Walter Leman, had long planned leaving Washoe for the East. Finally in June Pope and Leman boarded an outbound stage, Miss Howard having "backed out," a facetious reporter declared, because "Brigham would not respect the Pope and would freeze to her for his one hundred and twenty-fifth wife." Hence, Miss Howard was on hand to help Maguire's troupe with the "excellent bill" presented to a good house on June 2, the joint benefit night for Louis Aldrich, his wife, and sisters — Misses Mattie and Josie Aldrich.

Mme. Duret also stayed on in Virginia and, no doubt, on June 7 volunteered for the benefit of Washoe Engine Company No. 4 at Maguire's and the National Guard's benefit at Sutliff's, both gay with flags and "military adornment." In both instances the theatres were packed for "the most successful entertainments and dances." [1]

Besides the regulars, John Torrence and J. H. Leroy — making his Virginia debut as Old Pete — joined the Opera House troupe and helped present *The Octoroon,* "a sad and truthful commentation on the horrors of slavery." Though seats were well filled for the opening presentation, Burns and

---

[1] Enroute to the benefits, Comstockers took special note of Virginia policemen in their new gray uniforms, single-breasted with a row of black buttons, and the "official star plainly in sight."

June 7 was a wisely chosen date as the previous day Gould and Curry had paid a dividend of $125 per foot. Even so, the stock fell from $6000 to $2500, "a public calamity with bears taking advantage of tight dollars."

Maguire often were pressed to make ends meet. Nevertheless, when some gentlemen, raising some money for a man ill with rheumatism, asked for a free ticket to *The Octoroon,* Burns handed them 50 tickets, which raised a sum that kept the sick man for a considerable time.[2]

Although a caravan of camels heavily packed with goods and amusement merchandise left for Reese River, two hundred teams loaded with freight struggled between Gold Hill and Carson, and lamps were almost ready to light Virginia with gas, business — especially show business — was not good. "Maguire's has been doing a very poor business," reiterated the *Call* correspondent, "and Sutliff's but little better."

2

Even the ever-popular minstrels found it difficult to obtain employment. The McFarland Troupe and the Sam Able Company played Washoe too "with poor success" though the latter met hardships with pioneer theatrical fortitude. Arrested in Markleeville for playing without a license, Able's left town in the middle of the night on a two-horse cart, which broke down. Faced with jail prospects if they returned, the whole company trudged on into Carson — no little trek — and a few hours later were appearing at the "entirely remodeled and renovated, comfortable and elegant" Carson's Saloon Theatre. Though they also played other Washoe towns, the company returned to California "flat broke."

One group of jobless blackface entertainers, called themselves the San Francisco Minstrels, made a one-night stand in Genoa, crossed the Sierras, and headed for Portland, Oregon. A more optimistic group, deciding to remain with Washoe, rented Topliffe's Theatre; renamed it the New Lead; and presented melodeon entertainment, which the *Union*

[2] Maguire paid the funeral expenses of a child who died from burns at Maguire's San Francisco Opera House though the fire was no fault of the management.

reported as "extravagantly patronized" by those who got a "glass of beer along with the performance — both for 25¢!"

The borrasca clouds of hard times were beginning to gather and discerning people could have read meaning in the news item: "Theatres are not doing well here." But the change was gradual with bursts of activity and then lulls. According to a Virginia reporter:

> Times are hard only in a comparative degree, as gauged by a year ago. Gaming houses still do a fair business; drinking saloons are yet patronized; and the theatres, melodeons, and hurdy-gurdy houses are well filled nightly. . . Horseback riding is much indulged in by the fair sex. . . These, with fast men and fast horses, throng the chief thoroughfare, C Street, on fine days.

Embracing these "fine days" Sutliff renovated Music Hall and added to his troupe, "of whom the least in size but not the least in attractions by any means" was little Ida Gibson, who performed her parts "with the assurance of a full-grown actor," amazing audiences with her Shirley-Temple-like faculty of complete naturalness. The Fillmore sisters billed for days, however, did not appear in their double-dance because they had "nothing to wear" though with precaution they had sent their wardrobes by "fast freight" over the Sierras.

Other "additions from San Francisco" included Miss Jessie Weaver, whom audiences hailed with enthusiasm, applauding her jig, danced "in a masterly manner" and repeated the next night along with the entire Sutliff troupe, who had volunteered for Johnny Tuers' benefit. Washoites applauded Johnny in "his favorite plantation jigs and dances and his inimitable jokes and repartees," as they did for Tommy Peel's benefit, which was "equal to anything seen at Sutliff's for weeks past."

Miss Emma Hardinge now delivered her last two "farewell lectures," reaping such "good opinions" that eighteen gentlemen requested to hear her "yet one more time" in "America and Her Destiny." Other Comstockers filled Maguire's to honor Mr. Shreiner and enjoy J. Maurin's Spanish song, a guitar solo, and "The Nightingale Polka," "The Crown of Diamonds," and "Postillion" — all done by a full brass band.

Over in Genoa thirty ladies had Union Hall "decorated in a style which would have done credit to Virginia," suspended gilded cages of "handsome, warbling canaries" about the ballroom, and with their escorts and guests enjoyed the "mazy waltz and the soul-inspiring quadrille" and tried their "luck at the grab bag or post office." So "successful" was this "ball of the season" that weeks later the Washoites were still marveling at the more than $700 raised for the Sanitary Fund, which was "very good, considering the hard times." [3]

3

Wrestling and prize fighting demanded amusement attention. And businessmen, even along C Street, closed their doors from noon to three (indicating their absences by "Gone to fight" signs), rushed to Mill Street, paid the dollar admittance, enjoyed the wrestling, and helped decide who won the $25 to $150 prizes that were "played for in Cornish Style." Even the school boys turned amateur pugilists, "wrestling and sparring and using lingo peculiar to the prize ring."

On June 4 two thousand spectators paid admission of $2.50 each, crowded inside a tight board fence, but twice that number swarmed over the hills outside unable to get in, to witness the Davis-Daly contest. That the fight was arranged "regardless of expense" shows Washoe's regard "for such exhibitions" even when held six miles from Virginia. By the seventh round Daly "threw up the sponge," thus declaring Davis the victor, but the crowds were "disappointed at the briefness of the contest."

---

[3] Even with the hard times certain citizens of Dayton, desiring more than a bare building in which to worship, each paid a dollar admission, filled the Dayton Theatre, enjoyed a "grand Concert," and with the proceeds furnished the new Methodist Church. Father O'Reilley, noting this generosity, urged completion of the first church for Gold Hill.

Better satisfied were those fun-lovers who converged on Washoe City. Driving past the new courthouse and the church of Gothic style ("surely an ornament to the city"), they stopped at Winters' Race Track to enjoy the races and "Jim and his bucking mustang."

Commemorating the eighty-eighth anniversary of the Battle of Bunker Hill on June 17, Curry Engine Company brought their new engine into town "amid becoming ceremony and pomp preceded by the Euterpe Brass Band." Then they presented three silver trumpets to deserving fire chiefs and with Warren Engine Company and other Carson firemen paraded 225 strong.[4]

4

At Maguire's the "mother of 20 children" Mrs. George Chapman, contributing "something new and interesting," took a "substantial benefit." To recoup for poor houses Maguire now sent Frank Mayo back to Virginia to appear as the soft-voiced Dr. Savage in *Playing with Fire.* As Mayo had "crowds of friends," a "good house assembled." Of course, Mme. Duret (Mrs. Savage), Miss Howard (Mrs. Waverly), and Louis Aldrich (the susceptible Uncle Timothy) gave Mayo "excellent" support. Comstockers applauded the program the next night, too, and during the week of June 20 Mayo's Logardere in *The Duke's Motto* and his Robert Briarly in the sensational *The Ticket of Leave Man.*

Meanwhile Sutliff featured the Fillmore sisters — their wardrobes having caught up with them — O'Neil, and Billy Robinson, for whose benefit Daly and Davis appeared in a friendly set-to. The New Lead advertised a "tip top entertainment" and a "rush," which did not materialize, so soon

---

[4] Having named their company for the famous Dr. Joseph Warren, "the first distinguished martyr in the cause of American freedom," Warren Company paraded their fire engine "bright and handsome as a newly cast eagle," applauded the speaking at the pavilion, where by night, "newly decorated and elegant floors laid," they held the Grand Firemen's Ball, at which the San Francisco firemen's pin-up Miss Hitchcock, was the honored guest.

closed its doors. The building became Topliffe's again, Miss Clarissa and others going over to the Free Concert Saloon.[5] On June 24 the Masonic Order in full regalia paraded [6]; then on to Sutliff's for an impressive program and a Grand Ball.

To off-set Mayo's "extraordinary" presentations, Sutliff brought in Harry Courtaine, "universally acknowledged as one of the most accomplished actors on the coast," [7] who,

---

[5] The New Lead advertising with:

  Care to our coffin adds a nail, no doubt,

  While every laugh is sure to draw one out,

and boasting an "elegant stage and all the accomplishments of a complete melodeon," gave free concerts that included "violins, harps, banjoes, and bones for instrumental music and the services of Miss Clarissa, Jonesey — 'The Peep O'Day Boy,' Sam Chase, and other eminent artistes."

[6] In the northern part of Virginia a Mexican festival was in progress. Mexican riders, on signal, dug the huge rowels of their Spanish spurs into the flanks of half-wild mustangs, made jump starts, and raced to a designated line. A woman who "rode like an Amazon" headed one of the troops in a similar event. Wild hilarious cries and twirling lariats accompanied these stake races, the bucking that was "almost professional," and the other vaquero contests, all hugely enjoyed by Mexicans, Spanish, Negroes, Chinamen, "and many white people."

[7] That Harry Courtaine was well educated and accomplished, a linguist as well as a singer, there was little doubt. The actor was handsome too, being "blessed by nature with an elegant figure, and his movements on the stage were grace itself," observed the pioneer actor and theatrical writer John H. McCabe, member of the original company that played Sacramento's Eagle Theatre, first building of California (1849) put up expressly for theatrical purposes.

Courtaine could have been a star but for a personal weakness. Tom Maguire had brought the comedian and his wife Emma Grattan to California from England in November of 1857 to appear at Maguire's San Francisco Opera House, where Courtaine won friends in the cast. One day he started a drinking spree, which Maguire, having been appraised of the actor's weakness, cut short by having him promptly lodged in jail. Feeling such treatment unjust for a first offense, the company unfortunately secured Courtaine's release.

Less than two years later the *San Francisco Call* in making an appraisal of California actors, noted that Courtaine, "a light and eccentric comedian," was playing at the Bella Union and observed: "Mr. Courtaine has had it in his power to place himself in a much more elevated position. Pecuniary worth, uncertain."

The next spring his wife, an attractive actress of chambermaid and burlesque roles, unable to stand the strain longer, left him and California. From then on Courtaine's life was, to quote McCabe again, "by turns on the stage, in the gutter, and the county jail," which he occupied so often that a cell was named after him. He was also involved with other actors and managers in an assault and battery suit (Carson City *Daily Silver Age*, October 2, 1862).

During one of Courtaine's sober spells Henry Sutliff signed him to appear at though London-born, did "prefer the blawsted Hamericans, you know." As the new manager of Music Hall, Courtaine invited the ladies to a "Minstrel and Dramatic Engagement" on Saturday afternoons. The *Era* reported: "In Washoe the drama suffers from the mining depression," the Opera House playing to "fair business." However, from Courtaine's first night Sutliff's was "filled to its utmost capacity by enthusiastic audiences," finding the programs "varied, spicy, but chaste enough," the *Union* boldly declared Courtaine and troupe "to be the very best in town." But that critic soon admitted he was "charmed with Mayo's acting," called him "a deservedly popular actor," and lamented the termination of the actor's season as "a public loss to all who are fond of the legitimate drama."

Mme. Duret left the Opera House now, headed a small troupe of her own, and alternated evenings with Lee and Ryland's circus then in Washoe. The Friday the big top opened in Dayton, Maguire advertised "the re-engagement for a few nights only" of Frank Mayo for the "arduous character of Gaston in the Great Sensation play," *The Man with the Iron Mask.* According to Dumas' novel the brother mistreated by Louis XIV was the "famous prisoner known only to history as 'The Man with the Iron Mask,'" now a play in which the troupe displayed "very good acting," Mayo rating "a genius."

Saturday Maguire repeated the comedy of *The Stage-Struck Barber;* and Mayo as Jerry Clip did imitations of celebrated actors. For how many nights Mayo submitted to the sensational masking in *The Man with the Iron Mask* is uncertain, but coast papers reported that "Frank Mayo and Miss Virginia Howard are great favorites with the Washoites."

Music Hall in Virginia. Silverland seems to have been the change needed, for a time at least. Over the years Courtaine would appear on many stages. In May, 1877, he lay ill and not expected to live. His wife returned, took him East, and cared for him. Reform was by now impossible; yet to the last (October 1886), in London and destitute, he insisted he was "starting over."

July-August 1864

The Pinch of Competition

1

To the English tourist's remark that the Fourth of July would soon be extinct, any Washoite would have retorted with an old Yankee's quick reply, "See here, Stranger, when the resurrection day comes around, the first thing done in the morning will be to read the Declaration of Independence." And that instrument was read in every town, camp, and gathering, no matter how small, during the big celebrations that were "an honor to Silverland . . . the grandest ever gotten up on this side of the Rocky Mountains." [1]

---

[1] The birthday of the United States was a day to note in Washoe. "Let there be a meeting of the citizens," wrote "Fire Cracker" in the Carson *Independent* early in June, "and let them bring the old spirit of our forefathers to suggest a course of action, which should strike terror into the hearts of rebellion. Pistols, my boys, if you like." The committees published regular progress reports of their work.

No. 4 fire company promised to wear their massive solid silver shields and silver-mounted belts of Virginia-mined silver, weighing collectively "no less than 43 pounds." All fire companies polished their engines, drilled nightly, and practiced on their Virginia-made trumpets of copper and brass (silver trumpets were not adapted for rough usage).

"The Misses Aldrich," then supporting Mayo and Miss Howard at the Opera House, presented Eagle Company No. 3 with huge wreaths of flowers to decorate their engine. The firemen, feeling as "proud of such tokens as a general does of a victory," assured the ladies that after the parade they would retain the wreaths in their engine houses as "trophies of priceless value" along with the large spread eagle over five feet high, carved from wood especially to enhance the impressiveness of Eagle Engine in the parade. Engine No. 2 fitted Fremont's 12-pound cannon with a new carriage and on *the* day fired it to arouse Comstockers from their beds.

Under command of Major General Van Bokkelen, the Provost Guards fired the meridian salute of 34 guns; and again at sunset, the original 13. By the time the people had filled the streets, windows, balconies, and hillsides — any place to get a view — the parade was in motion. Splendid, patriotic, and military in bearing and spirit marched the Provost Guards, the Virginia Guards, the Emmett Guards, the National Guards, and the Washoe Guards. Behind them came the fire companies, nearly as smart and snappy (the nightly drills were paying off), and behind them moved "an appropriate Car of State" containing 34 young ladies. Through the Comstock streets, decorated with flags, banners, ribbons, and garlands, "arranged with studied care and cunning device," wound the procession. On scores of buildings new flag poles had been erected and new flags run up. One Union man had trouble with a Copperhead woman, who tried to prevent his flying the Stars and Stripes. "He should have shot her on the spot," rasped a Washoe editor.

In the afternoon salutes, parades, and the circus delighted everybody, as did the circus in the evening; a Grand Military and Civic Ball sponsored by the Silver City Guards; the "First Annual Ball of the Virginia Fire Department in the aid of the Charitable Fund at the New Pavilion with music by the Metropolitan Band"; and about a dozen lesser balls. Now, to wind up the Comstock festivities, came the fireworks: "Lincoln Rockets, Johnson Bombs, Grant and McPherson Candles, Constitution and Columbiad Crackers, Bengala Lights, Mines of Stars and Serpents, Floral Shells, Volcanoes, Batteries, and every known variety of Pyrotechnics."

Those of the boisterous lumber camp of Galena who had not gone into Virginia celebrated the Fourth sanely enough with a concert of vocal and instrumental music, patriotic readings, and a grand ball at night, the proceeds going to the Sanitary Fund, "a practical application of patriotism."

According to the *Humboldt Register*, the County Commissioners would meet at two o'clock in the Unionville courthouse on the 88th anniversary of American Independence. After the opening prayer, the clerk would "read a very modest bill for printing which Dr. Shang will say is cheaper than he expected." Other bills would be "cussed." Then the Commissioners would read the Declaration of Independence and an original poem, "Mitigating the Reverse," and applaud the fact that 13 teams had left the Humboldt salt mines loaded with salt that sold for one cent a pound in Virginia and Reese River.

Generally the Fourth passed off quietly in the Humboldt area, except for a few fights and an accident during the firing of the national salute, when powder that Frank Cole was pouring into the hole in an anvil exploded before he had time — "though he was tolerably lively" — to put the second anvil on top. Dances were held in Dun Glen, Star City, and Unionville, a fine supper enhancing the ball at Backer's Pioneer Hotel in the latter town.

As though preparing for the Fourth in Clifton and Austin — by now considered one town — two industrious young men, Oscar and Joe Fairchild, took over publication of the *Reveille*, changing it to a "handsomely made up daily." (Phillips, the former owner of the *Reveille*, left for his home in the East with $10,000 he had made in a year in Washoe. The *Call* reported it a "case of lottery.") The nation's birthday, therefore, started well with the usual salute and the raising of flags from all public buildings (the largest one flying over the firehouse) and many private residences, enhancing the evergreen trees and rosettes of national colors that decorated the streets.

The parade consisted of the Austin band, playing patriotic airs; eight pioneers with axes; Pioneer Ladder Company No. 1; a decorated fire truck upon which sat Miss Emma Hanchett as the Goddess of Liberty; another wagon drawn by four spirited horses carrying Eddy Davis as a small edition of a Yankee tar, and 13 little girls in white with tri-colored sashes, spangled with stars. At Bradford's Hall a large audience heard the Reverend Mr. Webber speak a prayer, B. P. Rankin

Among the attractions were Lee and Ryland's Great Equescurriculum and Camel Show, a mammoth company of eques-
trians, acrobats, and gymnasts, organized "without regard to
expense" by Mr. H. C. Lee, who, according to the blurbs, had
"secured the services of some of the most distinguished Eastern Artistes; and ALSO a host of California talent, which en-
abled him to produce all the elegant, sensational, and comic
novelties of the day" as he had in California since early May.

"The Camels are Coming, Ho! Ho!" cried Washoe news-

---

read the Declaration of Independence, and H. G. Worthington deliver the oration.
Other former California celebrators — though without fashionable attire since there
was "no fashion in Reese" — included Judge John Wattson, who "doffed that blue
swallow tail coat with the brass buttons," and Colonel F. Forman, the lawyer who
still wore the blue breeches of his military glory.

At near-by Big Creek (where Artemus Ward had experienced a near-scalping
by would-be Indians) the ladies entertained with an Independence Day ball,
which netted seventy dollars for the school building fund. The *Reveille* editors,
however, lamented the children's being deprived of noisemakers through an over-
sight in ordering fireworks, a fact the large dog population of Austin probably
appreciated. (Three days later the City Council levied a five-dollar-a-year tax on
canines and prohibited the holding of dog fights within the city limits, but allowed
hogs to run the streets.)

Over in Nye County, Ione's 800 inhabitants were so busy with building — already
50 places were doing business — and with gardening, farming, mining, and welcoming their first newspaper (the *Nye County News* published by Dr. Henry De
Groot) that the Fourth nearly arrived before the camp was ready. Some mines
already down 80 feet were rushing work to reach 150 feet and thereby win a
prize to be presented at a grand ball, at which nearly all the 50 females of the
area promised to be present. This last condition made Ione an attractive place for
bachelors. As a consequence, when dances, concerts, weddings, and patriotic
occasions came around, Ione merchants had an "unusual run" on white shirts,
socks, ties, etc.

On the evening of the Fourth, however, the people moved with dispatch. They
cleared the courthouse, erected a rostrum, improvised benches, decorated the walls,
and persuaded such prominent people as J. D. Dawson to act as orator, N. T.
Smith to be grand marshal, Judge E. C. Southworth to read the Declaration of
Independence, G. A. Swansey to recite Washington's Farewell Address, and De
Groot to offer appropriate remarks. A choir of the "best singers," including several
ladies, practiced appropriate music while a gunpowder committee "unlimbered a
couple of anvils" to serve as ordnance. Fortunately John F. Kidder had a flag of
respectable dimensions, which a committee ran up the pole on the apex of the
Bank Exchange and made sure "a gilded ball" at the top contained a copy of the
Nye County News "and other articles of virtue." Ione finished the celebration with
a public ball and "all patriotic things generally." (Ione City *Nye County News*,
July 2 and 9, 1864.)

papers. "We don't know what Equescurriculum means, but what's the difference so long as the play goes on?" Having had "the honor of appearing" the last of June "before the citizens" of Carson, Dayton, and Washoe City, and then for three exciting days, July 2, 3, and 4 — and possibly the next day too — Lee and Ryland spread their tents on the Old Patio Mill Grounds between C and D Streets in Virginia; charged $1.50 (dress circle), $1.00 (second circle), and half price for children under ten. Presenting the first "genuine circus" to reach Washoe, they "drew such crowds as had seldom before been seen in a place of amusement of the kind in this or any other country" in spite of dull times.[2]

When J. A. Wright "called for 40,000 able-bodied men" to attend his third mammoth gift enterprise,[3] the Washoites looked longingly at the big silver bar valued at $2000 and the stacks of $20 gold pieces, then packed Maguire's. Fortunately the lottery was over by the time Frank Mayo, Virginia Howard, and the other professionals came on stage for another July evening of legitimate entertainment. On Wednesday for Johnny O'Neil's benefit, *Dominique the Deserter* and *Temptation; or, The Irish Emigrant* were presented. July 10 and 11 brought out the "splendid play," *Jack Cade, the Captain of the Commons.* Frank Mayo personated Jack Cade, of course.

Mme. Duret and J. H. Leroy opened the Carson Theatre on July 7 and served *Hamlet, Prince of Denmark,* but one can appreciate the Carson *Independent's* criticism that to give *Hamlet* with two people only was a "bilk." Mme. Duret, as if acting on the rebuke, added Johnny O'Neil and Professor Millwood to her traveling theatricals. But after appearing at the Gold Hill Theatre, they decided the sorrowing prince had

[2] Writing in *The Californian,* Inigo (feature writer Charles Henry Webb) gave his explanation of the dull times and the cause of the fall in stocks: "They told me it was the 'Mother ledge,' " he jibed. "With more propriety, it might be called the Mother-in-law ledge."

[3] Enterprise man J. A. Wright was soon to have competition. — Margaret Watson, "Washoe's Gift Entertainment," *The Nevada Magazine,* December, 1946.

run his course, boarded their private conveyance, and headed for California.

Although the papers had been announcing that Emily Jordan was enroute to Washoe, Belle Divine is the actress named by the *Call* as "connected with the Opera House" and given star rating with Virginia Howard for Mayo's benefit. Josie Aldrich and others of the company also volunteered as did John De Haga and Mr. Levison, who sang a duet from *I Puritani.* What part Mayo himself played is unknown. Remembering his Hamlet and the interest it evoked during the tragedian's 1863 benefit, one cannot help wondering just what part Mayo played that last night of the season. No doubt, the occasion was pleasant and profitable since the troupe had been "very popular in the transmontane capital at the Opera House."

Several unpleasant things occurred at this time. D. E. McCarthy, then proprietor of the *Enterprise,* angrily published a card accusing Burns of selling his own box to McCarthy and then filling it with Burns' friends. "It is a pretty business all around," lamented the *Call* theatrical critic. The second unpleasantness was more serious. Miss Howard was "severely injured" when she was thrown from a buggy in Virginia. Gravely concerned that she was "quite ill," the people tendered her a benefit at the Opera House. Whether Mayo was still in Silverland is not known, but actors were on hand to assist Virginia when she recovered sufficiently on July 20 to play Laura Leeson at her benefit in Courtney's drama of *Time Tries All.*[4]

---

[4] As noted in their solicitude for Miss Howard, the Washoites were concerned about theatrical people and did not forget them when they were gone from Silverland. Comstockers now learned with sorrow that Nellie Brown had died of a broken heart in far-off China; that Walter Leman had gone to the Sandwich Islands to improve his health; and that Charles Pope had boarded the *Moses Taylor* for the East. They were interested to know that J. H. Allen was giving *The Duke's Motto* for his San Francisco benefit; that McKean Buchanan and his daughter were appearing successfully in the Louisville Theatre; that the play of *Box and Cox* was being read to Pope Pius IX; that amusement business was dull in New York but

While Miss Howard was recuperating from her injuries, Professor Grambbs used the Opera House for his "first grand vocal and instrumental concert," assisted by such "accomplished musicians" as Mrs. Wiley, Mrs. Chappell, Mrs. Ells, Mrs. Derwin, John De Haga, Mr. York, the Germania and Virginia Glee Clubs, and Schreiner's brass band.

2

During Mayo's engagement at the Opera House and Courtaine's at Music Hall, Comstockers with less money now sometimes had difficulty deciding which theatre to attend. When the Maguire troupers — without Miss Howard and a few others — left for California, thus removing the pinch of competition, Sutliff gave Harry Courtaine a farewell benefit too. (Had Virginia's many saloons proved too great temptation for "the prince of light comedians"?) With Courtaine gone, Sutliff put the burlesque-farce-dancing-gags-variety program back on the Music Hall stage. Here on July 14 the everpopular Johnny Tuers took another benefit, this time appearing as Black Donald. Pat Holland played Commodore Hurricane and a young lady actress, Capitola.

---

good in Idaho; and that the laughing lady, the indomitable Mrs. Leighton, though she had lost her manager-husband through death the November before, still made more *Fools of the Family* than any one, and when engaged for an Idaho season (during which she became "quite a lionne"), according to the Boise *News*, drove the troupe "four-in-hand into Boise in triumphant style, handling the ribbons like a Jehu."

Following the career of the strip-tease artist Adah Menken, the Washoites noted that "Adah never was satisfied after playing Mazeppa in Virginia as that exhibition gave her an enlarged idea of men and things." Comstockers also studied the California court case of the "People vs. Thomas Maguire et al.," in which managers and actors insisted that theatrical representations should not be considered noisy and barbarous; an exception, they humorously conceded, might be in the instance of an actor like McKean Buchanan storming the stage in *Richard III.*

Still unsatiated, Silverland noted that J. B. Booth had played at the Boston Museum during the farewell benefit of his brother John Wilkes Booth; that Lotta Crabtree was getting first-rate notices in New York; that Julia Hayne was doing especially well in the Northwest; and that Mr. and Mrs. Seldon Irwin, "Brigham's pets," were playing Marysville.

By late July Sutliff had "gotten up" and was serving an Ethiopian opera called *Oh, Hush; or, The Virginia Cupids.* Tuers — still considered the "soul of Sutliff's" — personated Gumbo Cuff, an irrepressible nuisance in the *Oh, Hush!* opera, a piece full of interesting and timely scenes of Negro life, replete with humor and characteristic songs and dances. On July 29 the troupers and appreciative Comstockers gave Henry Sutliff "a first-rate benefit," just in time, too, it would seem.

A few nights later (August 2) Music Hall narrowly escaped burning twice, but the Sutliff troupe and other employees plus the Lode firemen fought the flames on both occasions so valiantly that the theatre was saved. But Comstockers recalled that just a year before to the month, a valuable part of Virginia commencing at A Street had been burned black. Though some Comstock citizens offered a reward of $2000 for the arrest and conviction of any incendiary, almost every day Virginia was "afflicted with fires." Was the cut in miners' wages a cause? The hard times?

But now Sutliff's anticipated another danger. Laughter, hilarious and uncontrolled, floated through open windows of the Opera House, attesting to Comstock appreciation of a new troupe, "the finest of its kind": the San Francisco Minstrels. So while Henry Sutliff searched among San Francisco theatricals for an exhibitionist "of the Menken school" to compete with Maguire's, the Minstrels, who had intended "to remain but a few days," proved themselves not only "more than acceptable," but so "very popular" they had a "splendid run while in Virginia City."

With such end men as Billy Birch and Wambold, "both among the heaviest old darkies on the coast and chock full of fun," the minstrels could scarcely fail to please. As the *Call* critic aptly appraised, "If in sentimental mood, Wambold and Abecco assimilate with our feelings perfectly. If melancholy, Birch makes us cheery as a cricket. There is solace in Simonsen's violin *solos* and consolation in Coe's banjo variations. Shattuck's *bass* is bracing — he doesn't 'change his base' — and Lewis' dancing is light as sponge cake. Backus' imitations of the great actors he has seen and the roaring burlesque of 'The Runaway Husband' are trump cards that have 'brought down the house.' "

None anywhere had experienced the best in Ethiopian entertainment until he had seen and heard Sam Wells, Charley Backus, Coes, Simonsen, and the "wonderful singers" Wambold and Abecco in such tantalizing verses of "Git Along, John" as:

> Behind the hen house on my knees,
> I think I hear the chicken sneeze,
> Turkeys playing cards on a pumpkin vine,
> Goose chaw tobacco, ducks drink wine.
>
> Then git along, John, the fifer's son,
> Ain't you mighty glad your work's most done?[5]

Then the minstrels swung into such timely songs as "On to Richmond," "The Gallant Young Zouave," "The Union Forever," and "Abraham's Daughter," from which I quote, "An' don't you tink I orter?'

> Oh, de soldiers here, both far and near, dey
>   did git quite excited,
> When from deir bredren from de Souf to war
>   dey was invited.
> But it was to be, it is to be, it can't
>   be nothin' shorter,
> An' if dey call upon dis chile, I's bound
>   to die a martyr.
>
> *Chorus:*
> For I belong to de fire Zoo-Zoos,
> An' don't you tink I orter?
> An' I'm gwine down to Washington,
> To fight for Abraham's daughter.[6]

---

[5] Taken from Bryant's *Cane Brake Refrains as Sung by the Minstrels*, 1863.
[6] From a pamphlet in the library of the University of California.

Perhaps Sam Wells (the leader and most versatile member of the troupe), Billy Birch, and George H. Coes would do the nonsense song, 'Shoo, Fly, Don't Bother Me!" and the ballad, "Joe Bowers." Or Sam would sing alone. "Don't know any singer we'd rather hear than Sam Wells in a good, old-fashioned song," a California critic voiced Washoe preference too. "After the cooings of some of the sentimental balladists we wot of, it is refreshing to hear his deep but flexible voice roll out 'The Deep, Deep Sea,' 'The Old Oak,' or 'Rocked in the Cradle of the Deep.'" Then Sam would read conundrums, considered by some as the lowest form of humor, by other theatrical critics as clever entertainment.

3

Although Lee and Ryland's show had recently left Silverland, a new circus, one "to outshine anything of its kind yet seen," played Carson, Washoe City, Dayton, and Genoa before the proprietors of the venture that was "successful wherever they spread their tents in the mountain area," pitched their huge tent on Mill Street and promised Virginia three days of entertainment. Even the San Francisco Minstrels felt this pinch of competition and left for Carson, where they opened on the night of August 9.

Having been brought by Mr. Wilson from New York and Havana at "immense cost, thus enabling the management to produce elegant, sensational, comic, and entertaining novelties of the day," the Great Ella Zoyara Troupe, boasting a "reputation celebrated and world wide," was a definite addition to the show. No wonder the Comstockers, crowding the sidewalks and balconies, thrilled to the gaily caparisoned circus horses prancing to "the van's sonorous music blowing martial sounds"; then hurried to Mill Street, crowded under the big top with its "immense chandelier whirling and twinkling like a python in coils of fire" around the pillars that supported the canvas, and enjoyed "the finest event of its kind that ever visited Washoe or California."

Not the least attraction of each show was "the famous equestrienne," Ella Zoyara, no one being quite sure whether he-she was "indeed a woman or not." But it was a puzzlement upon which to place bets. Meanwhile Zoyara floated around the arena, leaped through any number of balloons, and pirouetted with "bewildering grace" as Kidd's "celebrated Brass Band" set the tempo and mood for each event. The charming Mlle. Eloise and other daring riders of the sawdust ring also reaped rounds of applause as did Ella's trained and educated black horse, whose intelligence intrigued all who saw her tricks.

The show was fast. Scarcely had the bareback riders left the ring than gymnasts Durand and Painter performed and the daring acrobatic team of Carlo and Ross swung and tumbled high over head. One member of a specialty team impaled his brother with knives and did other feats with a dexterity that "passed anything ever seen at a boarding house." In the comic department the "merry quibs" and songs of jester-singer Fred Wilson and the stunts and jokes of the clowns Aymar and Williams kept the Washoites rocking with laughter.

One night the "Prestidigitator, Martin the Wizard," inveigled some Comstockers inside Sutliff's to witness his sleight of hand. Mrs. J. S. Grantley recited to "large and delighted audiences" at the courthouse, but Wilson and Zoyara's Circus was the principal amusement magnet. On August 17 the circus played a benefit for the local firemen to a crowd that taxed tent capacity. Then on Mill Street the light from the whirling chandelier was out, the last peg pulled, and "the charming place to drop into of an evening" was gone.

4

But at Music Hall the "divinely beautiful" Maggie Field as an equestrienne excelled even the Mazeppa of Adah Menken — or so insisted the *Call*. Maggie was Henry Sutliff's new find, over whom San Franciscans had gone "mad." So now to "tremendous audiences" Maggie burlesqued *Mazeppa* in Virginia and could say with the lead character, "I was a goodly *stripling* then." Adah Menken might lead but she would not stand alone in "stripping." "Her example of immodesty," now moralized the *Call*, "has debauched the artists of the stage." Mazeppa was in the spotlight again.[7]

Could the San Francisco Minstrels — upon their return to the Comstock — compete with Maggie's Mazeppa? Yes. And night after night the people from Virginia and near-by and even from afar filled the Opera House and enjoyed such fun as the minstrels dispensed. For Coe's benefit on Sunday, August 14, the theatre announced "full attendance" while Music Hall even with Mazeppa was "thinly patronized." Perhaps the critic was right when he insisted that with the Menken's departure *Mazeppa* was finished, "for what manager would be bold enough to put it on the stage and look for paying houses after the Menken had played the Tartar — the cream of the Tartar — and exhausted all its attractions."

Sutliff also seemed convinced. When Miss Field's engagement ended, he re-hired the "old company so justly popular" (the Fillmore sisters, Kavanaugh, Quinn, Prescott, and others) announced that "Mrs. Jefferson Confederacy" —

---

[7] Having recently lauded Mrs. Perry in the role of Mazeppa on the stages of Silverland's theatre, the Washoites were pleased to note that her San Francisco debut in the same character was a success, even though the actress appeared slightly nervous at first when having difficulty with the "wild horse of Tartary." While Mr. Thorne was apologizing to the audience — and reading this, the Comstockers must have doubled over with laughter — the horse kicked through the curtain and "Thorne nearly landed in the kettle drum." Mrs. Perry rode and stripped, but she also received a *Call* rebuke:

PERRY'S MAZEPPA

One day on Lake Erie — you all know the story —
Brave Oliver Perry while fighting for glory,
The British fleet stripped; but playing for pelf,
Our Perry outdoes him by stripping herself.

Washoites also noted that Emily Jordan was likewise "determined to play Mazeppa." With five Mazeppas playing San Francisco, little wonder *The Californian* observed: "About the theatres there is but one thing to say, all are possessed of Mazeppa." And Silverland followed the fashion.

whom the *Old Piute* had thought a charming Mazeppa — had ceased to act that role, and further reduced prices. Even so the Washoites preferred the Minstrels. And the editor of the *Gold Hill News,* though he received no Opera House advertisement, unable to restrain himself longer, wrote:

> Our readers have doubtless noticed that shows and theatres seldom get a notice in our columns. . . We will here make an exception. The troupe of minstrels now performing at Maguire's Opera House, consisting of Billy Birch, Charley Backus, Sam Wells, and a host of other performers, is decidedly the best company that has ever visited Washoe.

Cognizant of the temporary successes of the *Mazeppa* burlesques at Music Hall, the Minstrels also launched into burlesque, but, instead of *Mazeppa,* did a local travesty of Wilson and Zoyara's Circus that caused the previously reticent *News* to chuckle: "We saw the show not long ago, and have had the laughing hysterics ever since. Go see it!" The advice was not needed; for the minstrels were having such "splendid success" that they stayed through the month of August, far beyond their intended "few days," and would have remained longer in Silverland except for a serious accident.

5

On Friday, August 26, Sam Wells was riding up the canyon toward the Opera House to keep an important engagement, the minstrel's own benefit. Suddenly his horse, frightened by a dog, reared or jumped, and threw Wells into the street with such force that Sam's head striking an awning post splintered the wood. Doctors Pinkerton and Bryant declared that Sam's skull was broken and that there was no chance of his recovering.

While their leader lay unconscious at his home on A Street in Virginia, the minstrels attempted to put on his benefit, but "the sad accident threw a gloom over the whole performance and much of the program was omitted," although, sympathized Comstock papers, the troupe did "as well as they could." On Saturday Wells regained consciousness and the minstrels, thus encouraged, gave an "entirely new lot of songs, dances, and things," hoping to please everybody as their manager would have wished. But the spontaneity was missing from both sides of the footlights. For three days longer the basso profundo lingered, but on August 30 "in the full flush of wit and humor and song . . . left the stage of life in mid-act while the pleased audience waited for his appearing."

Next day the minstrels — respecting the last request of their leader — disbanded and returned to the Bay city, where on September 4, "the remains of Samuel Adams Wells were consigned to Lone Mountain Cemetery." According to the obituaries, Wells was a great-grandson of "Old Sam Adams, the Father of the American Revolution," and left several brothers, one well known to the press of San Francisco, another, proprietor of the St. James Hotel in New York City, and an aunt, Frances Sargeant Osgood. As if it, too, grieved, the Opera House in Virginia stood solemn and dark. But, borne in on night winds across the sagebrush hills sensitive ears might have caught a conundrum, a choice joke, or snatches of songs in the rich voice of the basso profundo, rising above the accumulated laughter of many weeks of Comstock audiences.

Since they could do nothing for their favorite now, the people tendered a joint benefit, which turned out to be a "splendid entertainment," for two deserving Thespians: Miss Howard and Signor R. Abecco. "Miss Howard is too well known here to need any praise from us," wrote the *Old Piute.* "But it may not be amiss to mention that the recent severe accident, which she has suffered, has so entirely changed her plans for future actions, as to seriously embarrass present movements and the tribute that her legion of friends may pay to beauty and talent on Wednesday evenings will be heartily appreciated by the lady." The other beneficiary, the harpist and *tenore sforza* of the San Francisco Minstrels, also had "hosts of friends," who admired him as a superior artist and a finished gentleman.[8]

The only lighted theatre now in Virginia was Sutliff's. Under the direction of L. F. Beatty and then Max Walters, Music Hall was again "well patronized by the lovers of unadulterated fun," the melodeon performers giving a certain "nip" to their programs that funseekers found inviting. Max Walters' benefit included "an entirely new and original lot of farces, songs, and dances." [9]

---

[8] Had San Franciscans been as generous as the Washoites and given Abecco another benefit some nine weeks later, he may not have had to "take himself and harp off suddenly to Australia" under circumstances that hindered "his name being mentioned except with execration," for

> "The harp that once Eureka's halls
> With softest music thrilled,
> Now floats as freight across the main —
> Its harmonies all stilled.

> "Abecco, sadly o'er the rail,
> His loneliness regrets;
> Even as the creditors on shore
> His many, hopeless debts."

[9] Blackface entertainment was enjoyed in Reese River when the Austin Serenaders, a group of amateur musicians, raised the seats in Bradford Hall, engaged a local "photographist as well as painter" to do a fine scene and drop curtain, made such other improvements as to give Major Bradford's venture (seating 500 people) the appearance of a regular theatre, and launched into "a series of fine entertainments" during August. According to the *Reveille*, "the large and fashionable audience" — whether it totaled 500 the paper neglected to state — was delighted with the music, both vocal and instrumental, and "hugely enjoyed the Negro eccentricities of Rowe and Edwards."

The Austinites then decided that A. H. Beck, their "accomplished leader and teacher of the local bands," should have a benefit, for which Austin's glee club and brass and string bands volunteered. However, an "untimely rain" caused postponement until August 25, when the professor and his accomplished daughter, living up to "flattering press notices from the Mississippi Valley, St. Paul, and New Orleans," gave dramatic readings, which were considered "of the highest order of merit and worthy of patronage of all lovers of Tragedy or Farce." In spite of slow times, the Reese Riverites saw that patronage was provided.

Next, the Masons and Odd Fellows decorated their hall with evergreens, flags, engravings, and dancing lights; then engaged a "band of first-class musicians under the leadership of J. Varney" for a benefit dance to aid the charitable organizations of Austin.

After doing "full justice to all the food set before them," Company B, First

Regiment of Nevada Volunteers — as guests of Austin — paraded in full dress uniform and demonstrated "all the different evolutions and maneuvers laid down in Slott and Hardee's Tactic." The Volunteers then marched to Fort Ruby, their winter quarters.

One Sunday after the horse races and a foot race that involved "a fist fight," Professor Silliman, the widely travelled mineralogist, entertained "at the request of the citizens," who had offered Bradford Hall for the free lecture. Finding Bradford's crowded and hundreds more packed against the outside of the hall, Silliman led his audience into Main Street, climbed onto a wagon seat, and helped alleviate the feeling of pinched times by telling the "Sagebrushers" that "the Great American Desert, a Territory Incognita, thought by outsiders to be the fit habitation of rattlesnakes and savages, is really a land of great mineral wealth." Everyone went home feeling flattered and important.

Drifting About

1

Less than a week after its use for the boldest single-prize lottery of the territory, the Taylor gift drawing on September 8,[1] Maguire's was twinkling with lights and in use again. Stephen C. Massett drifted in to give his famous "Drifting About" lecture. The curly-haired globe-trotter was no stranger. Since the gold rush of '49, the "Jeems Pipes of Pipesville" had given San Franciscans regular entertainment in the little schoolhouse that faced Portsmouth Plaza. Writer as well as actor, singer, elocutionist, and mimic, "Steve" Massett had so "thorough a sense of the ludicrous" that he repeated "the most funny things as quietly as if he neither saw nor felt them to be so" — even President Lincoln said Massett's stories were as good as his own Springfield jokes.

Opening his serio-comic program with amusing remarks, much as Ward had done, Massett talked, but "not in the usual didactic style of travelers." Casually he injected "entertaining incidents and anecdotes" — of which he had an "inexhaustible fund" — inspiring the imagination and carrying his listeners along with him. Then Steve became a tricky-voiced mimic, launching into clever imitations of Edwin Forrest, McKean Buchanan, Anna Bishop (especially in the song, "Home, Sweet Home"), and an English tourist visiting America. The

---

[1] The prize? The "large and magnificent three-story brick building at C and Taylor Streets, valued at $60,000." This started a new fad in gift lottery. On New Year's day of 1865 two buildings were "given away": a two-story house of seven rooms and another building containing 20 rooms. Later real estate gift entertainments were even more ambitious. — Margaret Watson, "Washoe's Gift Entertainment," *The Nevada Magazine,* December, 1946.

"large and fashionable audiences" learned much, laughed at his jokes, and wept during the exquisite pathos of his reading of the sentimental poems, "Beautiful Snow" and "The Vagabonds."

Massett also sang. There were songs of his own composing, timely and fitting, changed as occasion required. He was a complete program in himself,[2] but it was during his "caricature of geniuses and exotic characters he had met" that he was interrupted by the most frequent applause in Virginia as elsewhere in Silverland.

2

Massett had scarcely left the Washoe mining metropolis when Blaisdell's Swiss Bell Ringers drifted in and took over the Opera House. Included in this accomplished and clever company were the Blaisdell brothers; Madame Julia Blaisdell, who was solo harpist; Frederick Buck, violinist; Frank Moore, flutist; Rudolph Hall, solo cornetist and clarinetist; and the tiny and petite, but certainly not the least of the unusual Swiss entertainers, little Clara Jenkins.

Besides playing their musical instruments, the Blaisdell's troupers performed on 239 bells (weighing from 12 pounds down to five ounces), which tinkled, jingled, chimed, and fairly sang out delightful music that "immensely pleased" the Washoites. But for little Clara Jenkins applause was not enough; the audience sent a "shower of half-dollars" to the stage that September 16. In fact, the small charmer received so many encores that the manager had to come before the curtain and beg the audience to let the show go on. Perhaps the *Gold Hill News* was right when it lauded "Little Clara" as "the best balladist and best character singer that has ever appeared on the Pacific coast."[3]

---

[2] San Francisco *Golden Era*, September 14, 1864.

[3] When four years later the troupe returned to Silverland, Little Clara was still the favorite. In spite of the "terribly sung" ballad by a Reese volunteer, Clara's benefit in Austin was a "decided and handsome success." — See *Reveille* for February 5, 1869.

Of the program only one complaint was heard: "Too short!" So the Comstockers took "seconds" on the bell-ringing and musical entertainment. They came again a third night too, and perhaps a fourth. Not until September 23 did the Swiss Bell Ringers entertain Carson City with their "melodious chimes." They also rang their bells at Dayton and at Washoe City.

3

On the heels of Blaisdell's melodious musicians came a young and unheralded violinist, Paul Julien, who arrived in California to be "enthusiastically praised by the interior press" as a "genius in his line . . . a vio-line — if a bad pun may be pardoned because it embodies a palpable truth." In Washoe, however, Julien got a different reception when he chose Maguire's for his opening concert, September 21.

According to the *Era,* the Opera House was crowded that night "with the beauty and fashion of the Metropolis of Silver Land." And although they approved the home talent parts of the program, the audience was disappointed. Was it the choice of numbers? The artist played classical selections that had pleased the Californians. Nonetheless, the Washoites did not consider it "an experience in life to hear Julien play 'Home, Sweet Home' and manifest their wonder and feelings without regard to a preservation of kid gloves." Hurt and angry, Julien retaliated by announcing that he would not appear again on the Lode.

Julien's pronouncement evidently was the shock treatment needed. The Comstockers did an about face. What would Californians think of them? The Washoites apprised Julien of their new sentiments, even going so far as to send him a public letter reassuring him that the conduct of certain Washoites during the artist's concert received the "unqualified reproval of all present . . . whose good opinion is desirable." "We solicit the pleasure of hearing you again and respectfully tender you a Complimentary Benefit," wrote the contrite and generous thirty-five Comstockers who signed the letter and, hence, also would pay all the expenses of the evening. Julien hesitated, but placated now by such "kind and generous sentiment," named September 24 as the date for a second appearance and promised "an entirely new and splendid programme."

The Saturday night arrived and so did the beauty and fashion of Washoe to again fill the theatre. After certain opening numbers, onto the stage strolled the world-renowned, the "greatest violinist of the age." He placed the violin under his chin. He played; and the Washoites — not wishing the world to think them uncultured — applauded.

A visitor from the Humboldt country, however, held no such compunction as his report to his home town paper showed:

> PAUL JULIEN. — You don't suppose we'd be in Virginia when the far-famed fiddler was having a complimentary benefit by particular request, and not go to hear him and see him? We didn't. A poster told us to "go early and secure a seat." To make a sure thing of it, we secured two, and then took a loose ticket for the theatre at large.
>
> The gentlemanly management soon discovered that we were there, and an artist was sent to the front to open a piano. He opened it pretty thoroughly; but since the recent mining panic a Virginia audience requires a full development of everything, and the artist labored diligently some minutes to expose the entire machinery. At length, the top was loosened, and carried off amid great applause. We were pleased to see the mechanic subordinate pursuits thus honored by a discriminating audience in this great city.
>
> Stadfeldt came forward and bowed backward, and seated himself within arms-length of the piano. He hammered, showed a partiality for the small end of the board, and played fast and stopped quickly, some two dozen rounds. A great deal of feeling but very little music in his performance. He was applauded. . . Mrs. Wiley sang a song. It was a great effort. We could see it.

It was time to bring Paul Julien to the stage and the Humboldt man did so in this manner:

> Paul Julien came down front. He was applauded for coming to the front. He bowed. He was applauded for bowing. He had one of those steel-pen split coats onto him. Did you ever notice how the stately raven's tail tips up when the raven dips up a bug? Paul's coat tail tipped up the very same. . . In some portions he did descend to a tune and the violin sounded melodiously. He is a complete master of the instrument, or he could never succeed in torturing so sweet toned a violin into the squeaks and squalls he brings from it. He stops occasionally, and the claquers applaud, while he wipes the neck of the violin with that white handkerchief from the tail of his coat. Then he bows. The Virginians then set up a din of clapping and yelling, and Paul appears unto them and bows. They applaud him for it, and he bows.
>
> The Beermania Society sung a fine chorus. Mrs. Wiley and Stadfeldt perform, and Julien comes back, and Studeman is dished up; and we leave long before it is out, thinking we have enough for a dollar, and that the dollar passed the wrong way.

Since the *Humboldt Register* was a weekly, the review of Julien's concert did not reach print until the following Saturday, but Julien had already played Carson and was well beyond the Sierra Nevada. That the musician appeared a third time at Maguire's is doubtful; and the *Call* editor, who had insisted that Julien's violin was the only passport he needed to public favor, judged that Paul and his colleagues did not make "too much money on their tour" of Washoe.

4

When the ladies in the Humboldt area held a dance at the schoolhouse that was the "greatest treat of the season," "the masculines" declared they were "willing to be trotted out again any time." So when politicians from Virginia [4] began "drifting about" and the male populace noted that half of the

---

[4] The fare from Austin to Virginia was $30, but to return over the same road and in the same stage one paid $10 more.

"packed Dyer Hall" were ladies applauding the speeches, they hurriedly "got the hall in readiness for a dance and didn't go home till morning." Perhaps the masculines were even willing to forego some of their Great Gander activities for dancing; but hardly on the night the Ganders — without a dissenting quack — elected Old Piute and Mark Twain to honorary life membership.

Saloonkeepers in Humboldt vied with one another in advertising "gay and efficient" barkeepers, billiard tables, talk that gives "tone," and quoted Lord Byron. The Telegraph Saloon offered $100 "in gold coin" — not greenbacks — to any player making the greatest number of billiard "rampses." [5]

5

A traveling correspondent "drifted" into Centerville (60 miles from Star City) to find a "vast encampment" with two stores, a hotel, over a thousand travelers, and a large campground completely covered with "immigrant wagons," as many at 234, some being those of the "family of John Brown of Harper's Ferry notoriety" and their fine stock, including three imported merino sheep.

The general ability of these immigrants to entertain themselves, greatly impressed the drifter, who later related, "We saw none, either male or female, who would not sing on the least invitation — the males having voices like hand-saws, and the females like nightingowls." For further diversion the travelers played pranks and jokes on one another and staged mock gun fights that were more realistic than "Hollywood Westerns."

Returning to Star City by way of Dun Glen, the roving reporter stopped at Jacob's Well, which boasted only two houses but such advertisements — stuck up in any conspicuous place — as "Travelers *must* patronize the bar or pay 12½ cents apiece for water for the animals."

---

[5] "Ramses" are now called "runs." Anyone then paying in greenbacks ran the risk of having his name published derogatorily in Washoe papers. To pay in territorial scrip was even more degrading as it was worth about 30 cents on the dollar.

October 1864

Theatrical Potpourri

1

No doubt, more disappointed than relieved that a bloody duel (involving Venetian daggers) had been abruptly called off, Comstockers found substitution at Sutliff's in some hair-raising entertainment (especially in the scalping scene) provided by some Indians. It all began when Chief Winnemucca and his family passing through the Lode towns received a gift of $25, thereby whetting the "High-Ugh-Muc-a-Muc's" appetite for additional dollars. The manager of Sutliff's made the next move. He persuaded the Chief and some members of his tribe to become actors.

And those who managed to crowd into Music Hall that night of October 5 were delighted. After the usual minstrel show, "the big chief of all the Pi-Ute nation" along with his daughters So-Me-To-a and To-Woo-To-Na (in English, Shell Flower and Lattice Flower), his fifteen-year-old son, and seven braves came on stage dressed in full Indian costumes with tomahawks, scalping knives, and all the other requisites.[1] "About six feet high, straight as an arrow, with a depth and breadth of chest which denotes great physical strength and quiet dignity and self-possession of manner," the formidable aborigine made an impressive entrance. His keen, unflinching, black eyes made as romantic and favorable an impression from behind the footlights as they had during conferences with the white men or his own people.

Then followed a series of tableaux representing a camp

---

[1] *Virginia Daily Union*, October 5, 1864.

scene, a council of war, a war dance, a scalping dance, and other phases incident to Indian life on the deserts, in the mountains, or along the rivers and lakes of Washoe. The climax of the show "brought down the house." In it the chief and other loyal native-born citizens captured a Copperhead just arriving over the Sierras and pulled off his scalp in a "highly scientific manner." The chief made a "grand speech," which his daughters translated. So popular was the entertainment that Max Walter persuaded the Indians to repeat their program the next night, again to a packed house.

Whether the Red Men entertained Gold Hill, Carson, and beyond cannot be determined. It seems they did; for local papers reported: "Our great Chief Winnemucca and his two daughters with a train of attendants" left Carson for Sacramento and San Francisco, where Jim Miller proposes to "show them up to the greatest possible advantage before the delighted citizens of that portion of the Pacific world."

A few weeks later the Washoites learned that the Sage Brushers, holding their San Francisco powwow on Sunday afternoon at the Metropolitan Theatre, were "abundantly greeted by the *elite,* the dark of the city," the legislators, the board of education, Officers Blitz, and Emperor Norton, who sat apart "clothed in his own stolidity." Everyone seemed impressed, especially with the coyote dance and the "horrors of the scalping knife." A few days later the friend of the palefaces "withdrew his mighty moccasins and pi-uted peaceably at San Jose and other California towns."

In Washoe though the Indian entertainers were gone, Music Hall continued "to draw good houses under the indefatigable management of Max Walter," who, determined that his public "should not lack for anything new and interesting," presented fine bills nightly.

2

Except for political meetings, the Opera House had remained dark from the night Paul Julien had tortured his violin until the season of Miss Belle Divine. According to the advertisements "T. Maguire, sole proprietor, and McGowan, stage manager," would for Miss Divine's benefit on October 10 present "for the first time" in Washoe the "elegant comic drama," *Giralda; or, The Seal of Love.* (Miss Divine must have played for some time before a benefit.) While the box office scrutinized all twenty-dollar greenbacks (many two's, crudely altered to twenties, were being circulated in Washoe), Comstockers filled the theatre to see "the beautiful young actress and vocalist" as Giralda, supported by an "excellent company," all of whom "acquitted themselves in their various parts very creditably." But the singing of little Emma, Miss Divine's seven-year-old daughter making her Virginia debut, "brought down the house," and showers of money coming from all parts of the theatre took the "infant balladist La Petite Emma, an amazing long while to pick up." One individual, however, became so excited with the "witching songs" of Emma's mother that he threw "a regular square $20 gold piece on the stage."

"An Olio of Gems" followed, and the evening concluded with the humorous *The Youth Who Never Saw a Woman,* Belle Divine appearing in her great character of Colin. Although visiting Major General McDowell was too fatigued from his long journey to attend,[2] military color was not lacking in the theatre that night; for some of the general's staff, Governor Nye, and the Guards were there to applaud Miss Divine as "a fine actress and estimable woman."

---

[2] That afternoon the band, playing "spirit-stirring martial airs," and the National and Emmet Guards in full uniform met the handsome, horse-drawn barouche carrying General McDowell, Governor Nye, and staff members; and escorted them through Gold Hill and into Virginia, where the Comstockers had awaited the General's coming for hours. When the famous military figure appeared on the balcony of the International Hotel and made a short speech, the crowds, including the soldiers, cheered until they were re-assured they would see the general during the evening's theatrical performance at Maguire's.

3

The two musical gentlemen who now came to entertain the Washoites, Ossian E. Dodge, "the world-renowned vocalist," and William Hayward, "the sweetest and best singer of the day," chose, among other songs, "a poetic gem" written by a California poet, set to music by Mr. Dodge himself, and sung by balladist William Hayward. Considered an artistic and harmonious blending of the heart-ballad with an invocation to the Deity, "God Grant Our Soldiers Safe Return" [3] had "euphonious rhythm and intensity of feeling" that was "in every way worthy the pen of the most popular writer in America," or so thought the editor of the *Union*.

While the *Call* reported that "those mis-called humorists and vocalists" performed at the capital and "the Carsonites were much dejected thereby," the *Carson City Post* insisted the concert was "of the very highest order of merit." And the *Union* editor, having had the "felicty of hearing the great Ossian sing about 15 years before," wrote that "his voice with its music we ne'er shall forget."

Glowing under such local praise, Dodge and Hayward "concertized" to full houses in Silver City, Dayton, and Gold

---

[3] The first verse of "the poetic gem" enjoyed by the Washoites or inflicted upon them — depending on your ear or point of view:

GOD GRANT OUR SOLDIERS SAFE RETURN
By Mary W. Richardson
I am sitting in my cottage
    With a heart so sad and lone,
While the night wind round me whispers
    In a bitter, wailing tone
Of the days that are departed:
    Ah! I was so blithe and gay,
For my lover then was with me,
    But now he's far away!
CHORUS
O, Our poor boys now are fighting
    Upon Georgia's burning plain.
But the war will soon be over,
    And we'll have them home again.
Oh, God grant us in thy mercy,
    All our dear boys home again!

Hill. By Saturday the two reached Virginia to learn that their agent had selected *not* the Opera House, but the probate courtroom, because of its superior acoustic properties, a point the *Union* critic felt should be considered in "a first-class, unequalled musical entertainment of the kind given by Dodge and Hayward."

In the face of the *Call's* report that "Old Hundred Dodge and ballad-ballasted Hayward disconcerted the patient people of Gold Hill, N.T., on the 13th and 14th and did the same thing again in Virginia City on the 16th," the *Union* lamented the smallness of the audience and unhesitatingly pronounced the program "the most meritorious entertainment of its kind that we have attended in this city."

After a second Virginia concert, the musical gentlemen and the praise-penning editor dressed themselves in protective clothing, and carrying lighted candles, descended hundreds of feet into the Mexican Mine, "dodged corners," scrutinized rich ore, which Superintendent Beckwith told them ran well over $2000 to the ton and would be shipped to Europe, and "climbed all sorts of queer ladders at the risk of their bones and precious necks where a small misstep might easily have dodged them into another world." In that event no further concerts, including the farewell one of October 20, would have been "inflicted" on the Washoites. But, added the *Call* critic derisively, "As the old lady said when she kissed the cow, 'Everyone to his taste.'"

Over the Sierras now came Martin the Wizard, who "hocus-pocused at Carson City on the 12th and 13th before 'respectable audiences,'" stated the *Call*, then facetiously queried, "Respectable in what respect? — in intelligence, behavior, or numbers?"

The "decidedly popular" place of amusement, however, continued to be Music Hall. "Gorgeous spectacles, fine little farces, the best of dancing, and the choicest singing served up in the best manner possible," would effectually drive the worry of dull times away. Johnny Tuers twisted "his lovely physiog" into more comical contortions than ever. Miss Clarissa and Mr. Kavanaugh sang their sweetest songs. Johnny Collins and Master Franklin in Ethiopian eccentricities "simply threw themselves away," and the lovely, seventeen-year-old Miss Florence sang in a voice of "remarkable sweetness." [4]

4

During the third week of October Comstockers found rich theatrical fare at Maguire's, which reopened for a season of legitimate drama with Charles Tibbetts as manager and a "full company" in *Leah the Forsaken*. Although a ratification rally was staged in front of the International Hotel and Sutliff's troupers did their best, the sensational forsaking of Leah as portrayed by the "highly talented" Miss Emily Jordan played "to a full audience of those who could appreciate true deserving merit."

Miss Jordan, the critic appraised, was "able to fairly individualize herself into the character assumed and becomes for the time being a pure, frequently loved Jewish maiden, full of native dignity and the deep Oriental warmth of her race, the audience being irresistibly drawn to her, . . . an actress of a superior order of merit." Lawlor acted Joseph "exceedingly well. Too well," the *Union* felt, "we consider it unpardonable, indeed, his deserting such a 'Leah' as was personated in Miss Jordan; *we* never would have done it in the world." [5] Miss Divine as the gentle unassuming Hannah

---

[4] A few short weeks after Miss Florence concluded her Sutliff engagement, the Washoites would be grieving her death in Nevada County, California. Lucy Brady was her real name, the sorrowing "local" told his readers, and added that he had been "well acquainted with her in Como, Palmyra District, N.T., where, as Mrs. Sam Case, she lived for several months." Of a happy, childish disposition, she was, said the *Union*, "one of those floweret waifs, cast early abroad upon the eddying River of Time. . ."

[5] But then the *Union* critic was not, like Frank Lawlor, a bridegroom of only a month. Lawlor had married actress Helen Mansfield.

and Mrs. George Chapman were "features of the play." A. R. Phelps was "A No. 1" in his part as "always," while Thayer and McGowan were "perfectly at home in their characters." After the forsaking of Leah, the audience insisted Frank Lawlor recite "Shamus O'Brien."

The following night Miss Jordan assumed the character of Aurora Floyd in the drama of the same name. Again a highly appreciative audience applauded her heartfelt portrayal, even if the *Call* did think that Miss Jordan, though very pretty, had too little pathos in her style. While the Hibernian Union Club at Odd Fellows Hall was holding a patriotic meeting during which Miss Stanton delivered "one of her eloquent lectures," Leah was forsaken again at the Opera House for the many who could not attend the theatre on Sunday. Although the *Call* ridiculed Miss Jordan saying she "launched the curse without necessitating a removal of *stays*," still Miss Jordan's Leah must have pleased the Comstockers; for they came yet another night to hear her.

Theatre-goers next night enjoyed "a play of sterling merit and intense interest," *The Ticket of Leave Man*, Washoites recalling that this sensational drama as done by Charles Pope and Virginia Howard had been well-received in Washoe as it had three hundred times (and was being repeated) in London. As given at Maguire's the scene was Paris. A couple met on the stairs, bowed, talked, and finally spent the evening together. A letter revealed that the heroine might not marry without her uncle's consent. The couple waited, won over the uncle, and after great preparation were married. Bridegroom Ernest then robbed the house of his new relatives and "skipped out with all his wife's money," arriving in America with $50,000.

Maybe it was the philosophy, the peculiar scenes and the unusual scenery, or the performance that made the play acceptable. Miss Jordan played May Edwards in her usual

fervent and feelingly effective style, various passages bringing tears to the eyes of many Comstockers. Of Lawlor as the
first-class swindler, the critic felt it was "useless to speak"
since this actor had "few equals in his peculiar line."

5

Emily Jordan in the role of Mazeppa! For Miss Jordan's
benefit Phelps (stage manager) and Charles Tibbetts (acting
manager) added new scenery and announced what Comstockers had been waiting to see. Could Emily Jordan possibly compete with the famous — or notorious — Adah Menken? The *Union* critic said yes; in fact, the Menken's Mazeppa, though it won for the actress "imperishable laurels,"
was "far inferior to Jordan's." Had Emily a better form or
more talent? "In beauty of body Miss Jordan is far superior,"
the *Union* insisted, but told ladies they could "rest assured
that nothing in Miss Jordan's representation will call a blush
to their brow as the immodest style of 'Menken' will be carefully avoided." Everything was arranged to insure success of
Miss Jordan's Mazeppa, including "an efficient police force to
preserve order." If a chaste performance, why the police?
Perhaps Comstockers had read the *Call's* review: "Miss Emily
Jordan withdrew her wardrobe and played a straight 'Mazeppa' at Placerville, assisted by Tibbetts for the nonce,
Tartarian Company."

The advertised October 20 arrived. Dodge and Hayward
sang their final concert at Carson. Sutliff's did its best. The
Eureka Benevolent Society held a dance "where enjoyment
reigned supreme" after the theatrical performances. But
Emily Jordan at the Opera House was *the* attraction that
Thursday night in Washoe. So great was the demand for
transportation that the management ran omnibuses along the
Lode. Even the *Enterprise* brusquely remarked, "We presume
all the seats in the theatre and some in the adjoining hay-
yard will be taken."

So, while Adah Menken (having left London [6] and her luxurious three-roomed, mirror-lined dressing room with its silk curtains, velvet carpets, a piano, rosewood furniture, marble bathroom and hot and cold water) played *Mazeppa* in the French language for the Parisians, Emily Jordan "under the assumed name of Cassimer" played *Mazeppa* in English "better than any one we have ever seen attempt it . . . before one of the largest audiences that has assembled at Maguire's Opera House for a long time," lauded the *Union*.

The "gorgeous scenery, the splendid tableaux with the lovely form dashing up and down the fearful mountain passes on the fiery untamed steed," plus the Abder Kahn of Frank Lawlor paid off at the box office with such success that Maguire had Mazeppa ride again next night even though Miss Grace Stanton, the lady refugee from rebeldom, lectured to the Second Ward Union Club and the soldiers, preparing to evacuate Fort Churchill for a new military station at the mouth of King's Canyon, were too busy to attend.[7]

For a Saturday matinee Miss Jordan played Mazeppa, and yet again in the evening, when the management, looking out over a packed house, were unaware of any competition in the political demonstrations along the Lode; the Copperhead celebration that embraced some 1700 "rag-tag and bobtail"

---

[6] Regarding the Menken's London season *The Californian* could not resist the following observation: "Englishmen generally pride themselves upon belonging to the *nil admirari* school, copying in as great manner as they can the stolidity and imperturbability of their cliffs. They stand before the pyramids and make no expression of wonder; they cross the prairies of the West and never raise an eyebrow in astonishment. But London has at last had a sensation; the side whiskers of our calm and composed cousins have at last been made to curl. Menken has appeared at Astley's, the fiery and untamed steed has been loosed on the boards of that great amphitheatre, and the habitués have been startled from their apathy. . ."

All the leading London newspapers (from the *Times* on) carried lengthy notices of the Menken's debut, and, strange to say, none of them were denunciatory.

[7] Bachelors read General McDowell's requisition requesting Governor Nye to raise enough companies of infantry to complete — with those already in service from Nevada Territory — a full regiment. Nye accordingly called for seven companies, each to have one captain, one second lieutenant, five sergeants, eight corporals, two musicians, one wagoner, and not less than 64 privates.

crawlers of the Democratic party parading with sagebrush brooms,[8] torches, and transparencies; or the "Grand Union Meeting" at Gold Hill, where "everybody and especially the ladies" enjoyed "an intellectual treat" in the lecture of Miss Stanton, who spoke before an audience so packed that the floor gave way and fell five feet, causing much confusion, no injuries, but considerable boasting that the Union party was "getting heavy."

After Sunday dinners featuring grizzly bear meat, Comstockers again packed the Opera House for another evening of *Mazeppa*. Five successive performances satiated even the Comstockers, so it is doubtful if the Menken-championing *Enterprise* was responsible for Miss Jordan's leaving. Nevertheless, note the *Call's* precipitation:

> . . . Having been outrageously Mazeppa-ed by the fair Emily, the *Territorial Enterprise* precipitates its ire upon the lady's airy "nothing to wear" impersonation of the character, and appeals to her, in the name of God, to blow her nose! Know, oh persecuted Emily, though it may be easier to show legs than ability, that an actress may "catch a Tartar," as well as a cold by so doing. Accept our handkerchief — and a petticoat. Be modest and you won't be pen-pecked.

6

Without Miss Jordan the Opera House troupe played *Uncle Tom's Cabin* Monday night, Frank Lawlor taking the part of Uncle Tom. Belle Divine "just growed" as Topsy, and La Petite Emma played the angelic Little Eva role, thereby

---

[8] The reason for sagebrush brooms and the scarcity of regular ones in the Democratic demonstration finally slipped out: a Copperhead collection of some $1,500 for the buying of good brooms had been lost in a San Francisco poker game by a "reprehensible rogue," who "got busted and skedaddled for parts unknown."

To liven the evening, the Democrats had hired the Metropolitan Brass Band, but the musicians wished it "distinctly understood that they are not of that party by any sorts of means, but utterly repudiate it and its principles." The band played such neutral airs as "When Johnny Comes Marching Home" for the Copperheads, but to prove their loyalty marched home to "John Brown" and "Rally Round the Flag."

winning "the hearts of all." Although the inclement weather kept some theatre-lovers away, *Uncle Tom's Cabin* was "well received and passed off in a highly creditable manner" in spite of the cold theatre.

On October 25 the Carsonites held "quite a large Union meeting." On the Comstock the irrepressible Union boys, marching arm in arm and singing "John Brown," made fraternal visits to all the Union clubs; then pushed into Sutliff's to watch Tuers, Collins, and the melodeon entertainers or found seats in the Opera House to welcome back the Washoe favorite, Miss Virginia Howard.

For her new Silverland engagement Miss Howard chose the sensational five-act *Camille,* which Maguire, with complete abandon, advertised as "the most attractive bill of the season." No small inducement was the promise of a warm theatre.[9] Needless to say, Miss Howard "drew a good house," the *Union* insisting she had "few equals" and "no superiors." Frank Lawlor, "fairly outdoing himself," appeared as Armand Duval; Mrs. Judah came on as Babilliard; and "the entire strength of the star company" assisted. Next night the Thespians presented Bulwer's *Money* to an appreciative audience.

To help the "gallant boys" of the Virginia Fire Department "get a big lot of hose and other fixins out of 'sock'" in the office of Wells, Fargo and Company, since the city fathers would not (or could not) pay the c.o.d. charges, Maguire's "star company" presented the "sensational and truly thrilling drama" of *Aurora Floyd,* Miss Howard portraying the heroine "in a lifelike manner" and Frank Lawlor winning fresh laurels as John Mellish.

Between acts — and *Aurora Floyd* had five — Miss Belle

---

[9] Few places in the world consumed as much firewood at this time as Virginia. Mills required six to 10 cords a day. Hoisting works, saw and planing mills, and other industries used quantities more. Already near-by canyons and hills were bare. Soon suppliers looked to the Sierra forests. Generally driven by Chinese, patient little donkeys carried wood into the Lode towns.

Divine sang a favorite ballad in her own unapproachable style; and Johnny Tuers (from Sutliff's) did "The Essence of Old Virginia" in a fashion "that brought down the house." The program closed on the laughable farce of *Forty and Fifty*, in which Mrs. Judah became Mrs. Lilly White and "sustained her well established reputation as an artiste of the first order of merit in her peculiar line." Reviewers, glowing under the evening's jollity, insisted that all the actors sustained their parts very well. McGowan possessed merit "that would adorn an even more presuming artist," Mitchel almost seemed a natural scoundrel, and Messrs. Phelps, Thayer, and Brown deserved special mention.

After viewing the "great national play" of *Putnam, the Iron Son of '76* with Lawlor as Lord Cornwallis, Miss Howard as Viola, and Mrs. Judah as Mrs. Starkham, the Washoites insisted Major Putnam must ride for them again and the Goddess of Liberty again predict the results of the Declaration of Independence. As *Mazeppa* had proved, Comstockers liked horses on stage (even without nude ladies) so enjoyed *Putnam* for a third night.

But the Opera House faced competition, mainly from Sutliff's. The evening of *Putnam's* opening, Max Walter presented Miss Isabella and other "talented performers" from the Bay, not the least attraction being Señorita Maria on whose "reappearance Virginia people congratulated themselves."

During the concluding days of October Charles Tibbetts of the Opera House arranged a series of benefits — besides the one helping the firemen get their fire hose "out of sock." On the 29th for her benefit Mrs. Judah appeared as Widow Green in *The Love Chase* and as Mrs. Cabbageall in *Putnam*. Sandwiched between benefits on the sixth night of her engagement, Miss Howard, supported by "the great combination company," treated theatre-goers to the nautical drama of *Black-Eyed Susan*. A repetition of the increasingly popular

Iron Son of '76 brought Lawlor again striding on stage as Lord Cornwallis.

The Comstock season of the "really excellent stock company" concluded with a farewell benefit honoring Frank Lawlor in *Jack Cade, the Captain of the Commons.* "A large and appreciative audience" packed the Opera House unwilling to miss seeing and hearing the beneficiary in Judge Conrad's great tragedy and in a recitation:

> Jist afther the war, in the year '98
> As soon as the boys wor all scattered and bate,
> 'Twas the custom, whenever a pisant was got,
> To hang him by thrial — barrin' sich as was shot.
> There was thrial by jury goin' on by daylight,
> And the martial-law hangin' the lavins by night.

So Lawlor began Samuel Lover's celebrated poem of "Shamus O'Brien," which with "masterly effect" Frank repeatedly had thrilled the Washoites.

> An' the bravest an' hardiest boy iv them all
> Was Shamus O'Brien, from the town of Glingall.

Lawlor concluded his recital with O'Brien's escape:

> The sodgers ran this way, the sheriffs ran that
> And Father Malone lost his new Sunday hat.
> To-night he'll be sleepin' in Aherloe Glin,
> An' the de'l's in the dice if you catch him ag'in.
> Your swords they may glitter, your carbines go bang.
> But if you want hangin', it's yourself you must hang.
>
> He has mounted his horse, and soon he will be
> In America, darlint, the land of the free.

The "entire galaxy of talent" concluded the evening with a favorite farce.

Next day the stock company took over the Carson Theatre for the week of the Nevada Fair. With the Opera House now closed, Comstockers were free to enjoy good music, good jokes, and "all that sort of thing," plus "Tableaux Vivants and Señorita Maria, all the rage at Sutliff's."

The Thirty-sixth Gun

1

Political events were rocking Silverland. Now was its chance to become a state (though as a territory Washoe had helped replenish the Federal treasury). Time was running out. How could the Nevada Constitution — modeled on the one written by an actor and others in 1863, but which now gave general satisfaction — reach Washington in time for Nevada's three votes to help pass the Thirteenth Amendment?

True, the telegraph line had been completed, but this method would cost over $3000. Yet this was the only way. To Frank Bell, a young Virginia telegrapher, went the initial job.[1] It was a tedious process. At each division the entire Nevada constitution was taken down in longhand, re-telegraphed, written again, and again re-sent on across the United States. Anxiously the Washoites waited.

Then, on the last day of October the operator on duty took down the reply: ". . . be it known that I, Abraham Lincoln . . . proclaim that the said State of Nevada is admitted into the Union. . ." It was an unusual entrance. But Nevada was in; and Company D proclaimed the joyous news by firing a "grand national salute of 35 guns," plus one more for the new Nevada. Leaving homes and businesses, gambling houses, and saloons, the people rushed into the streets and continued cheering "long after the military had left."

Nevada admitted! So, now to the polls! "Are the Union

---

[1] Margaret Watson, "$3000 Telegram," *Ranch Romances*, December 8, 1950, pp. 102-105.

men ready?" queried some Nevada newspapers. The question
was almost an insult. "Anyone wishing to bet that Abraham
Lincoln will not carry the new state can be accommodated
to the extent of $500 by calling at this office," challenged the
Union. Nevada would celebrate a three-thousand majority,
the people insisted, sang a new version of "Kingdom Coming," cheered Miss Stanton's patriotic lectures, and applauded
the addresses of Dr. H. M. Bien and Colonel C. A. Summer
directed to "all loyal hearted men." Professor Millington,
reopening his dancing school, found the people "too full of
politics" to attend.[2]

2

In Lander County the "up-and-doing" Union men held
enthusiastic meetings; lighted bonfires; paraded through
Austin with their bands, torches, and flags; cheered themselves "nearly hoarse"; and packed Bradford's Hall to hear
Nye, DeLong, Stewart, and Claggett. Grace Stanton, the
"good Samaritan and Florence Nightingale of the War," also
lectured on the "Battle of Shiloh" and "Life in the Hospitals."

The elections over, the Reese Riverites celebrated with a
torchlight procession of twelve hundred marchers and a "great
ball." Such as did not go, submitted to requisitions upon their
wardrobes by those who went. "Boots found strange feet and
vests were in demand."

People of Humboldt gave vent to their enthusiasm in a
"grand jollification" that lasted all day, well into the night,
and all the next day. Governor Nye set off the celebrating by
"announcing the birth of the new state" and offering "a
patriotic toast," which was answered by prolonged cheering.
With Lincoln's proclamation still in his hand, Nye "mounted
a table and addressed the crowd in elegant terms and patriotic
sentiment. . . All this time the Old Flag waved proudly
from Tom Ewing's pole and Torrey thundered with his

---

[2] However, after the elections they danced "a successful season" of "Four Hands
Round" and "Ladies Grand Chain" at the Gold Hill Theatre.

artillery." [3] Then as many as could, pushed into Vanhoven-berg's Hall for more speaking. Not until two in the morning did the people sleep, but by ten o'clock were on the go again helping Dun Glen, Star City, and Humboldt City with patriotic demonstrations.

Silver City set the Lode towns celebrating again with a fine procession. Virginia brought out the sprinkling carts and put on a Union demonstration so magnificent it eclipsed a like celebration of late October. Putting their Opera-House-laid plans into reality, the Comstockers came out in a "Grand Torchlight Procession" of 3500 people with two thousand torches, colored lanterns, and twirling mottoes.[4] Eight and ten deep with shouts and songs and music playing, the paraders surged from the Mouth of Six Mile Canyon to the top of Mount Davidson in so grand and splendid a sight no pen could do it justice, or so thought the *Union* reporter, who with others viewed the "dancing illuminations," the magnificent "river of fire," from a hill north of the Savage works.

3

November 8 was election day. At Silver City the Copperheads found the Confederate flag nailed to the floor at polling places so they "had to trample it under foot in exercising their privilege as voters." Virginia voted to music. The Metropolitan Band, having plastered the names of Lincoln and Johnson on each side of their band wagon, "enlivened the scene with soul-stirring national airs."

At last the voting places closed. Local papers "officially reported" 16,420 votes cast; 9,826 for Lincoln, first president to be re-elected since Andy Jackson, thirty-two years before,

---

3 Unionville *Humboldt Register*, November 5, 1864.

4 Such mottoes as "Union," "God Grant Victory," "Loyal is Nevada," and "Struck the Copperhead ledge; pinching out." ("That's so." agreed the *Union*, "They never were a regular sound lead.") During the parade the Copperheads already as "scarce as hen's teeth . . . slunk away abashed," but the Chinese stood amazed with mouths open while the "dusty Piutes must have wondered at this dazzling turn out of their brethern, the pale-faces."

and 6,594 for McClellan. Glory to Washoe! But Nevada was disappointed that she had not won the $1000-flag and the title of Banner State.[5]

At sunset a funeral procession passed "slowly and mournfully" through Dayton, Silver City, Gold Hill, and down C Street in Virginia, a band at its head playing "The Dead March in Saul," to bury in some imaginary grave "the last hope of the Democrat party." Aside from commenting on brooms having become very cheap, some of them "beautifully trimmed, and all that sort of thing," loyal newspapers could not "find it in their hearts to crow" over the Democratic newspaper, the *Daily Constitution* and the Copperhead defeat, except to remark that the McClellan Broom Rangers' headquarters in San Francisco had now opened, significantly enough, as a coffin shop.

At Silver City, Democrat loser J. D. Benson paid off his election bet in the presence of a committee of thirty men, a band, a glee club, and a hilarious crowd by sawing a cord of tough Washoe mahogany into convenient lengths and auctioning it for the manufacture of canes, picture frames, and other salable articles, the proceeds — amounting to "four or five thousand dollars" — going to the Sanitary Fund, labeled proudly as a gift "from the State of Nevada."

H. G. Blaisdel, the newly elected first governor of the Sagebrush State, "looking extremely hearty and feeling about three feet taller," hurried down to Carson along with the Gold Hill Artillery, the Silver City Guards, and the Silver City Artillery to fire a 36-gun salute and aid the jollification. Already the capital was illuminated. Candles shone in the

---

[5] Kansas, having the largest vote percent-wise of any state for Lincoln, won the coveted flag and honor instead. Brushing aside this disappointment, D. Narcross of Virginia manufactured the first flag to contain the full 36 stars though "Congress did not require" that the Nevada star be added until the next Fourth of July. A man in Silver City and another in Washoe City promptly ordered the Norcross flags to prove "our new State of Nevada to be nowise behind her older sisters in true loyalty."

windows; bonfires flared in the streets. Chinese lanterns, rockets, and all sorts of fireworks lighted the night. Carson citizens and guests marched and counter-marched through the streets; then pushed into the Pavilion for the addresses, which they finally adjourned with a grand flourish of music and "booming of the loud-mouthed cannon." The general hilarity kept up until midnight; a noisier and jollier time had never been experienced in Carson City.

4

But bonanza times were fading. Though not all the celebrating Washoites were yet fully aware of it, the thirty-sixth gun ushered in Nevada's statehood as the Comstock entered borrasca days.[6] Not without reason were such "Nursery Rhymes" as the following found in local newspapers:

> Sing a song of sixpence, a pocket-full of rocks,
> Half a dozen dividends cooked on our stocks;
> When the mine is opened nary gold you see —
> Isn't that a nice report to make a company?

As Washoe mining stocks skidded downward, Montgomery Street (the Wall Street of the West) was troubled; and on the Comstock Lode some mine superintendents forced Union men to quit their jobs, so as to hire Secessionists in their places — or so stated the *Humboldt Register*. What was more serious, however, was the fact that Nevada miners were finding it increasingly difficult to locate and bring out rich ore.[7]

---

[6] The *Enterprise* realistically estimated the indebtedness of Nevada at $358,000; taxable property at $80 million, which would yield only $240,000.

[7] Nevertheless, the San Francisco *Scientific Press* announced that several large Ferrand oscillating amalgamators had gone to Silverland, and that the returning teamsters hauled back potatoes. "A few years since we little thought that California," observed the Carson City *Post* proudly, "would ever depend on Nevada for any vegetable production."

Return of the Pioneers

1

With statehood attained it would seem proper to close this review of Washoe entertainment; however, before the end of Nevada's natal year old friends would reappear on the theatrical scene as if by plan to terminate fittingly the territorial phase of the Silver Theatre. While unknowingly awaiting these pioneer Thespians, Comstockers crowded the Opera House for patriotic celebrations; a gift enterprise; and various theatrical performances, including a concert benefit for a Mr. Maguire, popular member of the Virginia Glee Club, at which both the Virginia and the Germania Glee Club "acquitted themselves admirably." Judge Baldwin put the "ring of true metal" into his address, and the inspired audience joined in singing "The Star-Spangled Banner" and in cheering the "Old Flag." The evening closed on a note akin to wild excitement.

Remembering the actor's help in raising funds for them, the Virginia Fire Company tendered Johnny Tuers a complimentary benefit, which Johnny made exciting too, by performing the "Zampillaerostration," the grand gymnastic feat on the flying trapeze, making a huge leap of 125 feet from the dress circle to the back of the stage. Next, using a loaded revolver, he would shoot an apple from a man's head at twelve paces. No one volunteered to hold the target though Tuers was known as one of the best shots on the Pacific coast. Johnny Collins was finally chosen, but gave Thomas Mitchell the honor at the last minute.

"One of the favorite and peculiar sons of old Momus and Terpsichore   .   .   .   a rich card by himself alone," Johnny could have given the entire evening's entertainment, but Virginia Howard graciously volunteered to appear in two fine comediettas: *Nan, the Good-for-Nothing* and *The Swiss Cottage*. Who assisted the actress besides Jimmy Griffith and Mrs. Chapman remains unknown as Mrs. Judah, Mr. Lawlor, and the rest of the dramatic company (according to the *Era* anyway) had returned to the Bay. The Metropolitan Band, however, "enlivened the occasion," thus helping to make the November 6 benefit a successful Tuers farewell.

Diminutive Jimmy Griffith took a farewell benefit too, on November 17. The perennial favorite, Miss Howard, appeared in three of her best-liked characters and "by particular request in her perfect impersonation of the character of Nan, the Good-for-Nothing, supported by the entire strength of the company" (whoever they were). Comstockers who braved the weather — "first it blew, then it snew, then it thew, and then it friz" — were rewarded with "the thrilling Irish drama" of *Nora Crenia,* the comedietta of *Floating Beacon; or, A Sailor in Search of a Friend,* and, of course, *Nan.* The benefit was a success, the *Enterprise* observing that Griffith lacked one thing short of being a great actor, "every man cannot be as large as Forrest."

Saturday was to have been the benefit night of the pioneer actress Mrs. George Chapman. Selby's beautiful moral drama of *Robert Macaire; or, The Two Murders* and the amusing comedy, *The Enraged Politician,* with all the original music, along with other attractions were on the advertised bill, but the weather forced postponement, the *Union* admonishing Comstockers to restrain impatience until the following Saturday. However, this date turned out to be a disappointment too.

2

At the Carson Theatre many Carsonites enjoyed Gropius' "Grand Panorama of a Tour of Europe" and made plans for

November 24, the day set apart by President Lincoln for thanksgiving and prayer. Thanksgiving Day was "more generally observed than might be expected in this new country." Many places of business closed; churches held services. Besides "turkey dinners *a la mode* New England," Washoites enjoyed venison, hares, sage hens, rabbits, and quail at dinners and "convivial parties too numerous to mention." On Thanksgiving evening many Comstockers attended the dance at Armory Hall sponsored by Engine Company No. 4. While "rich, voluptuous music wafted from Millington's fiddle and the chief horn-blower poured forth rapturous sounds from the big end of his brazen horn," the National Guardsmen and their ladies floated past "in the mazes of waltz, schottische, and mazurka." Zephyr winds also celebrated, pulling down awnings and signs; then, growing bolder, snatched up a big 2,200-pound wagon of the Reese River Fast Freight Line, "carried it over the housetops and everything else and landed it about a mile away in Cedar Ravine, smashing it up pretty essentially."

Regarding business at the Opera House, the *Era* noted that "an occasional dramatic performance" was given by Virginia Howard, Jimmy Griffith, and a few others. Heavy rains, mud, and snow precluded "the idea of any one attending the theater" that Saturday evening of November 26 so the management again postponed Mrs. Chapman's benefit, setting the next Tuesday as *the* day. Again the weather intervened. Finally on Sunday, December 4, Mrs. Chapman would take her thrice-postponed benefit, but whether she actually did, or proved that, as the *Union* insisted," a patient waiter is no loser," was questionable, as yet another benefit would take place before the one honoring the mother of twenty children.

Another familiar face now appeared in Nevada, "a well-known, active, and useful member of the dramatic profession," P. M. Westwood, bringing with him "a reputation that had long been established" in Washoe. Recalling that Westwood had settled in Virginia with his family during the pre-territorial days and had built there Nevada's first theatre, The Howard, the Washoites greeted the pioneer actor with special warmth and appreciation, but with stabs of remorse too; for they never had given "P.M." a benefit. The Nevadans, however, intended to correct that unkind omission with "a grand volunteer benefit" on December 3. That first Saturday night of December the Comstockers shovelled the snow from D Street and away from the door of the Opera House, pushed into the lighted theatre, and filled the seats.

The program was well worth braving the snow, storm, and cold to be present; for Miss Howard, as promised, appeared in new leading characters, assisted by the faithful Mrs. George Chapman. Mrs. M. R. Williams and other volunteers presented the laughable pantomime of *The Four Lovers* and also assisted with *Family Failing*, a Virginia première. *The Stage Struck Yankee* completed an evening that seems to have been satisfying amusement-wise as well as gratifying to the deserving recipient, P. M. Westwood.

3

Following Philip Westwood's benefit, a dearth of theatrical, political, and other news caused by the wintry storms left Washoe newspapers so "hard up for items" that editors filled space with any likely or unlikely matter.[1] The colorful procession, ceremonies, and grand ball of December 7 dedicating the new I.O.O.F. Hall, "an ornament to this or any other city," located on Virginia's B Street afforded Washoe writers some-

---

[1] Hard up for news, editors filled columns of newspaper space with a supposed accident to De Quille. Rushing about C Street, "following his nose in search" of elusive news, the *Enterprise* local — according to the account — plunged headlong into a snowbank and had to be pulled out. The "hopelessness of his condition," his possible "death," and the following epitaph were included in the *Union* fabrication:

> Here *lies* the famous Dan De Quille.
> He *lied* on earth, he now *lies* still.
> His f-*lying* soul somewhere did soar
> There to *lie* forevermore.

thing to report and Joe Goodman an opportunity to compose and deliver the dedication "Poem." [2]

In spite of bad weather the energetic ladies of Nevada churches held money-making festivals: $1300 resulted for St. Paul's Church after the ladies had secured the assistance of Jimmy Griffiths in planning and executing a series of tableaux; $800 was netted for the Episcopal Church; and an unknown amount by the "colored people" for the First Baptist Church of Virginia. During the Orphans' Fair, Nevadans drank "patent lemonade," danced to the music of a Virginia band, and spun the wheel of fortune for chances, which included a "lovely" statue of Mazeppa lashed to a huge arrow instead of the famous wild horse that the Menken-championing De Quille "was, of course, too gallant a local not to buy."

4

Disagreeable weather made good business for Music Hall. Rather than cruise about the cold streets or loaf in the saloons, many men felt it cheaper to sit in a comfortable room, drink, smoke, and watch Señorita Maria dance,[3] Miss Florence and Miss Clarissa sing new ballads, Master Franklin and Johnny Collins do Ethiopian acts, and the entire company present *tableaux vivants* and the sidesplitting little pieces: *The Magic Statue* and *Sports of the Ring*.

---

[2] Goodman's dedicatory lines were:

> Amid the shock of millions, met in strife
> To save or sacrifice a Nation's life —
> Amid the crash of empires, swept away
> In quick convulsions or by slow decay,
> Whose massive fragments, fiercely downward hurled,
> Shake to their base the structures of the world —
> Amid the years whose suffering and crime
> Plow deeper yet the wrinkled front of time —
> We meet in Faith's eternal peace and youth,
> To rear a shrine to Friendship, Love, and Truth.

[3] Irritated at the *Enterprise* for calling Señorita Maria "a first-class pedal manipulator," the *Call* retorted that "the term would be better applied to a chiropodist." The *Enterprise*, it seems, was making so many derogatory remarks at this time that the editor of the *Humboldt Register* expressed himself as "considerably surprised . . . to find a very favorable notice of one Jesus Christ."

Then the "terrific clog dancer" Master Franklin took a benefit. "A representative specimen of the genuine, young, plantation darkey," the beneficiary appeared as the feature in the minstrel part of the evening. Two plays then held the spotlight: "the grand spectacular and side-splitting farce of *The Derby Races,* a play as full of ghosts as a California dog is full of fleas," and a piece involving magic, *Jocko, the Brazilian Ape.*

So popular were the Sutliff presentations that many men requested "the two great magic pieces" — *The Derby Races* and *The Magic Box* — be given as a Saturday matinee for their wives and children. Max Walter happily obliged, charging fifty cents, and children half as much. Two nights later the Washoites filled Sutliff's again for the first presentation of a new local burlesque — title not given — that was repeated with additional novelties and attractions.

Music Hall continued to be the Comstock attraction, the *Union* critic wondering "how Max Walter can afford to get up such a quantity and variety of glorious fun and amusement for the low price of fifty cents a ticket admission." Max wondered too, especially when firewood prices [4] soared to such heights that Comstock restaurants were forced to raise the price of meals — although beef in Carson sold at five and six cents a pound. Maybe living was cheaper in the new state capital. Anyway, on December 19 Music Hall closed and the troupe went to Carson "for the edification of the new Legislature of the new State of Nevada," which was then "for the first time 'dissembled.' " [5]

More snow drifted down over Silverland. Gay, holiday equipage appeared and the "merry laugh of fast young men

---

[4] Although since 1861 alleged and real finds of coal had been made and tested in the quartz mills at Dayton and Silver City, the 1864 discovery, soon known as the Newcastle Coal Company, was "apparently a species of lignite" and did burn in the company's stove, in some Nevada homes, and in some blacksmith's forges since it cost "less than half as much" as firewood.

[5] San Francisco *Daily Morning Call,* December 25, 1864.

and pretty girls mingled in musical cadence." [6] Other Washoites — on six-foot snow skis, such as those used by Snowshoe Thompson — arrived in Virginia, pushed past the cold, dark, and empty theatres on C and D Streets, and headed for the lighted saloons for mid-December diversion. Then, the Thursday before Christmas the Sutliff troupers came back to Virginia, bringing with them "several valuable diamond rings" with which to induce attendance at Music Hall. Admission was still only fifty cents, but to get a chance on winning a diamond ring an extra fifty cents was needed.

All churches as well as places of amusement were "going full blast" now, presenting dances, newly prepared Christmas programs, novelties, Christmas trees, Santas, and gifts. President Lincoln's Christmas gift, "the invincible" Sherman's capture of Savannah, was celebrated with wild cheering and the "setting off of a lot of rockets."

To the Comstock now came the "Panorama of Europe," which the Carson editor — who had seen "about every painted thing" exhibited in the United States — reported "a magnificent painting, a work of excellence . . . the best." After an extended showing in Carson, the Panorama moved on to other Washoe towns to allow audiences to wander "from the frozen regions of the Arctic Ocean to London, Paris, Lisbon, the Mediterranean, Constantinople, Moscow, and the port of Hamburg." So engrossing were those celebrated

---

[6] Comstockers found diversion of other sorts too. The anniversary dinner of the "landing of the Pilgrims at Plymouth in 1620" was held at Morton's Cider Manufactory on B Street. For its opening, the Nevada Brewing Saloon, opposite Maguire's, provided free, all the lunch and beer that patrons could consume. Two amateur "bruisers put on a milling match" in a Virginia brickyard. "A grand billiard tournament" began. Saloonkeeper Carl York held a "grand barbecue." At "A Grand Ball and Soiree" at Armory Hall, featuring Virginia's Brass and String Bands, the Emmett Guards and their ladies "danced all night till broad daylight," as many also did at Professor Millington's "Grand Soiree and Ball" at Silver City.

Surprise parties became "exceedingly fashionable in the gay and festive city of Washoe." Taking the "fair lady of the house" and the host by complete surprise, even routing them from bed, added to the "enjoyment and mirth" of those impromptu occasions. — Washoe City *Weekly Star*, December 31, 1864.

places, it was "some thing of a shock" to suddenly realize "you were still in Washoe City," Virginia, Carson, Dayton, or other Nevada town.[7]

5

Before some widely advertised gift enterprises could be given at the Opera House, an actor's benefit was held there. Harry Taylor — and "Who does not know Harry, the theatrical and musical individual, so well known in California as well as here?" queried the *Union* — took his farewell benefit, for which Virginia talent volunteered in "a stirring bill of attractions" on December 29.

Next night the Opera House was dark. But three following nights (December 31 and January 1 and 2) Maguire's glowed with special warmth and inviting lights. The reason? As agent for the Empire Gold and Silver Mining Company, Jim Stark had arrived from the East aboard the *Constitution* early in October, had gone out to his old home at Aurora, and from there to Carson and to Virginia. He was heartily greeted as "the most eminent tragedian," who had brought Shakespeare to the Nevada desert back in 1861. As with P. M. Westwood, Stark's arrival prompted quick action. Admiring the actor's "private virtues" as well as his "histrionic talents," Comstockers persuaded Stark to agree to perform for three evenings in Sir Edward Lytton Bulwer's "beautiful play in five acts, *The Lady of Lyons*," and to conclude the evening with "the laughable farce" of *Nan, the Good-for-Nothing*.

To enlighten any uninformed newcomers, the *Union* further recalled that though Stark was "no longer a professional actor, having retired from the stage some time ago," he was a member of "our first Constitutional Convention from Es-

---

[7] Martin the Wizard, who was "as migratory, if not as predatory in his habits" as the bird of that name, "essayed the power of his magic on the pockets of the Austinites, and straightway came to the conclusion that 'scads' there abouts were as far and few between as angels' visits. More *pocus* to your *hocus*, peripatetic Wizard!" concluded the *Call* correspondent.

meralda County," was an "earnest friend of the Union, and was a prominent candidate for Congress before our first Union State Convention." The Comstock writer went on to assure his readers that Mr. Stark would be "greeted by a large and fashionable audience, as his superior talents as an actor are well known." [8]

To properly present the pioneer actor, the management of Maguire's made changes and improvements, throwing open the doors of the Opera House "to the play-going public in a style that all Comstockers properly appreciated," it being their "last opportunity" to see James Stark before he returned East. With another pioneer, Miss Virginia Howard, as his leading lady, Stark portrayed Claude Melnotte in an any-thing-but-disappointing manner. Next night the tragedian and the "full and efficient company," including Miss Howard and Mr. and Mrs. J. D. McGowan, treated the Washoites to Kotzebue's domestic play of *The Stranger* and concluded the evening with the popular comedietta of *Box and Cox*.

Some in the audience, on those choice winter evenings of Stark's brief visit, had been in Washoe since its beginning, when a dearth of legitimate drama had sent them to saloons, gaming tables, and hurdy-gurdy to find diversion. Many now recalled it was "that mad wag" troubadour Mart Taylor, "Bobbin' 'Round" in the mines, braving Indians and bedbugs, who had brought the first professional entertainment to the amusement-starved miners, thus rating the title: "father of the Nevada theatre." Of that exciting summer of 1860 the miners recalled too, after the Indian wars when without fan-fare and with little more than their own ingenuity, the West-wood troupe, fresh from entertaining Johnston's soldiers in Utah, had built the first theatre to grace the Nevada desert landscape. That this playhouse, the Howard "above A Street," finished even before the mining camp could boast a news-

---

[8] *Virginia Daily Union*, December 30, 1864.

paper or had completely "lost its canvas appearance," had
been opened that memorable September 29, when "P.M.,"
his sister Mercy, and others of the Westwood Troupe had
"exceedingly well-rendered" the drama of *The Toodles* and
the farce of *The Swiss Swains*.

Of the next year, nostalgic memories recalled the Gruenwalds and a melodeon on C Street, and lame Ned Bingham
with his minstrels departing almost as James Stark and his
company had arrived along with the first of the winter storms.
What a rich theatrical season that had been! William Tell,
Hamlet, Othello, King Lear — as enacted by Stark — had trod
the Howard stage. Comstockers — everyone, not just the
cognoscenti — had filled the seats and clambered over the
roof to crawl in the windows to see the famed tragedian, the
lovely Nellie Brown, Miss Hamlin, Jimmy Griffith. Also there
was Harry Brown who tried "doing himself brown" in Comstock saloons, eventually bringing about the dissolution of the
"Washoe Star Dramatic Company," though not before Mark
Twain had done his biting local version of *Ingomar*, and Dan
De Quille his timely hit, *The Wheelers in Washoe*. Mrs. Stark
had come up from California to play the morally precarious
Camille and *The Lady of Lyons*. The Stark Troupe, early
Comstockers recalled, had taken time to open Topliffe's new
theatre in July of 1862; and not long after, Sarah Stark had
given up trying to dissuade her talented husband from for-
saking his histrionic profession for an Aurora mine.

The bonanza year of '63 was one Comstockers liked recalling best, perhaps; for a new theatre over on D Street had
claimed their admiration, attention, and attendance. True,
the opening of Maguire's Opera House came near being its
closing as Washoe Zephyrs set the theatre to creaking in its
storm-tossed and ship-like seams. Nevertheless, Julia Dean
Hayne — though "noticeably shaken" — had read Walter
Leman's poem of dedication and the troupe had played

Money to a rather anxious but attentive audience, loath to leave until the freshly painted curtain reproducing the beauty of Lake Bigler finally had been run down.

Frank Mayo had played his first Hamlet in that Opera House. Charles Pope and the beloved Virginia Howard had pleased Comstockers there, as had "Queen of Comedy" Mrs. W. H. Leighton, light-hearted Lotta Crabtree, McKean Buchanan, and J. B. Booth. There James Murray had displayed his Scotch genius, and Mrs. H. A. Perry had gaily danced for appreciative audiences. Naughty Adah Isaacs Menken had intrigued the Washoites for weeks by riding a "wild mustang" up the rocky stage crags, where later a disgraceful fight between over-tired actors had taken place. At Maguire's, too, such San Francisco Minstrels as Birch, Backus, Abecco, and Wells had induced joyous laughter, which had turned to tears of sorrow at Sam Wells' untimely death. Mr. Gridley of Austin had sold his sack of Sanitary flour from its stage, where Paul Julien later had tortured his violin.

And now with the close of 1864 the pioneer Thespians had returned as if by plan. What if Virginia's streets were "in a terrible condition"? The people struggled through them to the Opera House, scraped the mud from their boots, and filled the seats to enjoy and honor "the great tragedian and capital good fellow" James Stark as he fittingly closed the Silver Theatre of territorial times.[9]

---

[9] Was it his Comstock reception that caused James Stark to change his profession again? From Virginia he appeared in theatres in Salt Lake and Denver, eliciting notices of special praise. Stark returned to the histrionic profession and endeavored to recoup his finances by a trip to Australia. But audiences and tastes had changed. He returned again to California, only to lose title to mining property and to lose his wife through divorce. On May 11 while playing Virginia City, he was striken with paralysis.

For six years more Stark dragged on, the acting profession giving him bit parts. Then in New York, while Edwin Booth was playing Hamlet and James Stark, who had once been hailed as the greatest interpreter of not only Hamlet, but Othello, Richelieu, and others, was playing a negligible role in the same production that October 12, 1875, the curtain fell not only on Shakespeare's tragedy but on Stark's own. And the former Nevadan made his exit from the stage of life.

Appendix

Performances of Individual Plays

Be assured many more plays were performed in early Nevada than this list would indicate. Only those plays specifically mentioned in the newspapers, handbills, and programs are included along with the known date given. These dates, too, are often for only one of several performances in different parts of the territory. Extant information is limited regarding the repertories of nearly all Washoe-playing troupes, the Westwood company being the earliest example. Newspaper files are incomplete, and managers often changed programs for variety or from necessity. Though plays were sometimes known by two titles, only one for each is indicated here.

1860
September 28: The Swiss Swains; The Toodles

1861
March: The Last Chance in Virginia City
November 12: Irish Assurance and Yankee Modesty; William Tell

1862
February 22: Ingomar, the Barbarian; The Sage Struck Yankee
March: The Wheelers in Washoe
April: Oh, Hush; Po-ca-hon-tas
May 19: The Iron Chest
  " 27: Richelieu
June 26: Flirtation; Hamlet (Act 3); Richard III (Act 2); Romeo and
    Juliet (Garden scene)
Late June or early July: Camille
July 5: (same program as of June 26)
  " 26: The Lady of Lyons
September 4-5: Fool of the Family; Pride of the Market
      " 22: All that Glitters is not Gold; Fool of the Family; The
    Windmill

1863

July 2: Money
"   6: Barney the Baron; She Would and He Wouldn't
"   7: The Irish Tutor; The Marble Heart
"   8: Limerick Boy; Retribution
"   9: Limerick Boy; Ruy Blas
"   10: The Happy Man; Romance of a Poor Young Man
"   11: Fool of the Family; Oliver Twist; Retribution; Ten Nights in a Bar Room; Tom and Jerry
"   12: Oliver Twist
"   14: East Lynne
"   15: Barney the Baron; Flirtation; The Rough Diamond
"   16: East Lynne; Ingomar, the Barbarian; Much Ado About Nothing (selections)
"   17-18: East Lynne
"   19: Ireland as It Was; The Happy Man
"   20: Fool of the Family; Sketches in India; A Wife for a Day; The Woman in White
"   21: Ten Nights in a Bar Room; The Woman in White
"   22: An Object of Interest; Romance and Reality
"   23: Alice the Forsaken; Limerick Boy; Our Female American Cousin; Raising the Wind; Sketches in India
"   24: Faint Heart Never Won Fair Lady; Fool of the Family; Griseldis; Our Female American Cousin; The Widow's Victim
"   25: Idiot of the Mountains; A Kiss in the Dark; The Pleasant Neighbor; The Rough Diamond
July 26: Jack Sheppard
"   27: Fool of the Family; Hamlet
"   28: East Lynne
"   29: Lady Audley's Secret
"   30: Camille
"   31: The Three Guardsmen
August 1: A Glance at New York; The Irish Diamond; The Rough Diamond
"   3: Masks and Faces; More Blunders than One
"   4: Il Trovatore
"   5: The Rag-Picker of Paris
"   7: Romeo and Juliet; The Rough Diamond
"   8: Asmodeous; Sketches in India; A Wife for a Day
"   10: Captain Charlotte; Podijah B. Peasley; The Windmill

August 11: The Barrack Room; The Maid with the Milking Pail; The
   Yankee Pedlar
" 12: An Object of Interest; Willow Copse
" 13: London Assurance
" 14: Comedy of Errors; Swiss Swains
" 15: Uncle Tom's Cabin
" 16: Ireland as It Was; Ten Nights in a Bar Room
" 17: Comedy of Errors (condensed into 3 acts)
" 19: The Colleen Bawn
" 20: Rob Roy
" 21: The Colleen Bawn; The Yankee Duelist
" 22: Guy Mannering
" 23: Richard III
" 24-25: The Octoroon
" 26: Macbeth
" 27: Othello
August 28: The Irish Cousin
" 29: Guy Mannering; Retribution
August 31-September 4: The Duke's Motto
September 5: The Duke's Motto; My Aunt
" 6: The Stranger
" 6-9: The Blacksmith of Antwerp
" 10: The Duke's Motto
" 11: Fool of the Family; The Orange Girl of Venice
" 15: The Dumb Girl of Genoa; Ingomar, the Barbarian
" 16: The Dumb Girl of Genoa; Nick of the Woods
" 17: Andy Blake; The Serious Family
" 18: The Maniac Lovers; The Pride of the Market; The
   Swiss Swains
" 19: Black-Eyed Susan; The Irish Emigrant
" 21: All that Glitters is not Gold; More Blunders than One;
   Tom and Jerry
October 16: Bone Squash Diablo
" 17-18: The Ghost
" 20: As You Like It; The Bonnie Fish Wife
" 21: The Bonnie Fish Wife; Masks and Faces
" 22: The Loan of a Lover; She Stoops to Conquer
" 23: Court and Stage
" 24: A Duchess for an Hour; The Loan of a Lover
" 25: The Married Rake; A Roland for an Oliver

1863

October 26: The Merchant of Venice; The Swiss Cottage
" 27: The Honeymoon; The Married Rake
" 28: My Neighbor's Wife; The Soldier's Daughter
" 29: The Bonnie Fish Wife; Sharp Practice
November 2: Mazeppa (burlesque)
" 6: Love
November 23: Evadne
" 25: The Stranger; The Swiss Cottage

1864

January 4: Poor Pillicoddy; The Toodles
" 5: To Paris and Back
" 6: Ireland as It Is; Slasher and Crasher
" 8: Andy Blake; The Wandering Minstrel
" 14: Ireland as It Is; The Two Bonnycastles
" 17: The Phantom
" 18: More Blunders than One
" 21: Andy Blake; Old Soldier
February 17: Mazeppa (burlesque)
" 27-29: Mazeppa (burlesque)
March 2-5: The French Spy
" 4-7: The French Spy (burlesque)
" 7-19: Mazeppa
" 10-17: Alta Skeesicks Blenken (burlesque)
" 18-20: Blackeyed Susan
" 20-27: Dick Turpin
" 21: The Lake of Killarney
" 30-31: Aurora Floyd
April 2: Aurora Floyd
" 4-6: Leah, the Forsaken
" 6-8: Home for a Day (burlesque)
" 9: All that Glitters is not Gold; Mazeppa (burlesque); The Stranger
" 10: Leah, the Forsaken
" 11: Hamlet
" 12-14: Mazeppa (burlesque); The Ticket of Leave Man
April 15: The Brigands; Fanchon, the Cricket; The Taming of the Shrew
" 16: The Ticket of Leave Man
" 17: Faint Heart Never Won Fair Lady; The Robbers
" 18: The Four Bald Heads (musical extravaganza)

April 19: Fanchon the Cricket; The Quaker City; The Taming of the
    Shrew
"   20: Evadne; In and Out of Place
"   21: In and Out of Place; Still Water Runs Deep
"   22: A Day in Paris; The Married Rake; Perfection
"   23: Othello
"   24: Nick of the Woods; Pocahontas
"   25: Loan of a Lover; Pocahontas; The Rough Diamond
"   26: The Marble Heart; Po-Ca-Hon-Tas (burlesque)
"   27: Box and Cox; Ingomar
"   28: Box and Cox; The Wife's Secret
"   29: The Limerick Boy; The Wife's Secret
"   30: Irish Corroberee; A Kiss in the Dark; The Mormons; The
    Mormons (burlesque)
May 1: Charles II
"   2: Don Caesar de Bazan; The Honeymoon
"   3: A Kiss in the Dark; Richard III
"   4-5: The Octoroon
"   6: The Lady of Lyons; Paddy Miles' Boy
"   7: The Poor of New York
"   9: The Serious Family; The Wife's Secret
"   10: Richelieu
"   11: Damon and Pythias; Sketches in India
"   12: Macbeth
"   13: School for Scandal
"   14-16: Jack Sheppard
May 13: Green Bushes; The Mischievous Nigger
"   18-22: Cartouche; The Old House on the Bridge
"   21: The Dumb Belle
"   22: Cartouche
"   23: The Morning Call; The Queen of Abruzza; Robert Macaire;
    The Serious Family: The Water Witches
"   30: The Creole; Faint Heart Never Won Fair Lady
Before June 9: The Octoroon
June 18-19: Playing with Fire
"   20-21: The Duke's Motto
"   21-27: The Ticket of Leave Man
July 1: The Man with the Iron Mask
"   2: The Man with the Iron Mask; The Stage-struck Barber
"   6: Dominique, the Deserter; The Irish Emigrant

1864

July 7-8: Hamlet (with 2 characters)
"   10-11: Jack Cade
"   20: Time Tries All
"   25: Oh, Hush (Ethiopian Opera)
August 15-18 (?): Mazeppa (burlesque)
October 11: Giralda; The Youth Who Never Saw a Woman
"   17: Aurora Floyd
"   18: Leah the Forsaken
"   19: The Ticket of Leave Man
"   20-23: Mazeppa
"   24: Uncle Tom's Cabin
"   25: Camille
"   26: Money
"   27: Aurora Floyd: Forty and Fifty
"   28: Putnam
"   29: The Love Chase; Putnam

Bibliography

Angel, Myron, ed., *History of Nevada*. Thompson and West, Oakland, 1881

Bancroft, Hubert H., *History of Nevada, Colorado, and Wyoming, 1540-1888*. History Company, San Francisco, 1889

Brown, T. Allston, *History of the American Stage*. Dick & Fitzgerald, New York, 1870

Browne, Charles Farrar, *The Complete Works of Artemus Ward*. G. W. Dillingham Company, New York, 1898

Browne, J. Ross, *Adventures in the Apache Country, A Tour Through Arizona and Sonora, with Notes on the Silver Regions of Nevada*, Harper and Brothers, New York, 1868

Church, John A., *The Comstock Lode*. John Wiley and Sons, New York, 1879

Clemens, Samuel L., *Roughing It*. F. G. Gilman and Company, Chicago, 1872

Davis, Sam P., ed., *The History of Nevada*, 2 vols. Elms Publishing Company, Reno, 1912

Hazlett, Fanny G., "Historical Sketches and Reminiscences of Dayton, Nevada." *Nevada Historical Society Papers*, vol. III, 1922

Ireland, Joseph N., *Records of the New York Stage from 1750 to 1860*. T. H. Morrell, New York, 1867

Kelly, J. Wells, *First (and Second) Directory of Nevada Territory*. Valentine and Company, San Francisco, 1862, 1863

Leman, Walter M., *Memories of an Old Actor*. A. Roman Company, San Francisco, 1886

McCabe, John H., "Historical Essay on the Drama in California," *First Annual of the Territorial Pioneers of California*. W. M. Hinton, San Francisco, 1877

Mack, Effie Mona, *Nevada, a History of the State from the Earliest Times Through the Civil War*. The Arthur H. Clark Company, Glendale, California, 1936

Odell, George C.D., *Annals of the New York Stage*. Columbia University Press, New York, 1931

Powell, John J., *Nevada: The Land of Silver*. Bacon and Company, San Francisco, 1876

Pyper, George D., *The Romance of an Old Playhouse*. The Seagull Press, Salt Lake City, 1928

Riegel, Robert C., *America Moves West*. Henry Holt and Company, New York, 1930

Rourke, Constance, *Troupers of the Gold Coast or the Rise of Lotta Crabtree*. Harcourt, Brace and Company, New York, 1928

Simpson, J.H., *Report of Explorations Across the Great Basin of the Territory of Utah for a Direct Wagon-Route from Camp Floyd to Genoa, in Carson Valley, in 1859*. Washington, Government Printing Office, 1876

Taylor, Mart, *The Gold Digger's Song Book, Containing the Most Popular Humorous & Sentimental Songs, Composed by M. Taylor, and Sung by his Original Company with Unbounded Applause throughout California*. Marysville, California, 1856

————, *Local Lyrics and Miscellaneous Poems*. San Francisco, 1858

Vrooman, Gertrude S., "A Brief Survey of the Musical History of Western Nevada." *Nevada Historical Society Papers*, vol. III, 1922

Wemyss, F.C., *The Standard Drama*. William Taylor and Company, New York, 1854, or n.d.

Wright, William, *The Big Bonanza*. American Publishing Company, Hartford, 1871

————, *A History of the Comstock Silver Lode and Mines*. Boegle, Virginia, Nevada, 1889

Magazines and Newspapers

Alta California (San Francisco), 1849-1891

Ballou's Pictorial Drawing-Room Companion (Boston), 1858

Browne, J. Ross, "Peeps at Washoe." *Harper's Monthly Magazine*, vol. XXII

————, "Washoe Revisited." *Harper's New Monthly Magazine*, May, 1865

Carson Daily Independent (Carson City), 1863-1875

Daily Old Piute (Virginia City), 1864-1875

Deseret News (Salt Lake City), 1850-1899

Golden Era (San Francisco), 1852-1893

Gold Hill Daily News (Gold Hill), 1863-1882

Humboldt Register (Unionville), 1863-1876

Nye County News (Ione), 1864-1867

Reese River Reveille (Austin), 1862-1867

Rodecape, Lois Faster, "Tom Maguire, Napoleon of the Stage." *California Historical Society Quarterly*, vol. xx-xxi

Sacramento Daily Union, 1851-1905

San Francisco Call, 1860

San Francisco Evening Bulletin, 1855-1929

Sawyer, Eugene T., "Old-Time Minstrels of San Francisco." *Overland Monthly*, October, 1923

Territorial Enterprise (Genoa, Carson, Virginia City), 1858-1916.

Virginia Daily Union, 1862-1867

Washoe Times (Washoe City), 1862-1863

MANUSCRIPTS AND MONOGRAPHS

De Groot, Henry, "Sketches of the Washoe Silver Mines." Newspaper clipping in Scrapbook at Bancroft Library

Eastavan, Lawrence, ed., "San Francisco Theatre Research," Monograph. First Series, vols. i, ii, v, vi. W.P.A. Project 8386, San Francisco, 1938, 1939

Field, Isobel, letters of December 19, 1939 and January 16, 1940, Serena, Carpinteria, California

Folsom, Mrs. E. Florence, letters of March 8 and 18, 1943, Fresno

Lord, Eliot, *Comstock Mining and Miners*. Monographs of the United States Geological Survey, vol. iv. Washington, Government Printing Office, 1883

McCabe, John H., unpublished theatrical journal manuscript, Sutro Branch, California State Library, San Francisco

Miller, William C., "An Historical Study of Theatrical Entertainment Virginia City, Nevada." Unpublished doctoral thesis, University of Southern California, 1947

Watson, Margaret G., "A History of the Theatre in Virginia City, Nevada, 1849-1864." Unpublished master's thesis, University of Nevada, 1940

Index

Transportation: by stages, 30-31, 56, 59, 72, 76, 89, 107, 119, 170, 180, 186-87, 237, 245, 266; railroad, 32; pack trains, 32, 57, 62, 85, 108, 267, 294, 333; horseback, 38, 59, 149; wagons, 43, 59, 119, 240, 345; carriages, 45, 280, 294, 306; illus. of stage coach, 51; sleighs, 57, 215, 248-49; mail, 64; difficulties, 79, 83; for salt, 79, 203, 260; to Aurora, 108-09; oxen, 119, 235; accidents, 119, 280; buggies, 149, 280, 305; to duels, 179; to theatres, 217, 221-22, 330; humor during, 227; in Reese, 235; stables for, 276; costs, 321-22; barouche, 325

Trappers and traders: 14, 24

Tuckett (White) Mercy Westwood; biography of, 42-43; first lady, 46-48, 57, 352; in California, 58

Tuers, Johnny: at Niagara, 242; manager of New Idea, 262; at Maguire's, 277; at Sutliff's, 286, 288, 307, 328, 333-34; benefits for, 295, 306, 343-44

Twain, Mark: on Greeley story, 30; on *Ingomar*, 76, 193, 352; at Steamboat, 115; photo of, 161; in Third House, 161, 224; writings of, 169, 173, 202; on Ward, 224-28; gets letter, 237; on Menken, 256, 259-61; with Sanitary drive, 291; as "Gander," 322; *see also* Samuel Langhorne Clemens

Two Bonnycastles, The: 243, 358

Uncle John: 76
Uncle Tom's Cabin: 183, 332-33, 357, 360
Union Blues: 63
Unionville: 109, 173; *see also* Humboldt District
Unionville *Humboldt Register:* on activity, 110; about song, 171; on Twain's writing, 178; on Menken; 259, 261, 266; about Fourth, 302; about Julien, 320-21; about statehood, 338-39; about Secessionists, 341; regarding the *Enterprise*, 347
University of Nevada: 87, 160, 240
Utah Mine: 241
Utah Territory: *see* Nevada; Washoe

VEGETATION: weeds, 34; sagebrush, 34-35, 180, 270, 313, 332; flowers, 184; trees, 24, 195, 302, 333; vegetables, 208, 341
Vesey Hall: 219, 231, 267
Viola, Miss (balladist): 191
Virginia Cadets: 124, 138, 155
Virginia City: theatre in, 14; naming of, 27, 119; isolated, 28; appraisal of, 33-34, 45, 130, 197; Taylor in, 38; building in, 41, 44-45; first theatre of, 44; map of, 50; described, 53, 176-77, 197, 203-04; churches of, 53; first baby in, 57; martial law in, 63; governor in, 65; photos of, 70, 139, 142; saloons in, 83-84; recruiting in, 86; entertainers troubles in, 95-98; fires in, 97; dances in, 115; schools in, 123; billiard contest in, 132; Fourth in, 137-38, 143-44, 302; streets of, 202, 279-80; cemetery in, 219; money troubles in, 288; lights for, 294; dull times in, 295; boxing in, 296; and statehood, 339-41; amusements in, 349-52
Virginia City *Daily Constitution:* 340
Virginia City *Daily Old Piute, The:* lottery advertisement (illus.), 264; birth of, 285; Gillespie of, 291; on Mazeppa, 311-12; praises Howard, 313
Virginia City Guards: 102, 137, 301
Virginia City *Territorial Enterprise:* calls meeting, 55; suspended, 81; theatrical appraisals, 90, 186, 223, 226, 237, 259-61, 265-66, 330, 332, 344, 347; printing of, 93; on circus, 98; on Humboldt, 109; on dances, 114-15; on hangings, 116; on "feet," 118-19; on theatre's opening, 136; of war victories, 145-46; public correspondence, 156-57; new building, 176; De Quille on, 178, 346; about duel, 179-80; Twain on entertainers, 193-95, 224-25; staff of, 205; about Cushman, 210; McCarthy with, 305; Nevada's debt, 340; *see also* Carson City *Territorial Enterprise*
Virginia *Daily Union:* on the Howard, 46; on concert, 113; rivalry, 174, 179;